CATHOLICS ON LITERATURE

# Catholics
# on Literature

J.C. Whitehouse

EDITOR

FOUR COURTS PRESS

Set in 10.5 on 12 point Bembo for
FOUR COURTS PRESS
55 Prussia Street, Dublin 7, Ireland
*and in North America for*
FOUR COURTS PRESS
c/o ISBS, 5804 N.E. Hassalo, Portland, OR 97213.

A catalogue record for this title
is available from the British Library.

ISBN 1-85182-276-3

This book is printed on acid-free paper.

Printed in Great Britain
by Redwood Books, Trowbridge, Wilts.

*Makebelieve can be not a lie, but a truth in figure.*

Thomas Aquinas

*On the whole, all literatures are one; they are the voices of the natural man.*

Cardinal Newman

# Preface

The principal sources of the material included in this book are the works of Catholic creative writers, critics, scholars, philosophers, theologians and ecclesiastics. In the case of the first of these categories, much of the writing is copyright and of varying degrees of commercial value, and permission to reproduce it has been granted subject to payment. I acknowledge such permission with regard to the following authors: Georges Bernanos, 'Une Vision catholique du réel' (A Catholic View of Reality), 'Proust et l'écrivain catholique' (Proust and the Catholic Writer) and 'Le rôle de l'écrivain catholique' (The Role of the Catholic Writer) in *Le Crépuscule des Vieux*, © Editions Gallimard, Paris, 1956; Heinrich Böll, 'Kunst und Religion' (Art and Religion) in *Essayistiche Schriften und Reden,* vol. 1, © Verlag Kiepenheuer & Witsch, Cologne, 1979; Graham Greene, extracts from *Why do I write?* Percival Marshall, London, 1948, reprinted by permission of David Higham Associates; François Mauriac, '*The Detachment of the Artist*' in *Second Thoughts,* Darwen Finlayson, London, 1961, reproduced by permission of Phillimore & Co., Chichester; Flannery O'Connor, extracts from *The Habit of Being: Letters of Flannery O'Connor,* edited by Sally Fitzgerald, © Regina O'Connor, 1979, reprinted by permission of Farrar, Strauss & Giroux, Inc, New York; Jean Sulivan, extracts from *Morning Light: the spiritual journal of Jean Sulivan,* translated by Joseph Cuneen and Patrick Gormally, Paulist Press, New York, 1988; Evelyn Waugh, 'Felix Culpa?' and 'Literary Style in England and America', from *A Little Order: Evelyn Waugh, a selection from his journalism,* edited by Donat Gallagher, Eyre Methuen, London, 1977, reprinted by permission of Peters, Fraser and Dunlop, London. In the case of Shusaku Endo, François Mauriac, Flannery O'Connor and Evelyn Waugh, the firms or persons concerned were able to offer a reduced rate for the reproduction in an academic publication, and I am grateful to them.

My warmest thanks go to those authors, editors of journals and copyright holders who, in consideration of the non-commercial nature of this undertaking, have given me permission to reproduce material at either a purely nominal fee or, as happened in virtually every case, without charge. These are Joseph Majault, for permission to include my English translation of the foreword to his *L'Evidence et le mystère,* Paris, Le Centurion, 1978; Francis Mathy, SJ, for his 'Shusaku Endo: Japanese Catholic Novelist', originally published in *The Month* in May 1987; John J. Mulloy, for his riposte to Newman, *Is Christian Literature a Contradiction in Terms?* originally published in the *Dawson Newsletter* in 1984; Brendan Murray, SJ, for permission to use the late Patricia

7

Corr's collected articles *A Catholic Viewpoint: Modern Novelists,* first published as
a booklet by the *Irish Messenger,* Dublin, in 1966; Karl G. Schmude, for his 'The
Changing Accent of Catholic Literature', which first appeared in *Quadrant* in
1984; and last but by no means least Christianne Undset Svarstad for her permission to reproduce the English version of Sigrid Undset's two essays 'Truth
and Fiction' and 'D.H. Lawrence' from her collection *Men, Women and Places,*
published by Cassel, London, in 1939. I am also grateful to the editors of the
*Modern Language Review* and *Renascence* for allowing me to reprint my own
contributions to this book, which originally appeared in those journals.

Two friends of long standing, Dr John Sowden, formerly of the University
of Bradford, and Fr Matthew Rigney, of the English Dominican Fathers,
helped enormously with two of the translations in the book. The former made
very helpful suggestions in connection with my version of Heinrich Böll's 'Art
and Religion', and the latter translated from Latin Leo XIII's letter on literary
studies.

Every attempt has been made to trace possible copyright owners. The task
has been long, often difficult and occasionally unsuccessful. I trust, however,
that I have offended no-one. All errors or failings pointed out to me or the
publishers will be rectified in any later editions.

JCW, Bradford 1996

# Contents

*Appendix: Papal and Episcopal Reflections*

# Introduction

This anthology is an attempt to bring together thematically a scattered, unsystematic, and highly individual range of reflections by a variety of Catholics on the role and responsibilities of the writer, individual authors and their work, and the nature and characteristics of literature.

I am grateful to the Marxist academic and critic David Craig for providing, in the form of his *Marxists on Literature* (Penguin, 1975) one of the sources of the inspiration for it. To express this crudely: if jam tomorrow, why not pie in the sky? The two phrases each seem to represent a type of enduring human aspiration (or at least an expression of divine discontent) which have, in their own way, helped to shape what we think and do. Both Marxism and Catholicism are world-views whose characteristic systems of belief and action are international, whose greatest concentrations of numerical and active strength are now to be found outside the regions where they were first developed and applied, whose future is at best unclear and at worst problematic, but whose tenets include an assurance of their permanence, in one form or another, until the end of history.

The other source has been the writings of usually certain liberal humanists, not always of the atheist/agnostic variety, whose native intelligence sometimes seems clouded by prejudice or wilful ignorance, and who seem to say harsh and often contradictory things about Catholic literature. Some condemn it for its naivety and sentimentality and others for its bullying, limited, authoritarian and dismissive tone. The condescending nod Sartre's Roquentin is prepared to give it in *Nausea* or Martin Green's angry diatribes in his essays in *Yeats's Blessings on von Hügel* make one wonder whether Bernanos, Endo or Undset are really simple and gullible, or whether the hesitations, reservations and decent reticences of Mauriac or Böll do actually constitute fictional or critical harrassment. The fact that in such writers I see qualities which these critics have failed to notice, and which could be given the traditional but now unfashionable names of faith, hope, charity and wisdom, has lain at the root of much of my thinking on Catholic literature. It has also spurred me to compile this anthology.

As I suggest in my own contribution to this discussion, there is virtually nothing in the way of an official or unofficial Catholic theory of literature or even of a consistent specifically Catholic criticism. Nor has literature ever been seen by the institutional Church or individual Catholics as a means of converting the world, even if literary style or the Catholic equivalent of criti-

11

cal realism may have been proposed by certain ecclesiastics as useful aesthetic or moral aids in the Church's struggle to humanize mankind. What exists in scattered abundance, however, is a rich corpus of often idiosyncratic reflections by individual Catholic writers, critics and scholars on literature in general, specifically Catholic literature and individual works. What they have to say may sometimes be rather surprising and is rarely, particularly in the case of those writers of fiction we think we know best, as totally predictable as we might imagine.

There is no school of Catholic critics, no specifically Catholic way of criticizing literature, no judging it on agreed and formulated Catholic criteria. This is not to say that there has never been censorship, clerical or lay, in recent times in Catholic countries such as Ireland, Spain or Portugal. That censorship, however, was usually local and to a degree governmental in origin and practice, inspired by a desire to maintain the *status quo* rather than to restrict the citizen's reading matter to improving Catholic works. Indeed, in Spain there was a parental outcry against the study of papal encyclicals like *Rerum Novarum* in schools, as such directives were judged to be far too revolutionary. In Ireland too, Graham Greene's biographer Norman Sherry tells us, although the government banned *The Heart of the Matter* because it was 'indecent in tendency', the clerical membership of the Irish Censorship Board opposed the ban, and the only reason it remained in force for a few months was that the lay members were in fact in the majority.[1] Prudence may on occasion have been taken to excess by certain over-conscientious people (protecting the 'simple faithful' has always been a serious concern of the Church) and *proscription* too readily used. In that sense, Catholic censorship in the twentieth century has been more like that operating until recently in Britain, where the concern was, ostensibly at least, to protect wives, children and servants (another class of 'simple faithful'?). Perhaps the German Bishops' pastoral letter on *Realism in the Catholic Novel* is another example of such a preoccupation. *Prescription,* however, is a very different matter. It is to the critic, not the imaginative writer, that it is offered. In his unique address of February 1956, Pius XII pointed out the necessity, nobility and importance of criticism, raising and then attempting to answer the question of the function of the critic. The first element of his reply was to stress the necessity of an unprejudiced reading of the work in question, a refusal to write to please the author, the publisher or the public, a certain serenity, and confidence in his own judgement. He also posited three fundamental rules: the critic should write *sine ira et studio* (without fear or favour), be guided by the maxim *verbum oris est verbum mentis* (that the author is assumed to be writing sincerely), and *super omnia caritas* (charity above all). There are also some intelligent observations on the difficulty of establishing the 'clear, objective meaning' in works of fiction. This, the sole papal document on literary criticism, seems honest, charitable and even liberal.

1   Sherry, Norman, *The Life of Graham Greene,* Volume Two, London, Jonathan Cape, 1994.

I cannot find any theoretical writing by lay Catholics that presents an opposite point of view. The most that seems to be asked for its honesty, intelligence, imagination, perception and occasionally profundity and aesthetic competence. No doubt Catholic writers often feel that their faith gives them insights and understanding that are denied to other people (see, for example, Bernanos and Maritain on Proust) but that is not a feeling exclusive to Catholics. What they want is writing that tells the truth as the writer perceives it, and that is what they ask of themselves. That truth, it seems to me, is always a personal one, caught in its quiddity and idiosyncrasy and revealed effectively to the reader. It is not a vision of a better type of social organization or the end of history, but a vision of fictional lives in the here and now. In my own view they adopt (unconsciously, probably, because it is unlikely that they have read them) the views of Pius XII.

Paradoxically, the institution that after the publication of *Humanae Vitae* Michael Frayn once parodied under the name of the Carthaginian Monolithic Church has no official literary theory or doctrine and has not seen literature as part of a sustained effort to convert the whole world. With the exception of John Henry (Cardinal) Newman, who for obvious reasons has been treated as a writer rather than a cleric, few modern popes, bishops or other senior members of the ecclesiastical hierarchy have written on literature, and such documents as there are tend simply to extol it as an ennobling human activity, even if also as an undertaking which is perhaps essentially secondary to the work of evangelization. No didactic function is imposed on it, but it is sometimes seen (cf. Leo XIII's letter to Cardinal Parrochi) as a civilizing, enlightening and attractive embellishment to the primary tasks of the Church, as fine writing and an educated sensibility potentially at the service of instruction and persuasion. Its dignity and value are stressed, although there is little emphasis on its autonomy.

But what Maritain would call its 'end' remains uncertain. A close reading of the ecclesiastical texts reproduced here perhaps suggests that even if literature is seen as having both an aesthetic and a socially-critical function, and literary criticism is regarded as an activity of great worth, calling for the highest standards of impartiality, charity and careful, sensitive and intelligent exegesis, there is no suggestion of art for art's sake. The perception that literature can enlighten, illuminate and delight, however, is clearly present, and Maritain's view that all sublime art is Christian art and Bernanos's statement that mediocre art is a scandal are at least implicit in such writing.

Indeed, the former's *Art and Scholasticism,* which examines the nature of creative endeavour in terms of Thomist philosophy, is probably the most intellectually rigorous and stimulating Catholic writing at the highest level of generality and abstraction on matters of this kind. Its main area of reference and comment, however, is that of the visual arts, and it has very little to say specifically about literature. Consequently, there are no lengthy extracts from the book here, even though much of what it says could be profitably read as an exercise in the construction of a rational and comprehensive theory of art. What is particularly relevant to the matter in hand is the constant stress on the *disinterestedness* of art, the repeated statement that falsifying a work by forcing it to contain alien elements such as a desire to edify or disedify prevents it from reaching its proper end, and the declaration that (good, presumably) Catholic art is not clerical or confessional. In his own words, 'A Christian work would have the artist, as artist, free' (Maritain, 1930, 71).

Nor have Catholic writers – in the sense of Catholics who produce works of fiction – ever been anxious to assume the role of apologists, or even to accept it under protest. In many cases, notably, in recent times, those of Greene and Böll, they have even refused to be described as Catholic writers, preferring to be seen as Catholics who write. Even in terms of the strictest Catholic thought, they are right to do so, for a Catholic writer must primarily and essentially be a Catholic who writes: *operatio sequitur esse*. What we are shapes what we do, a point simply but effectively made by Chesterton in his *On the Novel with a Purpose*. At a less abstract level, their intuitive perceptions agree with Maritain's more abstract formulations: as writers they must be free, the 'end' of their art is the work itself, in its own formal and thematic necessity, not the edification of the faithful or the conversion of the world. In Greene's phrase, they reserve the right to write from the black squares. As writers, they are not to be the handmaids of the Church, or indeed of any other institution or system. In terms of Thomist thought, for so long the philosophical mode of Catholicism, they are quite justified in their stance, for such thought has always proclaimed the superiority of the speculative over the practical and the contemplation of the truth as the highest of human activities.

There was, but perhaps no longer is, a distinctive phenomenon called Catholic literature. Difficult to define but easy to recognize, such writing has been neatly described in the context of French society by Joseph Majault and more generally by Albert Sonnenfeld: 'There is something called the Catholic Novel: it is a novel written by a Catholic, using Catholicism as his informing mythopoeic structure or generative symbolic system, and where the principal and decisive issue is the salvation or damnation of the hero or heroine.'[2] Despite the difference between them (Majault refers specifically to a national literature but also to other kinds of writing than fiction, Sonnenfeld to a wider group of writers but restricts his observations to the novel) and ignoring for the moment the latter's closing assertion, which would be denied by many of the authors he refers to, the two offer a moderately useful if slightly imperfect working model. We we should see modern Catholic writers as those whose faith seems to have influenced (to varying degrees) their way of seeing and commenting on human life, and modern Catholic literature as literature with a Catholic dimension.

Catholic literature cannot satisfactorily be seen simply as a body of works

2   Sonnenfeld, Albert, *Crossroads: Essays on the Catholic Novelists,* York, South Carolina, French Literature Publications Company, 1982.

produced by 'Catholics who write'. Certain writers who are or were Catholics (Chaucer, Dryden, Pope) are not usually considered to be Catholic writers, whereas others (Newman, Greene, Waugh and Chesterton, Mauriac, Undset) usually are. The difference is that in the case of the latter group and others like them, certain factors come into play and to some extent force a literary identity on them. The chief of these is the presence in their work of a specifically (if occasional) Catholic element and its subsequent notice and discussion by critics and readers. This usually occurs in a society which is largely non or anti-Catholic, or where ideas and attitudes are immediately or distantly post-Catholic, as in the case of Bernanos in France, Greene in England or Undset in Norway, or in those which have never been Catholic to any but the most minimal degree, as with Shusako Endo in Japan. Where the ideas and attitudes implicit in a writer's work are in some ways different from those of the majority of his fellow-citizens, it tends to stand in a particular and easily-identifiable relationship to the rest of the literary culture.

In such cases, however, an extra and to some extent non-literary relationship is established between the Catholic writer and his readers. One danger is that the he might be seen by those who do not share his beliefs as an ideologue and by his co-religionists as an often wilfully and woefully unsuccessful apologist. Another is that perceptions of that kind may well provoke a certain hardening of ideas and attitudes on the part of the writer, making his work more explicitly 'committed' than would otherwise have been the case, particularly when read against the background of secularization typical of the nineteenth and twentieth centuries. Such a literature is likely to be conscious of itself as Catholic literature in the sense of being ideologically influenced by Catholic beliefs and attitudes. Those producing it will perhaps react in one of two ways to the situation in which they find themselves. One way would be to decide to appear 'truthful' and 'free', unwilling to be the mouthpiece of the official and institutional Church, and even to deny that they are Catholic writers. Another would be to accept that title and to produce works of theodicy or apologetics. However, whatever the reaction might be, works produced and illuminated by a Catholic sensibility are likely to be recognized by those who read them as being in a real sense Catholic literature and sometimes, because of this, to be judged on the basis of non-literary criteria.

My own view is that there is a valid distinction to be drawn between what for convenience I call Catholic *writing* and Catholic *literature*. The former I see as work intended, whatever its methods and approach, to persuade, influence and perhaps even convince. It is epitomized in theology, apologetics and polemics. The latter is fundamentally artistic, the fictional expression of idiosyncratic and subjective insights rather than general and analytical ratiocination. Some authors – notably the French Catholic writers of the first half of the twentieth century – produced both types of work. In their polemics, they were no doubt acting in a similar capacity to that of certain Marxist writers: raising consciousness, seeking a just order, urging a perspective. Although the purposes and meaning of *fictional* writing are hard if not impossible to establish, it seems to me that a novel, play or poem with a Catholic dimension is not necessarily or even probably a Catholic polemic. In a sense, Engels's talk of the struggle 'to make ourselves at home in the world' has a different meaning for Catholic writers, chiefly since they usually depict a personal and individual effort, often in terms of attempting to establish a satisfactory solution of what Mauriac and others saw as the paradoxes, opposites and contradictions contained in the human psyche and illuminating works of fiction. Nevertheless, it is at both the individual and the collective level a part of our aspiration towards relationships founded on more than mutual exploitation. The sense of a shared humanity is a feature of Catholicism and Marxism and, to particularize, Brecht and Böll have more in common than one might suppose.

The Catholic literature of the middle decades of the twentieth century represents an era of Catholic intellectual and literary history in which, as well as conviction, a belief in a certain objective and philosophical approach was dominant and was reflected in imaginative literature to some extent. It also provided an existential and imaginative approach parallel to the more abstract methods of the theologians and moralists.

The chief characteristic of such literature is perhaps seriousness rather than dogmatism. The latter may well be a permanent risk for the writer who has a consistent world view which he consciously accepts and which plays a part in his writing, and there is evidence that Catholic writers are not only aware of such a danger but also determined to avoid it. The real sense of the disclaimers expressed by Greene and Böll is almost certainly their determination not to be Catholic writers of the type exemplified by Bernanos's Pernichon or Wildred Sheed's Flax. Awareness and determination are not of course automatic guarantees of success, but it is possible that they will produce caution, restraint and honesty.

Precisely because it often contains an element of pious wonder at the mystery of man, such literature is often philosophically irritating to an increasingly secularized readership. It is possible to detect in reactions to it, particularly amongst the more astringently anti-sentimental and resolutely anti-deomorphic of its critical readers, a certain feeling that its portrayal of humanity is a little larger than life, rather more beautiful than true. It is also possible to suggest that such reactions are a by-product of philosophical antipathy rather than the result of reasoned investigation.

An impatience with the usually detectable and sometimes pervasive religious and moral dimensions of works which in some way are specifically Catholic – or in other words an ideological antipathy on the part of certain kinds of critics and readers – lies at the root of their reluctance to accept as truly humanistic a view of man and of human life and destiny which is positive and which, given its concept of man not merely as the measure of all things but as an image of God, is fundamentally hopeful. In the face of such a reluctance, the implicit or explicit traditional Catholic response will presumably be twofold. In the field of philosophical debate, it will state that to see man as the image of God is to give him a status and an eternal importance which he would never otherwise possess. In literary terms, it will portray human beings as selves, creatures of great value both individually and collectively, standing in a unique individual relationship with their Creator.

Since, in the twentieth century, writers of that kind have been operating in a post-Christian world, their work and its constituent ideology have both been noticeable. Indeed, the latter has often been singled out for special attention, either sympathetic or hostile.

In the middle decades of present century, Catholicism in literature seems to have dominated all other Christian sensibilities and to have attracted so much of the anti-religious criticism of religious literature that in the West to consider religion and literature means in fact to consider Catholicism and literature. It is hard to imagine a study of the modern Protestant novel or of twentieth century Baptist poetry. In short, when we talk of Catholic literature in our own day, we are talking of a literature marked by faith, or the tensions of faith, and noticeable as such in the surrounding secularized world. Such observations would hold good for many of the novels of what is now the older generation of Catholic writers.

In their novels, or at least in their most 'Catholic' novels, such writers were explorers, if not necessarily expounders, of their faith, illustrating the dramas and tensions of the truths of their religion seen in an existential and human context in all its confusion and messiness. Greene's Pinkie, his Scobie, his Mexican priest, Bernanos's country priest, Mauriac's Thérèse Desqueyroux may be fascinating or boring, sympathic or repulsive, attractive or appalling, confused and wrong-headed or perceptive and right, depending on our own temperamental and intellectual bias as readers, but they are all characters in an intense individual relationship with God in a situation seen and depicted in a religious perspective. Whatever kinds of lives they live, they are seen, even if it is fitfully, in the light of an understanding of that life that goes beyond the merely existential and incorporates a sense of another dimension. That suggestion, that exploration, that sense of religious significance are what, in my view, distinguishes Catholic literature.

What we might call the classical Catholic novel was in part at least the product of an era in which both the institutional Church and individual Catholics were distinct from the society surrounding them. Whether the differences were superficial or essential, they were markedly present. Clearly formulated dogmas requiring full and unconditional assent, teaching on matters of morality that required obedience under pain of sin, a liturgy and an international administration conducted in Latin, practices of piety familiar throughout the Catholic world and strange elsewhere, all helped to make the Catholic Church a separate and clearly recognizable institution wherever one went. The way in which individual Catholics ordered (or failed to order) their lives, the things they saw as right or wrong, their habits of religious practice or the way in which they rejected or temporized with their religion, were all characteristic of a particular kind of religious or spiritual sensibility. From that kind of pre-Vatican II Catholicism, we have moved on to a situation in which there are wide local and individual variations in ecclesiastical patterns, universal use of vernaculars, a new emphasis on the individual as a nexus of social relationships rather than as a being in a one-to-one relationship with his creator, and a massive increase, if we are to accept the findings of the surveys, in *selective* belief. Catholics now see themselves in a different way and live different lives. What was the norm a generation or so ago is now a survival from the past, and the overall result is that Catholics are no longer readily distinguishable from their non-Catholic neighbours or the Church so very unlike other benevolent and socially active institutions.

If that is the case, can Catholic literature of the kind produced by a Greene, a Waugh, a Mauriac, an Undset, have any chance of survival? If the dramas of individual sin and sanctity, individual salvation or damnation, individual hope or despair, individual faith or individual rejection of faith that they have given us were still being produced, would they have any profound meaning for today's Catholics or their secular neighbours? Would they in any sense still be dramas, or would they simply portray the inner struggles of eccentric and idiosyncratic egomaniacs? What place could the imaginatively contemplative approach we see in them have in a Catholic world so devoted to the active life? If the Catholic way of seeing human beings has changed, can pictures based on an older way still speak to our hearts and minds in the same powerful way?

My own guess is that they cannot. Or at least maybe they do not, since perhaps there are none. Anyone trying to write on Catholic literature of the last three or four decades has a very hard job. There are Catholics who write novels, Catholics who even mention Catholicism in their work, and writers who, as we say nowadays, come from a Catholic background. None of them has written anything that could be called a Catholic novel in the sense in which *The Power and the Glory* or *Kristin Lavransdatter* or *Brideshead Revisited* are indubitably powerful, and specifically powerfully *Catholic,* novels. Fiction informed by that older Catholic view of man as a creature of enormous individual worth, living in a special and dynamic relationship with his Creator and moving gradually towards salvation or damnation no longer seems quite relevant to the newer Catholic world of community and communications, a world in which we are urged to think in terms of social justice and in which sin goes largely unmentioned. Literature provides us with images of ourselves, and our situation is one of the factors that help create literature. Since we now see ourselves as social units, generally decent and naturally fairly good, the older picture seems a romanticization, a heightened and distorted idealization of the reality we see in our daily lives. Bernanos, however, that arch-Catholic novelist, told us that the average, decent, ordinary man is an illusion, and showed us in his novels the profound core of our nature and the uniquely individual nature of our experience. A way of seeing and reflecting on that nature and that experience has gone, in Catholic society as in Catholic literature, both of which are becoming increasingly like the society and literature of the deeply secularized world we live in.

That established and recognizable Catholic literature has certainly not flourished since the nineteen-sixties. The *aggiornamento* of the Church and the move from *verticalism* to *horizontalism,* the shift to a view of man less as an individual in a one-to-one relationship with his Creator and more as an element in society, reflect very wide-ranging and fundamental modifications of concepts and images of the human being that have had a marked effect on how we see and react to ourselves and others. In the Catholic Church as elsewhere, existence now seems to precede essence, to use Sartre's neat formulation.

The lexis, semantics and dialectics of Catholic thinking about human beings and the human situation have changed radically. Internally, it is no longer a case of *Roman locuta, causa finita,* and externally the Church no longer relates to the secular world quite so didactically. Within, it is more plural; without, more relative. However transient this set of new attitudes might be, or might have been, it has left its marks.

One of these marks has been made on the Catholic novel. Many newer Catholic writers (or writers who are to some degree Catholic) have for one reason or another rejected the older style of Catholicism without finding anything to replace it. At one end of the spectrum is an attitude combining both criticism and a kind of respect, or at least nostalgia. Examples might be David Lodge's *How Far Can You Go?* (1980) and Mary Gordon's *Final Payments* (1978). In both these books there is simultaneously a recognition that a former style of Catholicism has gone and that so far nothing has taken over from it. One result of this is a sense of affection and loss behind the sometimes not too gentle mockery and satire. At the other – the 'post-Catholic end' – are those who seem to have thrown out the baby with the bath water. Mary O'Malley's play *Once a Catholic* (1977) is a black farce, based on her London schooldays, in which everything Catholic is steeped in credulity, ignorance, venality, bigotry, sentimentality and repression, and the only way is *out.* A number of works, often by recent Australian writers like Desmond O'Grady's *Deschooling Kevin Carew* (1974), Ron Blair's *The Christian Brothers* (1976) and John O'Donohue's *A Happy and Holy Occasion* (1982) do much the same kind of thing. What is significant about such writing, as Karl Schmude's contribution suggests, is that while it is obsessed with Catholic subjects and scenes and with satirizing the older Catholic world, it cannot make the faith of that world believable. At the same time, contemporary, relevant, sociological, post-Council and conciliatory Catholicism seems to have little appeal. Newer 'Catholic' novels tend to give us a semi-fictionalized account of what it is like to be an unbelieving, secularized Catholic from a pre-Vatican II background. Even those which are still to some degree Catholic rather than 'Catholic' seem no longer to have the strongly individual identity of a rather older type of Catholic works. Who would take Piers Paul Read or David Lodge to task, as happened with Graham Greene, for mixing up theology and fiction?

Catholic fiction has seen a parallel shift to that taking place in Catholic

thought. There, the movement was from the paradigm of man as a creature
working out his own salvation to that of him as a nexus of social relationships.
Here, it is from a concern with ways of seeing human nature in the light of faith
to ways of portraying men and women in a dialectical and indeed often deeply
critical relationship to the Church and the Catholic cultural community that
had shaped them. But if it is parallel, it is a shift in the opposite direction. The
emphasis in Catholic thought moved from the individual to the community and
the collective. The move in fiction was from the community or the Catholic
ghetto to the isolated, newly secularized individual.

The older Catholic outsiders – Bernanos's Cénabre, Greene's Scobie or
Muriel Spark's Robinson – were still seen and presented from *inside* the old
frame of reference, as objects of pity and even love, as people who have gone
astray and for whose return one might pray. Their literary descendents in novels like *Final Payments* seems to have gone for good. The framework within
which their creators see and depict them has changed, and the ways of wishing them well are different.

I draw two very simple conclusions from my very simple reflections. The
first is specific and concerns fiction and Catholicism. Here, problems arise
when there is a shift in either or both. In Catholic thought, there was a change
in ideas about human beings and an epistemological shift in apologetics and
the notion of the *magisterium* and the consequent introduction of a new lexis.
In the Catholic novel, there was a movement away from a picture of human
beings working out their own destiny towards a presentation of them in a
dialectical and critical relationship to their formative culture, where the old
lexis – 'faith', 'grace', 'sin', 'salvation', 'redemption', 'hope', 'charity' – is largely
meaningless. To date, there is no clear sign of the emergence of what may
come next, a totally post-Vatican II Catholic novelist.

Any literature which to some degree draws on a system of belief almost
inevitably runs the risk of being seen as a defence of, or even propaganda for,
the creed it relates to. Both its critics and its partisans may adopt this attitude,
but perhaps the danger is greater when it is the latter who do so, since prescrip-
tions and censorship may be more  insidiously harmful than outright hostility.
A vitiated, emasculated and purely functional literature, serving externally-
imposed aims, is likely to produce reactions less vital and genuine than those
aroused by writing which manages to suggest the tensions inherent in any
deep and deeply conscious reflection on human life, experience and understanding. This, I think, is what Camus meant when he said in his essay *The
Myth of Sisyphus* that great novels are philosophical novels, that is, the opposite
of novels with a thesis. It is also what Catholic writers like Greene, Mauriac,
Bernanos and Böll have all said quite unequivocally, and what Newman
expressed vividly in his lectures on *The Idea of a University*:

> I say, from the nature of the case, if Literature is to be made a study of
> human nature, you cannot have a Christian Literature. It is a contradic-
> tion in terms to attempt a sinless literature of sinful man. You may gath-

er together something very great and high, something higher than any Literature ever was; and when you have done so, you will find that it is not Literature at all.[3]

Much of the unsympathetic criticism of Catholic literature stems from the not unreasonable perception that literature which recognizes an ideology as greater and more compelling than itself may well somehow present a distorted and falsified picture of human life in order to 'prove' or 'show' the rightness of that particular way of seeing 'man, the heart of man, and human life.' In other words, 'edification' may be the real aim, achieved at the expense of artistic and imaginative autonomy and integrity. Another source is the supposition (illustrated clearly and rather wittily in John Weightman's review of Conor Cruise O'Brien's *Maria Cross*) that Catholic writers are 'dramatizing frustrations that result from local or social personal prejudices, that is from non-essential forms of evil, and which would be seen as non-essential by keener intelligences'[4] and the implication that the whole problem of evil and sin is simply another way of describing sexual tensions, a series of *frissons* produced by the contemplation of fruit forbidden by their religion. If they do nothing else, such views at least suggest some of the complexity of the problem.

The varied texts from many cultures assembled here will, I hope, help to show that Catholic writers and critics have been aware of the problems connected with literature and religious faith and that, where there have been tensions and conflicts, they have had intelligent and thoughtful things to say about them. They will not, I believe, suggest a consensus, but they do indicate recurring imaginative, aesthetic, moral and theological concerns. Where Catholic literature and Catholic reflections on literature will go in the future is still far from clear, and the critical and reflective material still has to be produced and gathered. My aim here, however, has not been so much to predict future development as to illustrate the rich, varied and distinctly unmonolithic nature of Catholic responses to literature of all kinds.

The aim of this collection, then, is to show how literature has been seen by Catholic writers, critics, scholars, philosophers and clerics from all parts of the world over the last century or so, and to set out some of the main problematic features of the field. The texts themselves contain a wide range of views on literature in general, Catholic literature in particular, and Catholic reflections on individual works by both Catholic and non-Catholic writers.

There is no polemical intention, but simply a desire to show the diversity of creative, critical, theoretical, aesthetic and moral concerns and perceptions in a category of author or commentator too often seen as either rigidly conformist, over-anxious to disclaim allegiance to a monolithic system, or doomed to depict

3   Newman, John Henry, *The Idea of a University* (ed. Martin Svaglic), New York, Rinehart, 1960.
4   Weightman, John, *The Concept of the Avant-Garde,* London, Alcove, 1973.

human life in a paradigmatic straitjacket. That diversity should not be surprising, since Catholics are as temperamentally, socially, culturally and intellectually heterogeneous as the rest of their fellow human beings. Although it would be facile to expect a clear consensus, there are salient common features across the range: a concern with imaginative truth, with the proper purposes of literature, and with the necessary freedom of the artist.

*On the Writer*

# The Role of the Catholic Writer[1]

## GEORGES BERNANOS

One or two of the members of the editorial board of this review have kindly done me the honour of asking for what journalists in my country call a 'piece'. I could hardly refuse them such a tiny favour, but neither would I like the sight of my signature in an ecclesiastical journal to upset certain of its readers. Why not use the opportunity to say what I think about the role of the Catholic writer? I am quite aware that the question is not of interest to many people, and if I try to tackle it I am leaving myself open to a great deal of criticism. But, since I *am* a Catholic writer, I shall not be accused of meddling in what does not concern me.

I certainly do not believe that the Catholic writer is called upon to give sermons. It seems to me that in addressing the Vincentians I shall not surprise them if I say that eloquence does not seem to me to be the most evangelical form of apostolate. The only passage in the Gospels that might carry a faint echo of a kind of movement of divine eloquence is the invective against the Pharisees and − it is perhaps worth saying in passing − this is not a very tempting subject for a preacher. If he dared to treat it in depth, he would risk seeing his audience gradually thin out and delivering his concluding observations to an empty church ...

On the feast of St Augustine of Canterbury, one of the most illustrious patrons of England after St George, we recently had occasion to reread the passage from St Paul's letter to the Thessalonians, in which he speaks to his sons and daughters in a language so familiar and tender that many grave canons would hesitate to use it nowadays: 'But we became little ones among you, as if a nurse should cherish her children'. But it was also the language of St Francis, at a time when the Church seemed indeed much more like a nurse than a teacher of dogma and morality, even though she has never ceased to be both.

Perhaps circumstance impose on the Church the kind of reserve that a teacher should never abandon with his pupils, but the Catholic writer would be wrong to take the professorial chair himself. We are brothers speaking to brothers, not doctors of the Church or stewards. That simple truth has been forgotten far too often over the last twenty years. We have seen an increase in the numbers of such lay preachers and amateur theologians on whom the water of baptism has scarcely dried before they started commenting on St Thomas Aquinas or paraphrasing St John of the Cross without even bothering to learn their catechism. We must not confuse the Second Spring in France

1    From Jean-Loup Bernanos (ed.), *La Vocation spirituelle de la France*, Paris, Plon, 1975. This talk was given in Rio de Janeiro in 1943.

with such rowdy outbursts which, even if they have been beneficial at times, often bear the marks of an attack of literary snobbery.

Catholic writers cannot be part of the teaching Church, and the fault of a great number of religious is to see them as docile and punctilious collaborators, rather as when a teacher occasionally allows one of his pupils to take his place at the blackboard. The first duty of a writer is to produce good books, in the light of his own ideas of his art and the resources at his disposal, without special consideration for anything or anyone, for every book bears witness and hence must above all be sincere. An artist sees things more clearly than others and what we ask of him and have every right to demand of him is that he should say what he really sees, not what he would like to see or is ordered to see. If he cannot reconcile his vision and his faith, he should keep quiet. God is not honoured, or the Church served, by lies.

Within herself, the Church has always had to struggle against the tendency of certain religious orders to over-centralize everything, just as modern states claim to be able to do everything themselves. Unfortunately, those who want to control everything are eventually held responsible for everything, and the years that are to come will make clear to us the enormous harm to Christianity caused by the madness of putting budgets, police and propaganda at the service of the Kingdom of God. We Catholic writers lay claim to no special status. Our only ambition is to work freely beneath the gaze of God. Nor do we in any way exaggerate the importance of the modest services we can render. In this world, nothing is more important than saints or heroes, and God knows that we are neither. Sometimes we manage to create imaginary ones, who are no doubt unworthy of their glorious models, but whom God may sometimes use to stir in certain souls if not a knowledge of or even a desire for the divine, at least a curiosity about it and a sense of its absence.

We may have no exaggerated notion of the services we can render, but we are determined to render them, that is, to use the most precious of human rights, that of responding to God's call, of carrying out one's task, of being faithful to one's vocation – *vocatus,* called ... And above all, though we do not see morality and religion as in any way alien to us, being a moralist or a theologian does not seem to be a sufficient qualification to judge artistic questions. Mediocre art is a scandal, and even more of a scandal when it claims to be edifying. It is absurd and iniquitous to submit books to the judgement of illiterate ecclesiastics.

But what we find most unacceptable as writers is doctoring our witness to suit circumstances in order to further opportunistic scheming, even for the loftiest of purposes. If a religious is somethimes subject to the painful obligation of writing against his personal convictions, that is because of his solemn vow of obedience, and we have no criticism to offer. We, however, intend to take the risk and use our relative freedom to its utter limit. After all, that freedom belongs to everyone, and we can only give it up if we are specifically ordered to do so. Our modest task in the Church is to open the doors and windows and let a little fresh air in. If we get carried away and break the windows, if we are so bold that we tend to become foolish, we know that we shall hardly be handled with kid gloves and that no-one will miss the chance of pointing out how reprehensible we are, for I am afraid that we have never met with much indulgence at the hands of the masters and doctors ... Since we have already decided to deny nothing that a properly–constituted authority can legitimately ask of us, our conscience is clear and we hope that one day we shall be able to reply to the angel responsible for investigating the case of poor literary sinners that we have often been wrong, like everyone else, but have never refused our witness to anyone, friend or foe.

# Proust and the Catholic Writer[1]

## GEORGES BERNANOS  3

*And what is your own opinion of Proust?*
Proust's awesome introspection goes nowhere. For a time, it may seem to offer something to our expectations and by constantly opening up new perspectives to keep us on tenterhooks, it creates the illusion of a lesson it is about to provide but never does. The pursuit has all the power, and perhaps the desperation, of a hallucination. Proust's is a world of intelligent and libidinous animals, as complicated and polished as surgical instruments. I would go further than saying that God is absent from his work. There is not a trace of him to be found, and I think it would be impossible even to mention his name.

*You clearly see that as a drawback from an artistic point of view?*
Of course. Proust thought he could take up a stance of pure observation and that intellectually the state of grace was one of total indifference to good and evil. It might be possible to argue for such a claim if the moral law were imposed on us from the outside, but that is not the case. It is *in* us, it *is* us. Suppose that there is some non-human being of superior intelligence but with no knowledge of the problem of morality. We could also suppose that he is observing us and trying to understand us fully. I grant that for a time he would see the good as proper reasoning appealing to our intelligence and evil as a carnal appetite tending to undermine it. But we would quickly find out that that soon becomes no explanation at all. Once he came across the objection that good and evil are sought for their own sakes, loved and served, the whole argument would collapse. Man, at first apparently so simple, would become a

---

1    From *Le Crépuscule des Vieux,* Paris, Gallimard, 1956.

kind of incomprehensible monster. No, the fact of the matter is that *by remov-ing God and the Devil from his work the novelist risks losing everything:* they are characters he simply cannot do without. It's true that the naturalists got round the problem by changing man into an animal ...

*And with regard to moral theology ...*
Moral theology provides us with data we cannot do without, reliable bench-marks. If you have some acquaintance with it, it's hard not to burst out laugh-ing when some novelist makes great play of discovering what the humblest little priest has known for a long time.

*You think that the novelist can help the theologian?*
Obviously. A casuist can yield to the temptation of empty reasoning. A man with the gift of imagination, of creating, with what I would call an inner view of reality, offers the theologian an enormously important personal ability to see into life intuitively.

The novelist has a part to play as an apologist It is very true that we have been able to see Proust's work as beneficial, by virtue of the kind of anxiety that is the basis of the enormous intellectual joys he gives us. He awoke the desire to seek out, opened up the ground. In that descent into the depths, why should the Catholic novelist come second to anyone? It is up to him to lead the way. He has a torch in his hand.

# Art and Religion[1]

## HEINRICH BÖLL

The contexts of being a Christian are many and varied. Anyone using one of the abbreviations indicating membership of a Christian church under the heading 'religious affiliation' when filling in his tax return or having one marked on his income tax card is making a declaration that cannot but have its consequences. It is no-one's business to decide whether that declaration is true or false, for the human conscience is not open to inspection. Within very short periods of time – such as are known only to sprinters from the results of their practice runs – conversions can occur and be revoked, and even a gathering of the most gifted inquisitors could not presume to investigate a single con-

1   From *Erzählungen, Hörspiele, Aufsätze (Stories, Radio Plays and Essays)*, Cologne and Berlin, Kiepenheuer & Witsch, 1961.

science. Not until Judgement Day will it be clear whether the declaration on the tax card was correct or not. Declaring one's religion is a promise that is only rarely kept. Of course, there are those whose description of themselves as Christians becomes an adjective tacked onto their professions, and we have Christian drivers, druggists and decorators. Perhaps Christian drivers really do drive less recklessly than others, Christian druggists really do reject the heresy of a presumption of total hygiene, perhaps Christian decorators really do spare their customers the torture of living in an exhibition area instead of a home. A great deal happens in private and is never revealed to us. The authority we might call upon to make a Christian driver, druggist or decorator produce a certificate confirming his Christianity does not exist, but we can imagine one. The authority we might call upon to make an artist do likewise cannot even be imagined.

As long as the liberal arts were still the *artes liberales* and could flourish only within the closed circle of the Church, all artists were necessarily Christian artists. In those days, they expressed their anger unequivocally and sometimes crudely. The Franciscan Jacopone da Todi lampooned the Pope, Stefan Lochner consigned popes and cardinals to Hell, and on Gothic cathedrals many a gargoyle unambiguously turned its bare backside towards the bishop's palace centuries before Götz von Berlichingen put into words what those stone figures were merely trying to represent. In those days, however, great lords, perhaps because their power was more real, were still endowed with humour. They felt, and sometimes even were, in charge of things and took a relaxed view of breaches of discipline. They could punish and pardon; art and craft were seen as one and the same thing, and great lords trusted their own more or less robust aesthetic instincts.

Since then, quite a lot has happened and been acknowledged in innumerable treatises; the *artes liberales* have in fact become the liberal arts, to which Christians too are admitted. The Churches may have the right to establish whether someone is a Christian or not (a verdict to be confirmed or overthrown by the recording angel on Judgement Day), but not to establish whether someone is an artist. They can try to determine whether a particular work of art contains elements detrimental to faith and morals, or whether another fosters them. As guardians of faith and morals, they may have the right to do so, and the more clearly the purpose of such praise or condemnation is spelt out, the more pleasing it is. In matters of art, such praise or blame doesn't say very much. The endless argument about form and content becomes more and more meaningless and exhausting if the churches do not take into account the fact it is easier to cheat with content than with form. It is no coincidence that the further down the scale an artist is, the more carefree is his choice of content. One starts off with a representation of the Mother of God, writes a play about Judas, or tries to hew the great mystery of the Trinity out of a block of granite. All that was possible, moving and marvellous as long as the *artes liberales* were flourishing in the protection of the churches and the tradition of craftsmanship meant that there was a guaranteed minimum of form. It would all still be possible if the West were once again to be given a Saint Francis who was both a genius and a saint, but holiness and genius elude definition. As long as the theologians have to limit themselves to evaluating content, the tool of the trade most often recommended will be the one that is out of place more than anything else in the artist's workshop, the cliché. Even the things our fathers saw as revolutionary and least hackneyed, such as a critical approach and anti-clericalism, have long been mere stereotypes turned out not only by competent practised hands, and are now no more than a generally accepted stylistic device. Without a theology of art-forms, a label such as 'Christian literature' is merely emotive and inadmissible, at least in so far as it avoids differentiation. The writings of both Teresa of Avila and Theresa of Lisieux were certainly Christian literature. The former wrote  a powerful and elegant prose, and contemporaries and later readers alike accorded her a high and still uncontested place. In her autobiographical *History of a Soul*  which as a document has its *raison d'être,* the Little Flower of Lisieux used the kind of pallid and conventional prose available to any French girl of her time and class. Although they were of the same rank in terms of personal completeness, the gap between them as writers is as great as that between the prose of Bourget and Proust. Francis of Assisi composed the *Song of the Sun,* and Alphonsus Liguori also wrote, but comparing the two authors, both of whom were canonized, would be like comparing Everest with the gentle hills north-west of Bonn. Both of the latter can be described as 'elevations', which removes the problem of classification. We do something similar when we use the term 'Christian literature' and unthinkingly label someone as a 'Christian writer'. Such usages are tolerable on tax declarations alone, where a writer can describe himself as such under the heading 'profession', inserting under that of 'religious affiliation' one of the abbreviations indicating membership of a Christian church. Only the inland revenue is empowered to establish who is a Christian writer, and that body is bound to respect confidentiality.

As a free artist among free artists, the Christian is subject to the criteria of the art he has dedicated himself to. Even if all the authorities that grant or withhold recognition are perpetually controversial, at war with each other and use an ambiguous vocabulary, they are, despite all their varieties and weaknesses, nevertheless more competent than the one that simply does not exist, namely a theology of art. The relationship of a Christian to his chosen art is that of an isolated individual. As a member of one of the churches to which he has declared his allegiance on his tax declaration, he is subject to its rules like any other member, and the fewer privileges he accepts (such as that of being the licensed clown, the *enfant terrible* who makes people smile and shake their heads) the freer he is.

Gargoyles have been replaced by the achievements of modern plumbing, and now that the churches no longer have any authority, they are no longer subject to attack. So the sharp little jokes of the past are disappearing and survive only as kindly anachronisms. The churches no longer control art; it has escaped them, and their helplessness in the face of it is both touching and terrifying, since it increases to an almost unbearable degree the concomitant measure of freedom thrust upon the artist. He simply feels no longer affected by ecclesiastical judgements, for whether they are positive or negative, they always unavoidably lack differentiation and proven authority. He is alone, and yet must face up to daemons, good and evil spirits who watch over the mystery. Is he to betray his art, or the God he acknowledges? And if he betrays art by giving back less than he has been given, will he not be betraying God? Whether his talent be great or small, he cannot trivialize it by reducing it to the level of a kind of stock-in-trade that will protect him from temptation when the burden of freedom becomes too great to bear. The recognition that art is not the prerogative of Christians keeps him in a permanent state of schizophrenia. A non-Christian can declare himself free of all historical and social obligations, seeing art as everything, even God, his family and the world, thus achieving the total concentration that often produces great art. But confessing to being a Christian entails commitment, and anyone claiming to be both a Christian *and* a writer would need to know where this commitment is leading him. But he does *not* know, and no-one can tell him whether he is moving towards the meadows where the flowers of evil bloom or approaching the realms reserved for the innocent lilies of the field. As long as the mystery of art remains unsolved, the Christian has only one weapon, his conscience ... and yet he has an artistic as well as a Christian conscience, and the two do not always tell him the same thing.

Such problems do not concern Christians alone, but all artists who recognize responsibilities other than artistic ones. If they force an agreement between the two kinds of conscience, art suffers. One example of this is the writing and painting produced by socialist realism, and if the convergence is violently imposed, the result is that in harming art it also harms content by neglecting form. How the two are to be united remains a mystery. Half-truths are not possible, form cannot be sacrificed to content without betraying content. So the dilemma of being both a Christian and an artist and yet not a Christian artist also remains. Such a declaration is permissable only in one's dealings with the tax office, which keeps its secrets like our conscience, secrets which will not be revealed until Judgement Day.

# The Writer[1]

## GRAHAM GREENE

*(Letter to Elizabeth Bowen)*

When your letter came, I had just been reading Mrs Gaskell's *Life of Charlotte Brontë,* and this sentence from one of Charlotte Brontë's letters recurred to my mind. It certainly represents my view, and I think it represents yours as well: 'You will see that *Villette* touches on no matter of public interest. I cannot write books handling the topics of the day; it is of no use trying it. Nor can I write a book for its moral. Nor can I take up a philanthropic scheme, though I honour philanthropy ...'

Pritchett, too, I think, would agree with that, though perhaps it was easier for Charlotte Brontë to believe that she had excluded public interest than it is for us. Public interest in her day was surely more separate from the private life: a debate in Parliament, a leading article in the *Thunderer.* It did not so colour the common life: with us, however consciously unconcerned we are, it obtrudes through the cracks of our stories, terribly persistent like grass through cement. Processions can't help passing across the ends of our imaginary streets: our characters must earn a living: if they don't, what is called a social significance seems to attach itself to their not-earning. Correcting proofs the other day, I had to read some old stories of mine dating back to the early thirties. Already they seemed to have a period air. It was not what I had intended.

'The relation of the artist to society': it's a terribly vague subject, and I feel the same embarrassment and resentment as you do when I encounter it. We all have to be citizens in our spare time, standing in queues, filling up income tax forms, supporting our families: why can't we leave it at that? I think we need a devil's advocate in this discussion to explain the whole thing to us. I picture him as a member of the PEN Club, perhaps a little out of breath from his conference in Stockholm where he has been discussing this very subject (in pre-war times he would have returned from the Adriatic – conferences of this kind were never held where society was exactly *thick*). Before sitting down to add his signature to an appeal in *The Times* (in the thirties it would have proudly appeared with Mr Forster's, Mr Bertrand Russell's and perhaps Miss Maude Royden's), he would find an opportunity to tell us what society is and what the artist.

I'm rather glad, all the same, we haven't got him with us. His letters confirmed the prejudice I felt against the artist (there the word is again) indulging in public affairs. His letters – and those of his co-signatories – always seemed

---

1   From *Why Do I Write? An exchange of views between Elizabeth Bowen, Graham Greene and V.S. Pritchett,* London, Percival Marshall, 1948.

to me either ill-informed, naive or untimely. There were so many petitions in favour of the victims of arbitrary power which helped to knot the noose round the poor creatures' necks. So long as he had eased his conscience publicly in print, and in good company, he was not concerned with the consequences of his letter. No, I'm glad we've left him out. He will, of course, review us ...

We had better, however, agree on our terms, and as you have suggested no alternative to Pritchett's definition of society – 'people bound together for an end, who are making a future' – let us accept that. Though I'm not quite happy about it. We are each, however anarchistically and individually, making a future, or else the future, as I prefer to think, is making us – the death we are each going to die controlling our activities now, like a sheepdog, so that we may with the least trouble be got through the gate. As for 'people bound together for an end,' the phrase does, of course, accurately describe those unfortunate prisoners of the French revolution of whom Swinburne wrote in *Les Noyades:* they were flung, you remember, naked in pairs into the Loire, but I don't think Pritchett had that incident consciously in mind.

The artist is even more difficult to define: in most cases only time defines him, and I think for the purposes of this argument we should write only of the novelist, perhaps only of the novelist like ourselves, for obviously Wells will be out of place in any argument based on, say, Virginia Woolf. The word artist is too inclusive: it is impossible to make generalisations which will be true for Van Gogh, Burke, Henry James, Yeats and Beethoven. If a man sets up to be a teacher, he has duties and responsibilities to those he teaches, whether he is a novelist, a political writer or a philosopher, and I would like to exclude the teacher from the discussion. In the long run we are forced back to the egotistical 'I': we can't shelter behind the great dead. What, in *my* opinion, can society demand of *me?* What have *I* got to render to Caesar?

First I would say there are certain human duties I owe in common with the greengrocer or the clerk – that of supporting my family if I have a family, of not robbing the poor, the blind, the widow or the orphan, of dying if the authorities demand it (it is the only way to remain independent: the conscientious objector is forced to become a teacher in order to justify himself). These are our primitive duties as human beings. In spite of the fashionable example of Gauguin, I would say that if we do less than these, we are so much the less human beings and therefore so much the less likely to be artists. But are there any special duties I owe to my fellow victims bound for the Loire? I would like to imagine there are none, but I fear there are at least two duties the novelist owes – to tell the truth as he sees it and to accept no special privileges from the state.

I don't mean anything flamboyant by the phrase 'telling the truth': I don't mean exposing anything. By truth I mean accuracy – it is largely a matter of style. It is my duty to society not to write: 'I stood above a bottomless gulf' or 'going downstairs, I got into a taxi,' because these statements are untrue. My characters must not go white in the face or tremble like leaves, not because these phrases are clichés but because they are untrue. This is not only a matter of the artistic conscience but of the social conscience too. We already see the effect of the popular novel on popular thought. Every time a phrase like one of these passes into the mind uncriticised, it muddies the stream of thought.

The other duty, to accept no privileges, is equally important. The kindness of the State, the State's interest in art, is far more dangerous than its indifference. We have seen how in time of war there is always some well-meaning patron who will suggest that artists should be in a reserved class. But how, at the end of six years of popular agony, would the artist be regarded if he had been reserved, kept safe and fattened at the public expense, too good to die like other men? And what would have been expected of him in return? In Russia the artist *has* belonged to a privileged class: he has been given a better flat, more money, more food, even a certain freedom of movement: but the State has asked in return that he should cease to be an artist. The danger does not exist only in totalitarian countries. The bourgeois state, too, has its gifts to offer to the artist – or those it regards as artists, but in these cases the artist has paid like the politician in advance. One thinks of the literary knights, and then one turns to the plain tombstones with their bare *hic jacets* of Mr Hardy, Mr James and Mr Yeats. Yes, the more I think of it, that is a duty the artist unmistakably owes to society – to accept no favours. Perhaps a pension if his family are in danger of starvation (in those circumstances the moralists admit that we may commit theft).

Perhaps the greatest pressure on the writer comes from the society within society: his political or his religious group, even it may be his university or his employers. It does seem to me that one privilege he can claim, in common perhaps with his fellow human beings, but possibly with the greater safety, is that of disloyalty. I met a farmer at lunch the other day who was employing two lunatics; what fine workers they were, he said; and how loyal. But, of course, they were loyal; they were like the conditioned beings of the brave new world. Disloyalty is our privilege. But it is a privilege you will never get society to recognise. All the more necessary that we who can be disloyal with impunity should keep that ideal alive.

If I may be personal, I belong to a group, the Catholic Church, which would present me with grave problems as a writer if I were not saved by my disloyalty. If my conscience were as acute as M. Mauriac's showed itself to be in his essay *God and Mammon,* I could not write a line. There are leaders of the Church who regard literature as a means to one end, edification. That end may be of the highest value, of far higher value than literature, but it belongs to a different world. Literature has nothing to do with edification. I am not arguing that literature is amoral, but that it presents a personal moral, and the personal morality of an individual is seldom identical with the morality of the group to which he belongs. You remember the black and white squares of Bishop Blougram's chess board. As a novelist, I must be allowed to write from the point of view of the black square as well as of the white: doubt and even denial must be given their chance of self-expression, or how is one freer than the Leningrad group?

Catholic novelists (I would rather say novelists who are Catholics) should take Newman as their patron. No one understood their problem better or defended them more skilfully from the attacks of piety (that morbid growth of religion). Let me copy out the passage. It really has more than one bearing on our discussion. He is defending the teaching of literature in a Catholic university:

> I say, from the nature of the case, if Literature is to be made a study of human nature, you cannot have a Christian Literature. It is a contradiction in terms to attempt a sinless Literature of sinful man. You may gather together something very great and high, something higher than Literature ever was; and when you have done so, you will find that it is not Literature at all.

And to those who, accepting that view, argued that we could do without Literature, Newman went on:

> Proscribe (I do not merely say particular authors, particular works, particular passages) but Secular Literature as such; cut out from your class books all broad manifestations of the natural man; and those manifestations are waiting for your pupil's benefit at the very doors of your lecture room in living and breathing substance ... Today a pupil, tomorrow a member of the great world: today confined to the Lives of the Saints, tomorrow thrown upon Babel ... You have refused him the masters of human thought, who would in some sense have educated him, because of their incidental corruption ...

*(Letter to V.S. Pritchett)*

The last time I received a letter in this series I was reading the *Life of Charlotte Brontë:* this time the poems of Thomas Hood, and the change of mood may account for my uneasy suspicion that in my last letter I simplified far too much. Perhaps that magnificent poem, 'The Song of the Shirt', has unduly influenced me, for I am not quite so sure now that the writer has no responsibility to society or the State (which is organised society) different in kind from that of his fellow citizens.

You remember Thomas Paine's great apothegm, 'We must take care to guard even our enemies against injustice,' and it is there – in the establishment of justice – that the writer has greater opportunities and therefore greater obligations than, say, the chemist or the estate agent. For one thing he is, if he has attained a measure of success, more his own master than others are: he is his own employer: he can afford to offend; for one of the major objects of his craft (I speak, of course, of the novelist) is the awakening of sympathy. Now

the State is invariably ready to confuse, like a schoolmaster, justice with retri-
bution, and isn't it possibly the story-teller's task to act as the devil's advocate,
to elicit sympathy and a measure of understanding for those who lie outside
the boundaries of State sympathy? But remember that it is not necessarily the
poor or the physically defenceless who lie there. The publicans and sinners
belong to all classes and all economic levels. It has always been in the interests
of the State to poison the psychological wells, to restrict human sympathy, to
encourage cat-calls – Galilean, Papist, Crophead, Fascist, Bolshevik. In the days
of the totalitarian monarchy, when a sovereign slept uneasily with the memories of Wyatt, Norfolk, Essex, in his dreams, it was an act of justice to trace the
true source of action in Macbeth, the murderer of his king, and Shakespeare's
play has for all time altered our conception of the usurper. If at times we are
able to feel sympathy for Hitler, isn't it because we have seen the woods of
Dunsinane converging on the underground chambers of the Chancellory?

Here in parenthesis I would emphasise once again the importance and the
virtue of disloyalty. If only writers could maintain that one virtue so much
more important to them than purity – unspotted from the world. Honours,
State patronage, success, the praise of their fellows all tend to sap their disloyalty. If they don't become loyal to a Church or a country, they are too apt to
become loyal to some invented ideology of their own, until they are praised
for consistency, for a unified view. Even despair can become a form of loyalty.
How few die treacherous or blaspheming in old age, and have any at all been
lucky enough to die by the rope or a firing squad? I can think of none, for the
world knows only too well that given time the writer will be corrupted into
loyalty. Ezra Pound therefore goes to an asylum ... (the honourable haven of
the uncorruptible – Smart, Cowper, Clare and Lee). Loyalty confines us to
accepted opinions: loyalty forbids us to comprehend sympathetically our dissi-
dent fellows; but disloyalty encourages us to roam experimentally through any
human mind: it gives to the novelist the extra dimension of sympathy.

I hope I have made it clear that I am not advocating a conscious advocacy
of the dispossessed, in fact I am not advocating propaganda at all, as it was
written by Dickens, Charles Reade or Thomas Hood. The very act of recre-
ation for the novelist entails sympathy: the characters for whom he fails in
sympathy have never been truly recreated. Propaganda is only concerned to
elicit sympathy for the innocent, or those whom the propagandist likes to
regard as innocent, and this he does at the expense of guilty: he too poisons
the wells. But the novelist's task is to draw his own likeness to any human
being, the guilty as much as the innocent. Isn't our attitude to all our characters more or less – There, and may God forgive me, goes myself?

If we can awaken sympathetic comprehension in our readers, not only for
our most evil characters (that is easy: there is a cord there fastened to all hearts
that we can twitch at will), but of our smug, complacent, successful characters,
we have surely succeeded in making the work of the State a degree more difficult – and that is a genuine duty we owe society, to be a piece of grit in the
State machinery. However acceptable the Soviet State may at the moment find

the great classic writers, Dostoievsky, Tolstoy, Chekhov, Turgenev, Gogol, they have surely made the regimentation of the Russian spirit an imperceptible degree more difficult or more incomplete. You cannot talk of the Karamazovs in terms of a class, and if you speak with hatred of the kulak doesn't the rich humourous memory of the hero of *Dead Souls* come back to kill your hatred? Sooner or later the strenuous note of social responsibility, of Marxism, of the greatest material good of the greatest number must die in the ear, and then perhaps certain memories will come back, of long purposeless discussions in the moonlight about life and art, the click of a billiard ball, the sunny afternoons of that month in the country, the blows of an axe that has only just begun to fell the cherry trees.

I am sorry to return over and over again to this question of loyalty or disloyalty, but isn't disloyalty as much the writer's virtue as loyalty is the soldier's? For the writer, just as much as the Christian Church, is the defender of the individual. The soldier, the loyal man, stands for the mass interment, the common anonymous grave, but the writer stands for the uneconomic, probably unhealthy, overcrowded little graveyard, with the stone crosses preserving innumerable names.

There is a price to be paid, of course. We shall never, I suppose, know how many Russian writers have taken the same stand as Ivan Karamazov (one has only to substitute the words the State for the word God) and studied a long silence:

> This harmony has been assessed too dearly; the price for entry is already too high for our pockets. I prefer to hand back my entrance-ticket; and as an honest man I am bound to return it as soon as possible. So that is what I am doing. It is not that I reject God, Alyosha; I merely most respectfully hand Him back the ticket.

One mustn't, of course, forget, writing as I have just done, that at the moment the chief danger to us of Russia is the danger the publican represented to the Pharisees. We spend so much time as writers thanking God that we are not as the Soviet League of Writers, rejoicing in our freedom, that we don't see in how many directions we have already bartered it, in the interests of a group, whether political or religious.

I realise that I haven't taken up any of your practical and useful points on the question of the State's responsibility to the writer. But I remain intransigent. It seems to me unquestionable that if once writers are treated as a privileged class from the point of view of taxation they will lose their independence. What the State gives it can take away, and it is so terribly easy for a gift enjoyed for a few years to become a necessity. Once give us protection and we shall soon forget how we kept the wolf away in those past winters. And another danger is that privilege separates, and we can't afford to live away from the source of our writing in however comfortable an exile. I am one of those who find it extraordinarily difficult to write away from England (I had to do so at one time during the war), and I dread the thought of being exiled at home. It is possible, though I don't think it probable, that taxation might kill the novel, but it won't kill the creative passion. It may be that we are passing out of the literary period during which the novel has been the dominant form of expression, but there will still be literature. I cannot see why the poet should be affected by high taxation ... .

When you write of means other than State support for the novelist, I find myself more in agreement with you. Some kind of royalty collectable on library lendings is long overdue, but all the same don't let us make the mistake of treating the librarian as an enemy. He is our greatest friend. We have already emerged from the artificial book boom (that strange period when people bought novels) and are nearly back to normal times. In normal times it has been the library (I am not referring now to the public library) which has given the young novelist at least a basic salary. We must be careful not to kill the goose.

As for your proposed tax on the classics, I feel even more doubt, for who is to administer this fund if not the State? A committee of authors? But who is to choose the authors? In any one generation how many authors could you name whom you would trust to show discrimination or even common integrity? And as a matter of publishing fact, don't the classics already subsidise the living writers? A publisher's profits finance his work in progress. The best seller – or the classic – helps to finance the young author, the experimental book, the work of scholarship which cannot expect to show a return. There are certain publishers (we could agree on names) who never by any chance publish a book of literary merit, but these are not the publishers who are making money out of the classics. (I except a few mushroom firms who belong to the boom period and are dying with it.)

You may well ask, have you no plan, have you not one constructive suggestion to make? and my answer is quite frankly, None. I don't want a plan for literature. I don't want a working party, however high-minded or benevolent, to study the standard of life among novelists and decide a minimum wage. Even if by a miracle the State could be excluded from such a plan, I still don't want it. A plan can be taken over later by other authorities. Nor can a craft be trusted to legislate wisely for itself. Think of the Board of Film Censors which was set up by the industry itself, and consider how it has hampered the free development of the films in a way that would have been impossible to the Lord Chamberlain's office.

No, our life is too organised already. Let us leave literature alone. We needn't worry too much. Man will always find a means to gratify a passion. He will write, as he will commit adultery, in spite of taxation.

# The Intense Responsibility of Being a Writer[1]

## FRANÇOIS MAURIAC

For many writers this question does not so much as arise. If there is one dogma which has gained the support of the majority of writers in this century and the last, it is the dogma of the absolute independence of the artist. It seems to be agreed, once and for all, that a work of art has no object outside itself. It only counts in so far as it is gratuitous or useless: anything written to prove a point or to be of use is disqualified from the realm of art. Gide says that 'the moral issue for the artist is not that he should present an idea that is useful but that he should present an idea well.'

But we can be sure that this should not have to be said so persistently and so often by some writers if it were not vigorously contradicted by others. In fact, from the other end of the literary world comes a ceaseless protest against the pretension to absolute independence on the part of the artist. For example, when Ernest Psichari proclaims that one must write with fear and trembling under the eye of the Trinity, he is being the mouthpiece of all those who believe in the immortality of each individual soul, and therefore believe in the extreme importance of their writings as effecting each immortal destiny.

Then, between these two opposing camps, there is the huge crowd of novelists who fluctuate and hesitate. On the one hand they admit that their work is valuable only inasmuch as it apprehends living men in their completeness, in their heights and in their depths – the human creature as he is. They feel that any intervention in the unfolding of their characters – even to prove the truth of what they believe – is an abuse. They feel a sincere revulsion against falsifying life. On the other hand, they know that they are treading on dangerous ground, and that their intense desire to depict human emotions and passions may have an incalculable and permanent effect on the lives of many people.

Every novelist worthy of the name and every playwright who is a born Christian suffers from the torment of this dilemma. In French literature there is a famous example. Once in my holidays I followed the fashion of the time and wrote a life of Jean Racine. Racine is typical of the divided and hesitating writer who plays first into their hands of one camp and then into the hands of the other. The ultimate fate of a writer like him depends on the final decision. Everyone knows what agonizing fluxes Racine went through before he reached that decision. At the age of twenty he escaped from Port-Royal because his young genius revolted against the unbearable restraints imposed

---

1 From *God and Mammon*, London, Sheed and Ward, 1936.
The elements making up this chapter are taken from a conference on "The Responsibility of the Novelist." In a footnote Mauriac says: 'I would not write about it in quite the same way now. From now henceforward the whole question seems to boil down to the *purification of the source*.'

upon him there. Then, when Nicole, in his letter on *Les Imaginaires* made a violent attack on novelists and playwrights, Racine burned with rage. Nicole had written that 'the qualities of the novelist and the playwright, which anyway are not very honourable in the judgment of decent people, are horrible when considered in the light of the principles of the Christian religion and the rules of the Gospel. Novelists and dramatic poets are public poisoners, not only of the bodies, but the souls of the faithful, and they ought to hold themselves guilty of a multitude of spiritual murders.' Racine replied to this hard hitting with unparalleled verve and bitterness and venom in two letters which are not enough known. In our desire to excuse Racine for being unable to endure such inflexible doctrines without an outcry, we must be careful not to blame it on the inhuman rigour of the Jansenists. Nicole was only developing a doctrine of St Augustine; and Bossuet showed himself equally uncompromising in his letter to Père Caffaro on the subject of the play and the novel. Bossuet maintained that the success of plays and novels was due to the fact that people find in them substitutes for love and beauty and for their own feelings; and what answer can be made to that? The real reason why Racine was so furious with Nicole was because he was hurt to the quick. During the following years we can trace the struggle that he had with himself until finally, at the age of thirty-eight, he gave in and renounced for ever the depicting of human passions and personalities.

It is a renunciation that very few writers are capable of making, and Racine's renunciation was certainly not so easy as some people think. Is a man who is capable of writing and who has a masterpiece inside him at liberty not to give to the world? An author who gives up writing may do it because his belly is empty, as the saying goes, and he would only be able to repeat himself and copy himself. Self-repetition, in fact, is the occupation of most writers on the decline; even when they have given over everything that was expected of them and delivered their message to the world they go on regularly laying eggs because it is their job, and, after all, a man must live.

No human power, however, could reduce a man to silence during his period of fertility; there would have to be a supernatural power. We do not know whether Grace has ever been able to triumph over a writer who has writing-sickness. The conversion of a literary man is usually marked by redoubled activity and effort on his part. He wants the greatest possible number of people to read about the example that he gives to the world. We are still awaiting the miracle of a writer who is reduced to silence by God.

Actually, all the best writers are tugging at one rope. At one end of the rope there are those who are convinced that their work will be valuable only if it is disinterested and does not tamper with reality for reasons of modesty or edification, and at the other end there are those who have a feeling of responsibility towards their readers, of whom, in spite of their scruples, they want as large a number as possible. At one end there is the certainty that there cannot be a work in novel-form which has value outside absolute submission to its object – the human heart: there must be progress in knowledge of mankind, but whatever depths are found there must be no dizziness or disgust or horror. This is a certainty. At the other end there is only a sentiment, a feeling – at any rate for those who do not belong to a religious faith. For a Christian, eternity hangs in the balance if one soul is troubled or in danger of being lost. But while non-Christians are unable to stop themselves feeling a responsibility, in a dim way they have no difficulty at all in inventing sophisms to persuade themselves that their fear of scandalising others has no connection with reality. I should like to assure them, at this point, that their nebulous feeling corresponds with a very deep reality. We can say this: that although the whole matter seems more serious for writers with the faith, it certainly does interest the sceptics – and this, precisely because they only believe in man and know no reality in the world other than human reality.

A few years ago a review posed the question: 'Why do you write?' to the literary world. The majority of answerers merely tried to be witty; Paul Morand, for instance, said: 'To be rich and esteemed.' He was making fun of the whole thing by confusing immediate motives with deep motives.

The deep motive seems to me to lie in the instinct which urges us not to be alone. A writer is essentially a man who will not be resigned to solitude. Each of us is like a desert, and a literary work is like a cry from the desert, or like a pigeon let loose with a message in its claws, or like a bottle thrown into the sea. The point is: to be heard – even if by one single person. And the point is that our thoughts and, if we are novelists, our characters should be understood and loved and welcomed by other intelligences and other hearts. An author who assures you that he writes for himself alone and that he does not care whether he is heard or not is a boaster and is deceiving either himself or you. Every man suffers if he is alone, and the artist is the man for whom and in whom this suffering takes a physical form. Baudelaire was right when he called artists *lighthouses*. They light a great fire in the darkness, and they set light to themselves so as to attract the greatest number of their fellow-beings to them.

Artists, and particularly writers, are the most squeamish people in the world, and at the same time the most hungry for praise. Indeed it is impossible for writers to be sated with compliments – and they must not be despised for this because, as often as not, their great need of praise is due to a lack of confidence in themselves, and their longing for reassurance is due to a feeling that their work is worthless.

Of all the compliments that can be paid to a writer, there is one especially that will make him glow with pleasure, namely: 'You are admired so much among the younger generation.' Then his head positively swells, for though he may seem to be detached, what he wants above all things is to get the attention of the younger generation, and if he does not do this he considers he has failed in his mission. Nothing matters to him except that. He has got to reach others, and particularly he has got to reach those who are still capable of being influenced and dominated, the young mentalities which are hesitating and unformed. He wants to leave his mark on this living wax and imprint all that is best in him on those who are going to survive him. It is not enough for the writer who writes so as not to be alone merely to reach other people: he wants to make them replicas of himself: he wants his own image and likeness to be resurrected in them when he himself is in the grave.

We must not believe in a writer's false humility. The humblest writer aspires to nothing short of immortality, and the least pretentious clings to the hope that he will not perish altogether. Those who pretend that they do not care about what they write and only scribble their poems on cigarette folders do so with a secret hope that because these are lighter they will be carried by the wind to distant shores. The artist wants to escape from his desert during his life, but he also wants to escape from the solitude of death, and thus he hopes that something of what he has written — if only one line — should live, and that some youth — if only one — should hum a song he has invented to the end of the world. The ambition of an artist is not confined to wanting himself to live, but he wants his love to live too. He is audacious enough to impose on men of the future the vision of the face he has loved:

> Je te donne ces vers afin que si mon nom
> Aborde heureusement aux époques lointaines
> Et fait rêver un soir les cervelles humaines
> Vaisseau favorisé par un grand aquilon ...

But if the writer has so great a desire to reach and affect the largest possible quantity of people both in his own time and after it, surely he ought to feel a responsibility towards those he influences, even if he is not a Christian. And even if we abandon the word *responsibility* — which cannot have the same meaning for a sceptic as for a Christian — he still must feel *concerned* for those whose destiny he has perhaps altered.

Actually I know of no writers worthy of the name who are really not concerned — however non-religious they may be. I do not mean that this consideration has an influence on their work or moves them to control either their curiosity or the boldness of their depiction, for they always persuade themselves that a work which is true and in conformity with reality must necessarily be good. Flaubert had no desire for a title to fame other than that of demoralizer, and André Gide, nowadays, would not disown that same title. This does not mean that these writers intend to do evil; not at all, but they do not agree with us about the nature of good and evil. According to them a work which scandalizes is nearly always a work which sets people free. They see a writer as a sort of satanic benefactor who breaks the bandages of morality in which people are wrapped and restores liberty and ease to their movements. However, this is not the place to point out how these authors are wrong from the Christian point of view — how they do not take the dogma of the Fall of Man into account, nor the fact that man is born defiled, nor the virulent and terribly contagious element in the sores which literature is unveiling with increasing brazenness.

This does not take away from the fact that a novel is nothing if it is not a study of human nature, and that it loses all its reason for existing if it does not increase our knowledge of the human heart. Thus, should a novelist, however scrupulous he may be, falsify the facts of life and change the very object of his study in order not to offend or unsettle his readers?

I know that the question can be evaded in more ways than one; but we must not reassure ourselves with the hypocritical excuse that we are not writing for little girls, and are not bound to compete with Mme de Ségur or Mrs Molesworth. Unfortunately, readers who have attained the age of reason are often more dangerously disturbed by books than other readers. It is probably better to be read by little girls who have tea in the nursery and who do not know what evil is than by young people in full flush of youth. It would be difficult to imagine the sort of letters a writer can receive. After reading a book of mine called *Genetrix,* a boy once sent me a photograph with the words: 'To the man who nearly made me kill my grandmother.' In an accompanying letter he explained that the old lady resembled the heroine of *Genetrix* to such an extent that he had been on the very verge of strangling her during her sleep. How can readers like that be protected? Father Bethléem himself cannot do anything. The reading of imaginative literature should be forbidden to adults rather than to children.

It is seldom that writers who distort reality and depict untrue characters so as to be sure of not being immoral attain their object. For it must be remembered that they are not the only authors of their novels; the reader himself collaborates with them and often adds horrors without their knowing it. We would be amazed if we knew exactly what happened to our characters in the imagination of this or that reader who talks to us about our books. I think I can say with truth that no book has moved me more deeply than a simple and innocent novel called *Feet of Clay* which I adored when I was fourteen. It was the work of an old and virtuous woman called Zénaïde Fleuriot, and it was full of imagination and sensibility. The heroine had the lovely name of Armelle Trahec. She was young and red-haired with freckles on her face, and since reading about her I have distributed these freckles generously on the faces of my own heroines. Yet when a journalist asks me the names of the writers who have influenced me most, I quote Balzac and Dostoievsky, but I never dare mention Mlle Zénaïde Fleuriot.

This is a reminder that the devil never loses his rights, and it can well be imagined that on the Day of Judgment, though some writers will have to answer for the souls they have upset, others will be surprised by the unforeseen echo which their simplest works have had in other souls.

The collaboration between the reader and the writer, varying as it does with each individual, makes the question of good and bad books an almost insoluble one. I think that only a novelist is in the position to judge of it. For my own part I know by experience and by confidential admission that the book in which an excessive outspokenness has been detected – and doubtless rightly – and which has been most severely censured is also the very book which has had the greatest effect on people from the religious point of view.

We must not forget that the worst books as well as the best are double-edged weapons which the unknown reader plays with in a way we can never foresee. We cannot foresee whether the libertine and debauched element in the reader will be wounded or the good and pious one. Every human being makes his honey according to his recipe; he passes from book to book and from doctrine to doctrine, taking what is good for him. The young men who committed suicide after reading Goethe's *Werther* would have finished up by finding, somewhere else, an excuse for abandoning this mortal dizziness. Goethe cannot be held responsible for the death. Everybody re-creates what he reads after his own heart's-image, and moulds an idea of it which is valid for himself alone. I suppose it is my own peculiar feeling, but what stands out most vividly for me in the colossal and putrescent work of Proust is the image of a gaping hole, the sensation of infinite absence, and it is this chasm and emptiness – the absence of God in fact – which strikes me most about mankind according to Proust. I see this because I am a Christian; others may very well find satisfaction in these gloomiest of pictures. And that is why wretched literary people can still hope that the evil they have done will be forgiven because of the good which – often unknowingly – they have also done.

That is how I reassured myself. But sincerity with regard to oneself is the virtue of our generation, so we should be bold and face up to our vices. All I have said does not prevent our consenting to the professional depiction of human passions. Human passions are the object of our study, and we sell our books solely because thousands of people experience a kind of uneasy delight in this depiction of them. St Augustine confesses that he found in plays 'the image of his miseries, the love and the food of his fire ...' However, there is absolutely no need to write about obscenity in order to spread fire in the world. Bossuet said: 'Do you not feel that there are things which have no very specific effect, but which, without seeming harmful at first, put evil tendencies and dispositions into people's minds? Everything that provides food for the passions is of this dim origin. There would be only too much to confess if one examined oneself to find the causes of sin.' And he adds: 'If anyone could discern in a man a certain depth of sensual joy, and certain restless vague disposition for indulging the pleasures of the senses – tending nowhere and yet tending everywhere – he would know the secret source of the greatest sins.'

Can we honestly deny that it is nearly always this 'secret source of the greatest sins' which is probed by the writer? I am not saying that he does it on purpose or as the result of long premeditation. But in the light of this quotation from Boussuet we can understand better what André Gide means when he says that no work of art can come into being without the collaboration of the devil. The writer depends on this 'depth of sensual joy' in order to absorb and move his readers; he depends on this 'vague and restless disposition for indulging the pleasures of the senses – tending nowhere and yet tending everywhere.' The writer keeps up collusion with his adversary, the reader, whereas he ought to conquer him at any price. In every man – especially in every young man – and in every woman he has an accomplice personifying a desire for languor, a taste for emotion and a thirst for tears. Once again, I do not think there is a single novelist worthy of the name who thinks of that while he is writing and who deliberately sets out to upset people, but he is spurred on by sure instinct. All his art is concentrated on reaching the secret source of the greatest sins, and the more genius he has the more surely he will reach his end.

This question emerges: Must one stop writing even if one feels deeply that writing is one's vocation and that literary creation is as natural as breathing? Perhaps some doctor holds the key to the enigma; perhaps somebody somewhere knows the way in which a scrupulous novelist can escape from these choices – these three choices of either changing the object of his observation or falsifying life or running the risk of spreading scandal and misery among his fellow-creatures.

We may as well admit that a writer who is torn by this problem is hardly ever taken seriously. On his left there is only mockery and shrugging of shoulders – a refusal to admit that such a problem really exists. People deny that an artist has any other duty than to realise and achieve a beautiful piece of work, or that he can have any other care than to approach as near as possible to psychological truth. On his right there is an even greater misunderstanding. There is a total ignorance of the fact that he has scruples or high motives at all. It is difficult not to have a choking feeling the first time pious reviewers treat you as a pornographer and accuse you of writing obscenity for the sake of making money. When I was young and naive I felt an insuperable desire to pour out my heart to some distinguished and holy people about all these difficulties, but as soon as I had begun I realised that they made no essential distinction between me and, for instance, the author of the *Revue des Folies-Bergères*. I am not really shocked by their attitude, for I can understand perfectly well that people who are specifically in charge of souls are faced with an infinite number of problems wihich are far more urgent to them than the aesthetic problem, and it would be ludicrous for me to feel indignant with them on the grounds that they do not consider aesthetics to be as important as I do.

One Catholic writer has realised the importance of this problem and made a real effort to solve it. I could not follow Jacques Maritain's train of thought in all its complexity, but I shall quote a few lines taken from *Art and Scholasticism* in which he delimits very exactly the sphere of the novelist who is worried by his responsibility. 'The essential point,' he says, 'is not to know whether a novelist may or may not portray a given aspect of evil. The essential point is to know at what altitude he is when he makes this portrayal and whether his art and his soul are pure enough and strong enough to make it without conniving with it. The more the modern novel plunges into human misery, the more are superhuman virtues demanded from the novelist. For example, to write the work of a Proust as it should be written would require the interior light of a St Augustine. Unfortunately, it is just the opposite that has happened, and we see the observer and the thing observed – the novelist and his subject – rivalling one another in degradation.'

This is what Jacques Maritain says, and everyone will agree that he puts the question very well; everyone, that is, except the novelists.[2] However, he does not take into account the real point, since he neglects to consider the fundamental laws of novel-creation. He mentions the 'observer and the thing observed.' In fact he compares a novelist bending over the human heart with a physiologist bending over a frog or a guinea-pig. According to Maritain, the novelist is detached from his subject in the way the man in the laboratory is detached from the animal whose stomach he is delicately dissecting. I, however, hold that the operation of the novelist is utterly different from that of the experimentalist. As far as the novel is concerned, Jacques Maritain has stopped at the old naturalistic ideas. It is a condition of art that the novelist should connive with the subject of his creation, in spite of Maritain's warning, for the real novelist is not an observer, but a creator of fictitious life. It is not his function to observe life, but to create it. He brings living people into the world; he does not observe them from some lofty vantage point. He even confuses and, in a way, loses his own personality in the subject of his creation. He is one with his creation, and his identification with it is pushed so far that he actually becomes his creation.

It could easily be argued that if a novelist keeps the superhuman virtues that Maritain would have him keep, he could never write about evil people. His characters could not be wicked if they came from a creator who was good and pure. A good tree does not yield bad fruit. Let the novelist busy himself with his personal sanctification and nothing scandalous can emerge from his mind. True though this may be, it is worth mentioning in passing that the practice of superhuman virtue is not easy for mankind in general nor for nov-

---

2   Since I wrote this, Jacques Maritain has replied to me in the *Roseau d'Or* (No. 30): 'Does it mean that, in my opinion, the novelist ought to cut himself off from his characters and observe them from outside in the way a scientist in his laboratory follows the experiments he has set going? No, of course not. Would the character exist if he did not live in the author and the author did not live in him? It is not in virtue of a simple metamorphosis, but rather in virtue of a deep analogy, that it is proper to place the art of the novel in the theological light of the mystery of creation properly speaking.'
    And further on: 'The part of the novelist is not that of the scientist. The scientist is only responsible for notions, is only concerned with truth. He only addresses himself to a limited public of specialised readers.'
    'The novelist is answerable for an almost unlimited influence. Only rarely do his readers consist of those for whom his message is made (who are probably few in number). He knows that. He bewails it. He profits by it. The *unlimited* nature of his public makes the problem more and more difficult ...'
    Further on Maritain denounces me for a tendency to Manichaeism, and writes: 'The Blood of the redemption, which can turn a man into a friend of God, can also, if it touches them, exorcise Art and the Novel.'
    I am aware to-day of how much I owe to the deep charity which Maritain has shown to me in these pages of the *Roseau d'Or*.

elists in particular. In that case, would not a deeply virtuous man refrain from writing novels? For if he is a real artist he will not feel capable of producing insipid though edifying stories without a trace of human truth in them, and at the same time he will know very well that a living piece of work is bound to cause trouble. It is probably true that a novelist subconsciously resurrects in his characters the desires which he himself has repressed, and the temptations which he himself has overcome; thus, just as admirable men often have unworthy sons, the best novelist may find that he has re-incarnated his own worst elements in the sons and daughters of his brain. That is why a fervent Christian feels justified in describing passions from 'on high' – for example in a sermon or a treatise – whereas he does not in a novel where it is not so much a question of judging and condemning them as of giving them flesh and blood. Nothing, as we know, can prevent a fire from burning. Henri Perreyve, when he had just left school, wrote a letter to Charles Perraud in which he referred to 'this vice of lustfulness which word alone makes our seventeen-year-old hearts grow weak and faint.' If the mere mention of the word makes these young people grow faint and weak, what can be the effect of descriptions of the word – even if they are restrained descriptions?

Somebody may say that vice is not the only thing to write about, and that though man has his rottenness he also has his greatness; there are beautiful characters whose history can be written. Indeed, I am far from sharing Gide's opinion that good literature cannot be made out of fine sentiments, and that the worse the characters are the better the book. Nevertheless, it certainly is not easy to make good literature with only good sentiments, and it is almost impossible to isolate the good from the bad so as to make an edifying portrayal. The ambition of the modern novelist is to apprehend the whole of human nature, including its shifting contradictions. In the world of reality you do not find beautiful souls in the pure state – these are only to be found in novels and in bad novels at that. What we call a beautiful character has become beautiful at the cost of a struggle against itself, and this struggle should not stop until the bitter end. The evil which the beautiful character has to overcome in itself and from which it has to sever itself, is a reality which the novelist must account for. If there is a reason for the existence of the novelist on earth it is this: to show the element which holds out against God in the highest and noblest characters – the innermost evils and dissimulations; and also to light up the secret source of sanctity in creatures who seem to us to have failed.

Some people, however, have succeeded in overcoming their natures. The saints form material for novelists as much as any other living people. Why should not we portray saints just as Benson, Foggaro, Boumann and Bernanos did – or tried to do? On the other hand it could be maintained that on this very point of sanctity the novelist loses his rights, for if he tries to write a novel about sanctity he is no longer dealing purely with men, but with the action of God on men – and this may be an extremely unwise thing to try to do. On this point it seems that the novelist will always be beaten by reality, by the saints who really have lived. St Francis of Assisi, St Catherine of Siena, the big and little St Theresa and all the great mystics, are witnesses to a reality and an experience which is infinitely beyond the power of a novelist.

Whenever a novelist has tried to re-create the way of grace, with all its struggles and its ultimate victory, he has left an impression of arbitrariness and misrepresentation. Nothing is more elusive in human life than the finger of God. It is not that it is not visible, but its imprint is so delicate that it disappears as soon as we try to capture it. God is inimitable, and He escapes the novelist's grasp. I am sure that the exceptional success of Bernanos' novel, *Sous le soleil de Satan,* is due precisely to the fact that its saint is not a real saint: this tormented and agonized hero wanders too near the edge of despair. Or suppose, if you like, that the hero, Abbé Donissan, is a real saint; then Bernanos, with his novelist's instinct, meets that supposition by finally discovering in him the secret failure and deviation which, in spite of his heroic virtues, relates him to sinful humanity. The reason why most novelists have failed in their portrayal of saints may be due to the fact that they have drawn creatures who are sublime and angelic but not human, whereas their sole chance of success would have lain in concentrating on the wretched and human elements in their characters that sanctity allows to subsist. And this is the special realm of the novelist.

When I read the lives of the great saints I was always worried by their manifestations of humility, which seemed to me excessive. It seemed to me that people at such a height of perfection and practising such heroic virtues could not have been absolutely sincere when they announced how wretched and unworthy they were and strived to debase themselves below everyone else. But now I am convinced that sanctity means, above all, lucidity. 'One must know oneself to the pitch of being horrified,' Bossuet wrote to the Maréchal de Bellefonds. As the saints advance in the double knowledge of God and of their own souls, they get such a piercing vision of their unworthiness that they abase themselves and annihilate themselves by the most natural of instincts. It is not enough to say that they believe themselves to be wretched: in fact they *are* wretched, and it is precisely their sanctity that makes them see it so lucidly. They see what man, as compared with the light of God, really is even when sanctified, and they are horrified.

Thus even if a novelist devoted himself entirely to depicting the souls of saints, he would finally get back to the human – that is, the dangerous – element in man. He could not avoid the abysses lying in his way. There is often a sort of vanquished and frustrated viciousness at the source of people's lives. This has been said about some great revolutionaries and some great heretics, but it is equally true of very good and holy men.

Thus it happens that the novelist, caught between two fires as he is with all these difficulties, sometimes experiences a temptation to which, I must admit, he very rarely yields: the temptation to be silent – to be silent, to finish with these heavy and gloomy disclosures, to refrain from presenting the world with creatures who are diseased and who spread their disease, to make the sacrifice that Jean Racine made and which we admire so much.

Bossuet said that there was no greater difference than the difference between living according to nature and living according to grace. If the novelist is religious he suffers from this divergence, which upsets all Christians, in an especially sharp and tragic way. How could he consent to silence? And if he cannot come to a solution on this point we must remember to take into account the poor and sordid motives which attach a man to his job – especially when his job, as with the job of literature, flatters his vanity and his liking for a halo and at the same time brings him various sorts of advantages. But the necessity which obliges a genuine man of letters to write must not be forgotten. He cannot not write. He follows a deep and imperative need. We cannot smother the restless and importunate germs inside us; they demand life and we cannot know beforehand what sort of souls they will have. Our sincerest critics ought to ponder and try to understand Goncourt's affirmation: 'One does not write the book one wants to.' No, we do not write the book we want to write; alas, we write the book we deserve to write. Our judges come down on us as though our work were entirely dependent on our own free will, as if we made a deliberate decision to write a good or a bad book, tell an edifying story or a scandalous one. They do not seem to have the remotest idea of the mysterious unforeseeable and inevitable element in all creative novel-writing. The urge to write in a man of letters ends up by becoming a monster-like necessity which cannot be frustrated. Some time ago there was an amusing drawing that a hat manufacturer used as an advertisement: it consisted of a machine with a live rabbit going into it at one end and hats coming out of it at the other. It is like this that life, with all its hopes and sorrows, is engulfed by the novelist, and nothing can prevent a book emerging from this perpetual receiving of impressions. Even if he withdraws from the world and shuts his eyes and stops up his ears, his most distant past will begin to ferment. His childhood and youth alone is enough to provide a born novelist with an immense amount of literary nourishment. Nobody can stop the flow of the river which flows from us.

There is no doubt that our books have a deep resemblance to ourselves, and we can quite rightly be judged and condemned by them. Novalis' axiom, 'Character is destiny,' has often been repeated. And so, just as there is a close bond between a man's character and what happens to him during his life, so there is a similar relationship between a novelist's character and the creatures and events brought into being by his imagination. This is not to say that he is any more the absolute master of these creatures and events than he is of the course of his own fate.

People of my calibre complicate the 'drama of the Catholic novelist.' The humblest priest would tell me, like Maritain: 'Be pure, become pure, and your work too will have a reflection in heaven. Begin by purifying the source and those who drink of the water cannot be sick...' And I give the last word to the priest.

# The Detachment of the Artist[1]

## FRANÇOIS MAURIAC

During the summer of '39, when Paris was in a tumult of public tension, a Cézanne exhibition at the Orangerie acquired, by force of contrast, a special significance. I was troubled and divided in mind whenever I went to see it, but each time I came away with a renewed conviction that the artist's vocation springs fundamentally from his selflessness. And Cézanne reminded me that the more people surrender to violent partisanship the more they need the disinterested detachment of a few men.

It is a wonderful thing that Montaigne should have meditated on man and the human condition in the midst of the darkest of religious wars. The bloody horror of that conflict fortified him in his mission as observer and witness. He was the one attentive reporter in a country gone mad: 'Others mould man,' he wrote, 'but I set him forth.' He never claimed for a moment to do more than to describe us or to set us forth, yet it is he who actually moulds us by offering us an exact image of ourselves. Thanks to him, we can slip through the net cast by progressive Plans and benevolent Systems to ensnare us. And man as he truly is – man as Montaigne and Pascal saw him, the creature of flesh and spirit – must always be able to escape those fearsome fishermen.

It is Montaigne's business and not ours that he wrote the *Essais* only for his own pleasure and had no particular desire to help his fellow man. During the 'thirties it was fashionable to berate Paul Valéry because he pretended to care about nothing but the technique of his art, about the poetic means he used, and his own awareness of them. In the same way, some people scoffed at Proust because he was unable to do more than 'watch himself feel or think or speak'. His monstrous curiosity, which was neither selective nor critical in the strict sense, was accounted a near crime. But why does it matter to us what the impulse may be that makes a man write as he does? Suppose that *Jeune Parque* did result from the experiments of a man absorbed by problems of prosody, and the *A la recherche du temps perdu* from the use a sickly man made of his cloistered solitude. We are none the less indebted to them for a portion of our greatest wealth – wealth that has nothing to do with gold bullion meticulously weighed and stored in a vault but that is actively, nourishingly, endlessly creative.

Our young people today insist that we must 'think with our hands', that is, with a view to acting directly on our fellow men. They profess that intellectual

---

1   From *Second Thoughts: Reflections on Literature and on Life,* London, Darwen Finlayson, 1961.

labour must be directed towards a concrete end. According to them, the gratu-itous has had its day, and the people expect their mentors to supply only useful facts and directives. I wonder if they really believe that Montaigne and his kind did not influence human affairs? I wonder if the gratuitousness of a work is not often the measure both of its potency in depth for human beings as well as of its ability to endure in time?

The truth of the matter is that the action of a Montaigne is not like a bombshell's. It is easy to follow a man's trail in the political and social realm. The furrow turned up by Karl Marx, for example, is visible to the naked eye. But the saunterings of Montaigne or Pascal or Proust, the obscure modifica-tions wrought on the élite of mankind by Mozart or Cézanne, are of another order and escape our grasp. What was conceived in a spirit of contempt for the immediate by men who stood apart from their times and were indifferent to its preoccupations, classifications, plans, and systems – this is what proves with time to be quite literally overwhelming. How many of the great, eternally alive and potent books were born of some personal, unknown drama and had no connection with the contemporary concerns!

There are, as we all realize, some of the other kind. We know the type of creative person that some of our young people are demanding but cannot find among their elders nor, struggle as they visibly do, can they call forth, deliver, indeed forcibly rip from themselves. A lyrical philosopher like Nietzsche comes to mind: a man who would not think the search an end in itself, and who would be convinced that he held a monopoly on the formula to ensure human happiness. Or perhaps a poet, the heir of a Péguy, whose inspiration springs from the earth and, far from being soiled thereby, is nourished and enriched by all the passions of the moment.

I have always thought that this philosopher-poet was born some forty or fifty years ago, and that he is resting today somewhere between the sea and the Vosges or in the shadow of a wooden cross at Salonica, or in the Dardenelles, or down, down on the ocean floor – unless God, who knows what he might have become, has granted him the burial under the Arc de Triomphe that he would have been awarded after a long life filled with glory had he not been killed at the age of twenty.

## A CRITIQUE OF CRITICISM

If one is to believe them, the majority of my fellow writers do not bother to read what is published about their books. In my own case, neither time nor habit has been able to dull the pleasure it gives me to run through press clip-pings every morning. I don't think that I tally up my score out of any particu-lar professional vanity. More than once I have not even finished some fervid eulogy, whereas I will re-read a 'panning' two or three times if it throws any light on my book or on myself or on the personality of the critic.

What hope could there be for a writer who is nearing the end of his life but who is still unable to judge his own judges impartially or to benefit from the flood of contradictory opinions that assails him every morning?

I make an effort to read each critic with an open mind, except for the very few whose judgment is corrupted by concerns alien to literature. (From long experience we know that the book section in this or that paper gives the exact temperature reading of our relations with whatever political party the paper represents.)

If you read heavy doses of criticism – and that is the only way it is administered these days – you encounter many conflicting opinions, but one very definite impression emerges none the less. With a few notable exceptions, critics condemn and reject what is most particularly and intimately the writer's own.

In this connection, I might say, I find it significant that the critics should be nearly unanimous in reproaching one author I know quite well for his choice of characters. The hero of *Les anges noirs,* Gabriel Gradère, is blood brother to a Carco gangster. As Carco would envisage him, Gradère would be anything but frightening; actually, he would seem almost normal because his situation would not raise any question of eternity. Carco possesses the unique gift of making dope-trafficker, pimp, or blackmailer seem familiar and close to us.

I do the opposite. In spite of myself, I invest a metaphysical dimension in all my characters, and this makes for uneasiness in the reader. I am a metaphysician who works in the concrete. I exploit a certain gift for creating atmosphere to make the Catholic universe of evil palpable, tangible, pungent. The theologians offer us an abstract idea of the sinner; I present him in flesh and blood.

So when the critic complains about my characters, his criticism misfires because my people are everyday people. He should really not belabour them but me and whatever it is that makes every creature I put my hand to develop instantly into the dreadful and indefensible thing called 'a Mauriac character'.

Similarly, when the critic decides that you are not a real novelist and your novel is not a true novel, when he undertakes to demolish you totally by comparing you with Balzac or Dostoievsky, he is rejecting precisely that which differentiates you from these great forbears – your self.

To tell an author who claims he has written a classical tragedy: 'Your play is not a classical tragedy, because it has fewer than five acts and does not observe the three laws of unity' is legitimate, but it is absurd to base the canon of the novel on Balzac or Tolstoy or Flaubert, and to exclude from the category of 'novel' any book that departs from the type that criticism considers – on its own authority – the one and only true novel.

It is precisely differences and deviations that give the novelist his chance to survive. No one should construe this as vanity. Every literary period, I believe, jettisons the bulk of its fictional cargo and, accordingly, our individual chances of surviving are minimal. But if we writers had the good luck to reach a remote shore of the future, it would be thanks to everything in our work that is irreducibly our own, even to the very faults that limit us and prevent our measuring up to our predecessors.

Today no one thinks of reproaching Manet for having painted Manets. But while Manet was alive he was reproached for being Manet. 'When will Monsieur X paint happy lovers and normal, decent people? When will he write novels as long as Dostoievsky's? When will he concern himself with social problems? When will he be less facile? When will he follow a bent other than his own?'

An author can be more or less affected when such charges and demands are levelled at him. (Especially if a critic says severely to his face, as happened to me the other day: 'Your book tells me things about you that I had never suspected.' Now I don't have a strangler's hands, but instinctively I thrust my hands deep in my pockets!) Yes, under the influence of my critics, I have often dreamed of writing the story of a saintly little girl, a sister of Thérèse Martin. I have fancied that Mozart, who opened the gates of his paradise to me, might suddenly let loose in my books a flock of angels who would not be black. But the moment I set to work, everything becomes coloured by my abiding concerns: my most beautiful characters move into a certain sulphureous light that is peculiar to me and that I do not defend – it is simply mine.

'M. Mauriac has signed the decree that condemns him to be M. Mauriac for life,' one young upstart wrote recently about my latest book. Is this a death sentence? No, it is a life sentence – or, more exactly, a parole. What saves an author in literary terms – if he is to be saved – is his absolute inability to be anyone but himself. An artist who can be someone other than himself, who is all painters or all writers in turn, is lost before he starts. How could he last if he does not exist? Only to the extent to which the conscious will enters into my writing (out of scruple, a fear of shocking the reader, etc.) do I feel threatened.

In my opinion, a good critic who must judge an author will not insist that he be someone else; he will look to see if in the work under consideration the author was able to remain faithful to the laws of his own universe, if he employed only his own native gifts and did not resort to formulas or fashions. The critic should demand that the novelist does not deny himself, that he does not puff himself up in order to imitate anyone. In my view, it is reprehensible for the critic to indulge in invidious comparisons to demolish the work he is examining, for our problem as writers is not to follow in the footsteps of the great masters but to realize, each one of us to the full, the modest artist that he himself is. May each of us try to exhaust his own potential without trying to exceed it – that is what every good critic should demand of us. No universal law exists that allows him to damn us. A good critic looks for no touchstone beyond the author he is studying.

If a genuine writer produces a failure, it is never because he has broken this or that rule of the genre, for there are no recipes for the production of a good novel; he fails because he has been unfaithful to the secret code that allowed Colette to write *Chéri* for example, and Chardonne to write *Les destinées senti-*

*mentales.* The Code Colette is without value for Chardonne, and if Colette ever ventured into the atmosphere of Chardonne's environment she would die of asphyxiation. Let us be judged – if necessary, let us be condemned – by our own law alone.

# Excerpts from his spiritual journal[1]

## JEAN SULIVAN

I don't believe I write because of the need to share secrets. I prefer to tell stories, to give emphasis to a narrator and some characters while I watch from backstage. My personal journal is mixed in with my books. My preference would be to speak neither about faith nor about myself, but of men and women who set out against the night, of highways and skyscrapers, of the rejects of society, of love, its wounds and cures, in the secret hope that the absolute would offer a sign in spite of me. But many readers, including believers, have written to say that my books have helped them go on living. It is for them that I am writing this. A line of Bernanos has always haunted me: 'The writer is only the steward and dispenser of goods that don't belong to him ... If he fails in that duty he is less than a dog.'

Why say *If?* It may only be because a deeper knowledge of a writer's subjectivity is liberating for others, encouraging them to become joyously what they are. But also because of a forgotten truth.

To restrict oneself to ideas without ever referring to oneself is nonsense. Yet that's what many thinkers do, never committing themselves. They want us to believe that in the moral and spiritual order there is a logic of ideas that goes on apart from living experience. A humility that consists of not speaking about oneself while identifying with great ideas is the worst kind of pride.

Nevertheless, I must confess, I, too, have often had the temptation to write my book on *Faith* or *The Future of Christianity* from the outside. How peaceful it would be to become invisible behind the smooth pane of the writing, to play with ideas and show how they all fit together while letting the reader think that everything has taken place in a purely impersonal realm. A fine deception. It's what specialists do who build intellectual structures from which they pretend to be absent. Which is why they never finish gabbing about 'the crisis of our times' or dream about the future instead of speaking to us directly. [9–10]

1   From *Morning Light,* New York, Paulist Press, 1988. (Page references are given at the end of each extract.)

I write in order to breathe, to enlarge my space, to meet brothers and sisters, to practise a new kind of freedom. [27]

Human beings are not looking for just anything but for the absolute, even when they believe they are turning away from it, or when they unknowingly repress it in a search for material things. Every passion is an arrow aimed at the other shore. Literature speaks of the passionate experience of those purified in the fire of consciousness and risen from death. It is an interior demand, a movement of the body, emerging from the hand more than the head. Ideas, even when they are about the future and about eternity, speak only of death. Literature – at least when it tries to avoid complacency – is able to capture everything that rises. The only kind of writing that interests me is one that opens up on the impossible and the unknown. Such is my way.

It is only one way. According to it, to read, as well as to write, is to emigrate.

School and society as a whole fail to teach us how to read. They teach us to hold on and grab. Reading is completely pointless if it doesn't teach us to understand life, especially the burning passion of life itself. Of course, in order to read it is necessary to have roots, to experience in oneself the earth's heartbeat, but to read is also to reach out. Books that answer the need for nostalgia or merely offer knowledge can be read only with the intention of staying put. The Gospel, however, plunges us into the openness of the instant. It is the book of rebellion. To read it is to be born elsewhere.

Sometimes the word is indirect. It speaks of what is on the edges of reality in order to make those who listen aware of themselves. What is deep within us is beyond speech and can sustain itself only in obscurity, linked to an image, to the idea in its original state of excitement. Besides, to speak of what's deep down as against what's external no longer has meaning. The Word puts us in a state of grace, receptive to a discovery that will be unique each time, never definitive. It is always beginning. [27-28]

The warrior of the spirit, who knows that meaning is always in a state of suspense, expresses himself through paradox, humor and parable. When, through fear of solitude or because of a flabby notion of charity, he comes to adopt the language of the tribe – a language which inevitably aims at permanence – his betrayal is greatest at the moment he is most applauded. If he refuses to take the broad and illusory path of 'communication' it is because our everyday wisdom, with its lazy language of adaptation, offends him. He pierces our sleepy consciences and becomes in turn ironic, enigmatic, a killjoy. People start calling him paradoxical, destructive, or even crazy. [29]

I write every morning at daybreak. If language weren't so inadequate, I would have run out of things to say. But the Word never fails God, even though the very last words on the cross are words of abandonment.

How I'd like, for once, to make a book out of trees, water, roads, skyscrapers, crazy love, and poor people who march in the night, and let the Word speak for itself. The invisible in the visible, the absolute in the tangible, nothing else. Instead, it will seem that I'm trying to philosophize. If you only knew how little I cared about abstract syntheses and ideologies! But I promised to show you my way. It's one approach. *Andiamo.*

Every morning I write for you while the trucks roll into the city. If I wrote at noon or evening, moderation, that daughter of fatigue and fear, would guide my hand with a deadly sweetness. I have decided to place my confidence in the youth of morning. When we will no longer have anything but a small plot of earth to grow dandelions, there will still be mornings with their violent hopes. Everything is a beginning. I'm not trying very hard to pick up loose threads for fear that what I've already written should take over for me. Don't ask whether I'm repeating myself. I'm speaking about love. Don't look for order. Or look for order in yourself, in the heart of the source. But be suspicious of the order that passes directly into your head and to which you readily submit. Interior unity is infinitely stronger and more real than one born of logic and stylistic processes. Let the single dream of your life be to wake yourself up. Don't be stiff-necked, or I'll be forced to turn teacher and give you formulas. [85]

I've always had two kinds of readers. Some are primarily concerned with subject matter and are asonished or scandalized by the somber stories that my books seem to present in colloquial, irreverent language. They are often the same people who were impressed by my first books, which were more nostalgic. And there are others, who read me with their lips, who breathe in unison with me, and tell me that I help them survive.

In my desire to be brief I haven't told the whole truth about how I got into literature. Because of the admiration I had for the writers for *Nouvelle Revue Française* in its great days, I took up writing with the intention of composing beautifully polished novels or essays, of creating complex, lively cultural objects for contemplation, in which the writer pretends to be absent. Mirrors. An elegant and lofty aestheticism – something that could be read with one's eyes, composed for the pleasure of a detached intelligence. And in the background as motivation, the stupid idea of glory and posterity that school and TV puts in the hearts of French boys and girls. To speak, some day, from that pedestal.

With so many images and ideas in my skull I apply myself to be like the great writers I admired. I have a little success, begin to get recognition, even win a few prizes. I keep going. The polished objects crack, my fine passages get all mixed up, living faces begin to obsess me, and a word emerges that breaks the harmony. Imagination seemed like child's play, a pathetic entertainment for fashionable women. My vanity survived but my hope of glory was destroyed. The concern for posterity is a false lure, a terrible absence. It's here, now, that glory exists, in this tiny fragment, each instant of life, death, and resurrection.

Where does the word come from? That's not my problem. I trust it. That's what I've tried to say.

From the start I feel close to all those whom society has marginalized – tramps, addicts, freaks, even 'establishment' types, empty of spiritual substance and beginning to realize it. They live in the midst of steel, glass high-rises, highways that have become cemeteries, sex shops, and the rubble of human failure. But at the same time I notice with amazement that a song of freedom flows through everything, a paradoxical joy more powerful than my pain and mediocrity, the hope which those who bear it within them say they recognize.

What is surprising is that when I first began to write, skeptical and anxious to imitate others, believers in general applauded me. Now that hope plays her music in me, carelessly mingling with an existence that is simultaneously horrifying and wonderful, some believers just switch off.

Precisely because the word is immemorial and timeless, it can only be expressed in the instant. To remain in a dream of the past or the realm of ideas is to compromise with death. Since the absolute has become incarnate, how can one not be present at each moment of time, with its particular style, in the uncertain, irrational and painful flux of life, as well as in the bright lights of cities and in every human creation, in order to reveal that perhaps there are cells of purity even in the midst of Vanity Fair and that all things conspire toward unity and joy? Not to be contemporary leads inevitably to betrayal. [99-100]

And what about artists or writers? Because they have insufficiently shed the child within the adult, they try to rediscover the original impact of things by going beyond the dead text to connect up again with living gestures. They make use of words while exorcising them, they rid them of sedimentation, and turn them against themselves in order to break convention. In spite of the pressures of habit and mental laziness they give expression to a unique encounter. Their writing is simultaneously word. In such writing individual words have flesh, a face of their own, they tremble with every movement of the body. To be read is to be eaten. The best reader is the one who transforms the work totally into herself, enjoying her own music.

In the spiritual order there are no professors, only discoverers who reveal to others while they gradually renew themselves. They're the ones whom we try to re-enact within ourselves, who start us on our way without even wanting to. They hold no worldly authority; their only authority is that of *authors* – that is, those who engender, nourish and increase life. Not people who know how to manipulate others. [144]

# Truth and Ficton[1]

## SIGRID UNDSET

On the face of things, it would seem that for a writer of fiction at least it might be impractical to follow the maxim that an old Norwegian farmer's wife once handed out to me, as the principle on which she had been brought up and in her turn had brought up a large family of fine men and women: 'Never tell a lie. And don't tell a truth, unless it's necessary.'

It is a principle that has worked out very well in our peasant communities. It makes for honesty and courtesy. It makes people develop an agreeable art of conversation about the weather and the crops and the facts of your neighbors' life that are known to everybody already. It prevents people from talking too much. I have found it developed to perfection among Englishmen. And recently, here in America, I have had the privilege of meeting some quite charming New Englanders, who also practise the same principle. They were so kind, but so very reticent, I felt almost as if I were among my own people again.

After all, I think the maxim of old Gurø Dalsbøe is a very good principle to live after, even for the writer of fiction. That is, if the writer of fiction wants to be a creator of living art. Of course the very word 'fiction' is rather equivocal, like so many words in our present-day vocabulary, which has suffered from generations of loose thinking and the abuse of catch-words. So you often meet the word used as if fiction were the opposite of facts. Some kinds of fiction are, of course. But even that kind of fiction need not necessarily be the opposite of truth. Facts must be true, but they are not truths, just as wooden boxes or fencepoles or doors or tables are not woods, the society of living growing trees from which come the wooden implements.

Practical people may handle facts without knowing the truths they stem from, as a baby may sit in his high chair and enjoy his meal of porridge without knowing a thing about the tree from which his chair was fashioned, or the wheatfield and the cow that were the sources of his meal. Of course, we hope that Baby may live to experience the delightful meeting with woods and wheatfields and cows. And we may hope that the practical people who handle facts may some day make acquaintance, at least with some of the truths that facts stem from. And true fiction, if you see what I mean by that, must necessarily handle facts, but its chief concern must be with the truths behind the facts – the wild mountains from where the tame stories of the pavement and the cultured stone of statuary were quarried, the living woods which yielded the material for lumber mills and carpenter shops and pulp for the million

1    From *America*, 67, 1942.

tons of paper we use or abuse. The facts then become things of secondary importance to the writer, even if they are things of primary importance in practical life. Nevertheless, they are not origins; they originate from something.

To the Catholic writer the whole world of facts and truths behind the facts will appear in relation to the Ultimate Origin from which everything emanates – the mountains from which stones are quarried and ores are mined, the woods that give us timber and blueberries, the jungle of civilized or uncivilized life, where human beings roam or flutter and sometimes remember, and sometimes forget, and as often as not do violence to themselves and others in a futile attempt to deny that man was created in the Image of God, and to shake off the dreadful responsibility which is implied in the idea, that whatever you do may have consequences in all eternity.

We know that everything in this world, things animate and inanimate, are ultimately dependent on God. I do not mean that we always think of it – nobody ever could manage to think always of more than a fraction of the things he knows. But I hope, to all Catholics, it is always the submerged knowledge that prevents us from certain aberrations of thinking, as the submerged knowledge that the sea is deep and cold and very wet prevents us from turning to the right or to the left when we have to board a ship by way of a narrow gangplank. We do not consciously think how very unpleasant it would be to tumble over, but we walk straight all the same.

After all, I think the advice of my old countrywoman is very good advice for writers of fiction, too. Never tell a lie. And just tell the truths you have to. In fact, a writer – one who has a genuine urge to express himself in writing – may perhaps be described as a person who has got to tell truths more often, and to tell more truths than the bulk of the people, who may get along very well when they stick to the facts of everyday life, cultivate kindness and reticence, never tell lies, and tackle the truths behind the facts only on the rare occasions when they have to do it.

But remember, never tell a lie. Not even the lies of kindness, the lies to black out hideous or painful or discouraging truths. They are the kind of lies that represent the greatest temptation to people of good will, and they are certainly not so morally revolting, maybe they are less sinful too, than lies told for coarsely selfish reasons, reasons of greed and concupiscence. At least, I hope they are less sinful, for I shudder when I think of how often I have told that kind of lie, and still oftener have I thought them and tried to kid myself into believing them, even if I don't think I have committed them to writing very often.

But they grow upon you; you get into the habit of resorting to them, oftener and oftener. To perpetuate them in writing – I should say, try to perpetuate them – is usually very damaging to a work of fiction, for most readers find out, as soon as the interest of novelty has passed, if a story is untrue, untruthful. Don't you know all these stories about a spectacular conversion of a hardened sinner, by Catholic authors as well as, or even more frequently than by authors of the other Christian denominations? The conversion of a hard-ened sinner is such a tremendous miracle, what with God being Almighty, and the sinner yet having his free will, that I think very few writers of fiction are able to deal adequately with such a wonderful topic. I would say, let us leave it to the theologians – and don't expect all of them either to write well or clear-ly about it. Another thing: religious vocations are not too common anywhere, except among the characters of some Catholic writers of fiction, and their sto-ries are not always quite convincing.

And tell the truths you have to. Even if they are grim, preposterous, shock-ing. After all, we Catholics ought to acknowledge what a shocking business human life is. Our race has been revolting against its Creator since the begin-ning of time. Revolt, betrayal, denial, or indifference, sloth, laziness – which of us has not been guilty in one or more or all of these sins some time or other? But remember, you have to tell other and more cheering truths, too: of the Grace of God and the endeavor of strong and loyal, or weak but trusting souls, and also of the natural virtues of man created in the Image of God, and image it is very hard to efface entirely. Even in the times of genuine paganism, in the times before the Incarnation of Our Saviour, when mankind in perfectly good faith wove their creeds and myths about the Divinity they were aware of, and the Powers they sensed behind the pageantry of spring and summer and autumn and winter, behind the procession of living things from the womb of the mother to the grave, through health and illness, passions noble and evil, through joys and griefs – even in those times the hands that fumbled honestly for the truths of the Beyond succeeded in touching them, as was afterwards revealed in the daylight of Our Lord.

It is true, that the old heathen had also discovered the presence of the Devil, pure and personal Evil, and that many of them worshipped him through witches and wizards and magicians, in the hope that one might strike a bargain with the lower powers, while the higher, the good ones, would be less easy for man to understand or come to terms with. The worship of devils had already had a long history, when a group of Germans decided to dedicate themselves to the Power who encourages men to murder, treason, cruelty and wallowing in all kinds of moral filth, offering them in return Overlordship on Earth, and the accumulated riches of generations of other people's honest labor.

But it is equally true, that even in Pagan times, wherever men believed in Supernatural powers who were on the side of honesty, uprightness, justice, who sometimes even encouraged mercy and forbearance, and more often than not were considered the wardens of family loyalty and filial piety, those who lived these beliefs forged treasures of beauty and moral grandeur that have come down to us through the ages. And it is an interesting thing to notice how these heathen people, after their conversion to Christianity, when they tried to live up to their new faith and love their neighbors as themselves (they did it very imperfectly, of course, just as we do) how they then always tried to foster and partake with their fellowmen the things they had considered the best in life, since old heathen times. The expansion of freedom and personal liberty among ever widening layers of the population among the British and Scandinavian people, the creation of new and gorgeous Church festivals and times of merrymaking in the Latin nations, the conversion of tribal mysticism into the mysticism of the Saints among the Germans of the Middle Ages, are such fruits of the Faith among people, who had loved freedom or festivals, or mysticism, from the beginning of their histories.

We Catholics have the wellspring of Truth to draw from, and we are the heirs to the accumulated truths of pre-Christian ages. To us, it should not be fiction *versus* facts, but fiction should relate facts to truths, through knowledge, imagination, intuition and conscientious work. It should really be our rule, never to tell lies, and to tell the truths that must be told – the truths we need not tell should always be implicit behind our work.

*On Individual Writers and Their Works*

# Introduction to Newman's *Callista*[1]

## ALFRED DUGGAN

A great many historical romances have been written about the early Christians, and most of them follow a well-beaten path. And experienced reader of fiction will recognize it. There will be a beautiful maiden, as virtuous as she is fair; she is either a Christian or well on the way to conversion. She falls in love with a sturdy, manly fellow-Christian. In the background, as light relief, is a worthy member of the Church who cannot always keep all the Commandments, a strong man who seldom turns the other cheek but makes a useful bodyguard in a time of crisis. Even farther in the background are the famous saints and martyrs, who cannot be ignored but whose fate would mar the tone of the happy ending. From the tinsel of *Quo Vadis* to the infidel wit of *Androcles and the Lion* the pattern is familiar.

Newman chose to follow the same pattern. Callista is the usual virtuous Christian maiden, Agellius the usual sound homespun Christian hero, his brother Juba the usual Christianized average sensual man. But from these customary ingredients Newman made something quite extraordinary.

In my time I must have read some hundreds of historical romances, and *Callista* does not remind me of any of them. It is unique, like the mind that composed it: unique, astringent, remorseless, unforgettable.

Before yielding to its fascination the reader must overcome certain obstacles. One of these is the language in which it is told. For this experiment in what he may have considered a frivolous type of literature Newman, who was born in 1801, employed the language of his undergraduate days, not of the 1850s in which it was written. Contrast it with the contemporary prose of Macaulay, and note its archaism. The language is undoubtedly a barrier.

Yet the language of the Romantic Revival, though strange to us, was an accurate and learned tongue. Newman used it accurately. Every word means what it says, and is employed in its normal dictionary meaning. It may not be what we expect, but we have no difficulty in construing it. Presently we no longer construe it into modern English; we begin to think in it, as a foreigner learning French or Spanish at last begins to think in the alien tongue, instead of translating in his head what he wishes to say. By this time we can appreciate the accuracy and versatility of the author.

At first the dialogue in particular may seem literary and stilted. The author is determined to show forth a point of view with complete accuracy, and his characters choose their words as no one ever does in normal conversation. But there is a possibility that one character at least is drawn vividly from the life. It may very well be that in Juba's tirade in Chapter IV we hear the voice of some

---

1    From Cardinal Newman, *Callista* (1855), London, Universe Books, 1962.

daredevil Fellow who long ago disturbed the Senior Common Room of Oriel; there are traces of colloquial expressions as they might be rendered from memory by a man who had never himself employed slang to make his meaning clear.

It is important to bear in mind Newman's aim in writing this novel. In the first 'Advertisement' of 1855 he says that it is written 'from a Catholic point of view'. By 1988 he underlines this: *Callista* is 'specially addressed to Catholic readers, and for their edification.' He is not trying to convert the heathen, or to bring heretics to acknowledge the jurisdiction of the Pope. He is trying to recall to the minds of fellow-Catholics a picture of the Church as it was in the third century, and to teach them how they should behave in time of persecution.

Throughout the work there is an obvious element of autobiography. Young Agellius attempting to practise his religion alone, without the Sacraments, without counsel or advice, without human encouragement, must be Newman himself at some stage of his career. The arrival of Bishop Caecilius and the comfort of his presence is another obvious parallel. But the clearest element of personal experience must be the arguments put in the mouths of the heathen.

They are absurdly weak arguments to address to a rational man, and they must have infuriated Newman when he heard them advanced in favour of the Anglican establishment. But we may be sure he heard them, for sometimes they are still to be heard. There is first the argument of patriotism. Will you forsake the faith of your ancestors, the faith of your contemporaries, the faith which was held when your country became great? Will you set yourself up as the only wise man in a community devoted to the search for wisdom? You must be devoured by pride if you think you are the only one in step. That is Newman at Oxford, just as much as it is Agellius listening to his guardian. The appeal to Roman greatness answers the appeal to the greatness of England under Pitt and Wellington. In other words, it is the duty of a patriot to be wrong, if his fellow-countrymen are wrong.

The second argument is the argument of Indifferentism. Do your duty by your fatherland and your neighbours; live honestly and keep your contracts; leave this world a little better than you found it, and don't promote discord by too curious speculation concerning the next; there are many good pagans and many bad Christians; conduct is more important than religious belief. Combined with this is the appeal to a reasonable happiness. Enjoy yourself in this life, without doing demonstrable harm; since the very existence of a future life is most doubtful.

This combined appeal to selfishness and self-respect is always with us.

Curiously enough, Newman never mentions the most powerful argument for paganism. A Stoic might say: 'We also worship one supreme Creator. We also teach the Brotherhood of Man. We regulate our lives by a moral code as high as yours. But we are excused from believing that unlikely story about a man who was God, and came to life after being dead.' It was the argument which in fact carried most weight in the fourth century, but perhaps in the reign of Decius it had not yet been elaborated; or perhaps Newman considered that the little provincial market town of Sicca would not contain educated and humane philosophers.

The book was written to tell us – us Catholics and not the unbelievers – what the Church was like in the third century. The picture is not entirely what we might expect.

The first shock comes as early as Chapter II. We would suppose that a convert would be encouraged to remain faithful to his wife. Not at all, says Newman; if she practises magic it will be the duty of a Christian husband to get rid of her. Whether he would then be free to marry again is not stated. Strabo did not.

Note also that Agellius the virtuous Christian owns an aged Christian slave. Presumably it would have been a meritorious work of charity to free him; but it was not an imperative duty. The ownership of slaves is normally a dangerous temptation to cruelty and oppression, but it is not wrong in itself. That is quite out of step with the sentiment of the nineteenth century, and indeed of the twentieth. Newman was never influenced by contemporary opinion.

If we read *Callista* carefully we get a deep insight into his extraordinary mind, all the more startling because the revelation is unconscious. When Agellius is sick he is comforted by the knowledge that the stranger who nurses him is, not merely a fellow-Christian (that we might expect), but a 'Christian ecclesiastic.' Only Newman would value so highly the Sacrament of Holy Order. Yet he is perfectly aware that even bishops and priests may fall away from the Faith. In this account of the dwindling of the Church in Sicca he fairly rubs our noses in the disagreeable truth.

Newman is no democrat. The lower orders, if pagan, are unmitigated scoundrels, idle ruffians whose chief pleasure is plunder and destruction. It is taken for granted that the owners of property will hate and fear them, and will rejoice at the opportunity to massacre their enemies with the full sanction of the law. In Sicca there are no honest citizen cobblers, in the surrounding countryside no industrious respectable yeomen.

But to a modern reader the chief novelty is his picture of paganism. Consider the village festival described in Chapter XXIV. Imagine how Poussin would have painted it, and recall that Poussin was a devout Catholic. We can see the tall herm, topped by a merry bearded face, the leafy trees which bound the smooth greensward, the pretty little garlanded lamb, the sturdy rustics, their limbs glowing with health, who caper in an innocent country dance – all under a golden sun. The scene breathes innocent, unsophisticated merriment.

What Newman sees is 'the hideous brutal god, with yawning mouth, horned head, and Goat's feet', presiding over a scene of slaughter which will presently develop into an orgy. Human nature in the raw must always be fallen human nature.

In the same way, the outward signs of paganism must always seem shocking to a Christian. When Agellius visits Sicca he is nauseated by sight of the pagan temples, where we might feel only an innocent archaeological curiosity. As regards the general run of humanity this seems to be a fault of observation. Surely a Catholic who lives near a Hindu temple decorated with phallic sculpture, and must pass it every time he goes into town, will presently grow accustomed to the impudicity and pass it without a second glance? But to Newman himself the shock would never weaken, and he gave the same characteristic to his hero.

The main theme of this remorseless book is an exploration of the duty of Catholics in time of persecution. The harsh outlines are never softened to accommodate a timid reader. *Extra Ecclesia nulla salus.* With the fate of the heathen we need not concern ourselves. The wretched Christian who was driven by fear to worship the ass was lynched all the same, and went straight to hell; the Tertullianist heretic who provoked his persecutors was in little better case. Bishop Caecilius may hide, to preserve the Apostolic Succession; any condemned Christian may escape from prison if he can, for he has already borne witness to the Faith. But in the ordinary way martyrdom is neither to be sought nor to be avoided. It is to be endured, without complaint.

The full rigour of Divine Justice is deployed before us. It was God's plan that the people of Sicca should be afflicted with locusts, and they ought to have acknowledged His Justice. Cases of diabolic possession figure in the Gospels; therefore a witch may send a devil into a man, and later the man may be healed by a qualified exorcist. Callista was a successful sculptor, carving images of the Olympian gods as did many Catholic sculptors of the Renaissance; but as soon as she has been converted she is disgusted by her loathsome trade. The only happy ending imaginable to the author is entry into Heaven; Callista is duly tortured to death, and her sufferings are related with a clarity unusual in a novel of the period, when authors so often took refuge in talk about 'nameless horrors' and similar evasions.

I have already described this book as remorseless. Well, thinking about the Four Last Things is not very pleasant, but we all ought to do it. Newman wrote for those who shared his Faith; and our Faith, though it brings comfort, has its frightening side. To read *Callista* will put the fear of God into you, and that is not a bad thing. It is not a book that anyone can easily forget, though the memory of it may sometimes bring nightmare.

# Shusaku Endo: Japanese Catholic Novelist[1]

## FRANCIS MATHY

Shusaku Endo's latest novel *Scandal* (1986) begins with Suguro, the hero of a number of Endo's semi-autobiographical novels and stories, about to receive still another literary prize. As he listens to a fellow novelist make the presentation speech, Suguro, now in his late sixties, reflects with great satisfaction upon his long career as a novelist. He feels that with this latest novel everything he had been aiming at all through the years has been achieved. His life and his writing have at last reached a point of harmony.

Now entering his sixty-fifth year, Endo himself must be feeling a similar satisfaction. In the first place, he has been by any standards an eminently successful writer. He has written over thirty full-length novels, even more books of non-fiction, including several biographies, over a hundred short stories, a handful of plays, and newspaper and magazine articles too numerous to count. And he has been richly recompensed for his work. His books have sold well and many of them have gone through many editions. A large number of his novels and stories have been made into movies and television dramas. Being shown in Japanese movie theatres at this moment is the movie made from one of his earliest novels, *The Sea and Poison,* which the movie critic for one of the Tokyo English newspapers called 'the most powerful Japanese film of the year (1986) – indeed, for considerably longer'.

Endo has also been rewarded by critical success. His very first novel, *White Man,* received the coveted Akutagawa Prize, a prize for new writing that has often launched its recipients on to successful writing careers, and since then he has received many additional literary prizes. He is currently president of the Japan PEN Club and is even considered by many to be the writer most likely to receive a Nobel Prize in literature, should the Nobel committee train its sights upon Japan again in the near future.

Abroad too his reputation is steadily growing. Beginning with the English translation of *Silence* in 1969, a number of his works have been made available in English: *The Golden Country* (1970), *The Sea and Poison* (1972), *Wonderful Fool* (1974), *A Life of Jesus* (1978), *Volcano* (1978), *When I Whistle* (1979), and most recently *Samurai* (1982) and *Stained Glass Elegies* (1984). The latter two are now available in Penguin Books.

The novelist mentioned in the first paragraph begins his presentation speech by referring to Suguro's uniqueness in being a Christian writer in a country like Japan, whose cultural climate is so resistant to theological thought. 'From the first, Suguro agonized over how to get Japanese, who had no ears for it, to listen

1   From *The Month,* May 1987.

to the story he most wanted to tell – the story of God.'[2] Suguro wrote a number of stories based on materials from early Japanese Christianity: he dramatized the pitiful lot of the Christians as they were mercilessly pressed to abandon their Faith. For thirty years his constant theme has been: how can Christianity, a foreign import, be made to harmonize with the climate of Japan?

For the speaker, Suguro's most laudable quality has been that he has never sacrificed literature for religion. He has not made literature religion's handmaid. 'As a writer, he was continued to probe those ugly, unpleasant, even hateful parts of man that his Faith must condemn. He has been able to discover meaning and value in what he calls 'sin'. In every sin, he demonstrates, is to be found a hidden longing for life, a yearning to find a path out of the suffocating air of the world as it is today. It is here that the uniqueness of Suguro's literature is to be found'.

The above is undoubtedly Endo's own estimate of himself and his works. He considers himself a Catholic writer in the tradition of François Mauriac and Graham Greene, to both of whom he acknowledges a great debt of gratitude. (On a recent ten-day visit to London he spent most of his time wandering about the streets of the city, *The End of the Affair* in hand, retracing the steps of Sarah, and even a casual reading of *Silence* will reveal the great influence of *The Power and the Glory*. No wonder Greene has called Endo one of the greatest living novelists.)

Shusaku Endo was born in Tokyo in 1923 but spent his early years in Dairen in Manchuria. When his mother and father separated, Shusaku went with his mother to live in the house of a Catholic aunt in Kobe. There under the aunt's influence, Mrs Endo soon became a Catholic herself and also had her ten-year old son instructed and baptized. In university Endo majored in French literature and became especially interested in the works of twentieth-century French Catholic novelists. As one of the first post-war students to go abroad for study, Endo was able to pursue this interest further at the University of Lyons. Illness forced him to interrupt his studies and return to Japan, but it was while he was in France that he decided to become a writer. He already had in mind the plot of *White Man,* which was to initiate his career as a novelist. This novel, as mentioned above, won him the Akutagawa Prize and he began work immediately on his second novel, *Yellow Man.* Other works followed in quick succession. But his career was interrupted for several years while he battled with tuberculosis. He underwent a series of operations and had a close brush with death. It was after his recovery that he wrote his first short story that made use of early Japanese Christian materials, 'Unzen', and followed this up with the novel *Silence* and the play *The Golden Country.*

To understand what Endo was trying to do in *Silence,* and, in fact, in most of his work, it is necessary to take a closer look at his early experiences in Kobe and France and to see how the writer was shaped by them. Endo's bap-

2    Translation of Endo, unless noted, are my own.

tism, like that of Suguro in 'My Belongings' in *Stained Glass Elegies,* had been a
mere formality. As he has stated on several occasions, he soon became aware
that, in being baptized, he had been attired in a Western-style suit that did not
fit him and which he had not chosen. While in his teens, he had tried again to
get out of it, but always unsuccessfully. Finally, he had decided to restyle it into
a Japanese kimono more to his taste.

While in France, he became even more aware of how alien Western
Christianity was to his Japanese temperament. In an early essay, he maintained
that the Japanese are insensitive to God, sin, and death, and he wondered how
it is possible to make Christians of a people who dislike extreme ways of
thinking about evil and sin and who are totally indifferent to the question of
the existence of God. Japan, he averred, is a moral 'mudswamp', a metaphor
which was to pervade his works. When Fr Ferreira, the apostate priest in
*Silence,* is trying to convince a young confrere to apostatize, he tells him that
Japan is a mudswamp, that the Faith could never take root there. The seeds that
are planted may germinate and grow, but soon the roots begin to rot and the
leaves to turn yellow and wither. A Japanese official tells Ferreira, in *The
Golden Country,* that he has been conquered by 'mudswamp Japan'. 'The
Christian teachings', he adds, 'are like a flame and will set a man on fire. But
the tepid warmth of Japan nurtures sleep'. Almost all of Endo's novels are concerned with this 'mudswamp Japan', and several of them contrast the tepid
warmth of the mudswamp with the penetrating flame of Christianity. It is no
exaggeration to say that one of the main concerns of his novels has been to
show that there can be salvation also for the denizens of the mudswamp.

But the symbol of the mudswamp does not derive solely from Endo's speculative ruminations on the differences between East and West. It has more personal roots. Endo's mother could by no stretch of the imagination be
considered a 'mudswamp' character. She was made of the stuff that saints are
made of. A woman of strong will and passion, she threw herself with great
energy into whatever she undertook. She began her life as a convert with this
same passion.

A slightly fictionalized but generally accurate account of those early days in
Kobe is given in Endo's short story 'The Shadow Figure'. In her great desire
for sanctity the boy's mother places herself under the direction of a young
Spanish (in reality, German) priest of very much the same passionate temperament as herself. Learned, handsome, well-groomed, and with a very attractive
personality, this priest soon becomes a powerful influence in the boy's home.
'Like a nun', the narrator writes, 'she imposed on herself and on me a life of
strict prayer. Every morning she took me to Mass and whenever she had time
she said the rosary. She even began to act as if she were thinking of bringing
me up to be a priest like you'.[3] (In fact, Endo has written somewhere that

3   *Japan Quarterly* (Tokyo, Asahi Shimbun), Vol. XXXI, No. 3 (1984) pp. 169 (transla-
    tion by Thomas Lally, Yumiko Oka and Dennis J. Doodlin.)

when he was a middle-school student he did for a time consider becoming a priest.)

The priest would come to the boy's home once a week and his mother would gather people of the neighbourhood to listen to his stimulating talks. The boy found these soirées boring and even painful. But more painful to him was the discipline that this priest began to demand of him. He was getting poor grades at school. (Endo writes that he himself began middle school in the top A class and fell one class each year until he wound up in D and graduated 116th in a class of 118). The priest, by way of imposing discipline on the boy, had his mother get rid of his beloved dog, who was for him the only being who could share a boy's inexpressible loneliness.

> It was typical of you to act that way. Weakness, laziness, sloveniness – you hated these things more than anything. A man should grow strong. He has to make efforts. He has to train himself both in life and faith. You never said that in so many words, but you put it into practice in your daily life. Everybody noticed how zealously you carried out your mission work and how earnestly you devoted yourself to theological study. You were above reproach. Everyone (just like my mother) respected your noble character. I alone, mere child that I was, began to be irked by your irreproachableness ... I could not conform physically to your ideal of life. I do not try now to excuse myself for those days. All I want to say is that your kindness and enthusiasm brought good results to the strong but were harsh on the weak, and at times meaninglessly inflicted suffering on them.[4]

A sickly boy, ungifted in studies, Shusaku could not but realize the tremendous gap that separates the naturally strong, like his mother and the priest, from the naturally weak. If as he grew older he had given up his Faith completely and accommodated himself to an easier life, it would not have been strange. In a magazine interview Endo once stated:

> There were many times when I felt I wanted to get rid of my Catholicism, but I was finally unable to do so ... The reason for this must be that it had become a part of me after all ... Still, there was always that feeling in my heart that it was something borrowed, and I began to wonder what my real self was like. This I think is the 'mudswamp' Japanese in me. From the time I first began to write novels even to the present day, this confrontation of my Catholic self with the self that lies underneath has echoed and reechoed in my work. I have felt that I had to find some way to reconcile the two.

4    *Ibid.*, pp. 169-70.

But this was not the only reconciliation that had to take place. Endo seems to have had a love-hate relationship with his mother's confessor. The man had become a kind of a father to him. When, after graduation from college, Endo did not immediately find a job, the priest took both Shusaku and his brother to help out with his new work as editor of the Japanese edition of *Catholic Digest*. So it must have been a great shock to Endo when this very strong priest, a veritable avatar of God the Father, left the priesthood and religious life and married a Japanese woman. How could such strength and such weakness in the same person be reconciled?

Endo's speculative concerns about the distance that separates East from West, and his more personal concerns outlined above, are at the heart of two of his early novels, *Yellow Man* and *Volcano*. In both, the moral apathy of the Japanese characters is contrasted with the ferocious struggle between good and evil that takes place in the spirit of a foreign priest, who eventually loses the struggle and gets involved with a Japanese woman. *The Sea and Poison* is also about the Japanese mudswamp: the moral apathy of a group of doctors and nurses who conduct fatal medical experiments on captured American airmen during the war. But it was when Endo began to do research on early Christianity in Japan that he came across material exactly suited to his purpose.

Endo admits frankly that from the first he was not interested in the kind of Christians who held firm to their beliefs and convictions and refused to apostatize. 'My concern lay rather with the weaklings who compromised their convictions and stepped *fumi-e* because they were forced to do so'. Still more exactly to his purpose was the strong man Jesuit Provincial Christopher Ferreira, who had not only given up his Faith and married a Japanese woman, but who had also helped the persecutors in their attempt to stamp out Christianity. From this material Endo fashioned the novel *Silence* and the play *The Golden Country*. In stepping on the face of Christ, thereby apostatizing, both Ferreira (in the play) and his younger confrere Fr Roderigo (in the novel) discover a new and different Christ, an Oriental Christ, who understands their pain in sinning and continues to love them all the same. By stepping on the *fumi-e* Western priests become naturalized citizens of the Japanese mudswamp and all are saved by the all-understanding love of Christ. This, Endo seems to hope, is a Christianity that the Japanese will be able to understand and accept.

Catholics in Japan were greatly offended by the novel, not so much by the unorthodoxy of the climax, in which Christ himself urges the priest to go ahead and sin, assuring him that he understands his pain in stepping upon the face of the one who is dearest to him, but rather in the fact that the writer completely falsified history in warping it to his theme.

The missionary enterprise in sixteenth- and seventeenth-century Japan was one the Church has a right to be proud of. In less than a century as many as 700,000 Japanese (out of a total population of only twenty million) from all strata of society became Christians, and their faith was strong enough to support an estimated fifty to sixty thousand in their choice of martyrdom over apostasy.[5] It had also been strong enough to preserve itself in hidden settlements until the end of the 19th century when the missionaries returned to Japan. Endo, with no historical basis and solely for the purposes of his theme, suggested that this early Christianity had not been a true Christianity but an Oriental deflection from it. 'The God the Japanese pray to in our churches is not the Christian God, but a god of their own making', asserts Ferreira. 'Our God, when he came to Japan, like a butterfly caught in a spider's web, retained only the external form of God but lost his true reality and became a lifeless corpse'.

In proposing his solution to the seeming incompatibility of Western Christianity and the Japanese sensibility, Endo became an elitist in reverse. It is the weak and sinful that have first crack at salvation – not, it is to be noted, the sinner who repents of his sin and attempts to do better, but rather the one who continues to sin but feels pain in doing so. These are able to reach a high level of love. The priest in *Silence,* after stepping on the *fumi-e,* reflects that he loves Christ now in a completely different way from before. 'To come to know this love, everything that has taken place was necessary'. In short, sin born out of love leads to a higher sanctity.

It is not surprising that Endo should next have attempted a life of Jesus, depicting a Saviour who is completely powerless except to love, one who could work no miracles but continued to love. Perhaps to emphasize the overwhelming degree of Jesus' love, he involves all the apostles in Judas' betrayal: they are all equally guilty. But Jesus forgives and continues to love them. The final image of Jesus that emerges from the book is that of a joyless man with tired and sunken eyes, but eyes that overflow wiith love more profound than a miracle, even toward those who had deserted and betrayed him. Not a word of resentment passes his lips as he gazes with sadness at those who have hurt him.

One Japanese critic reviewing *Silence* had written that the face of Jesus on the *fumi-e* 'is the mother's face in Japan. I know nothing of Mr Endo's personal experience with his mother, but their relationship is depicted in Jesus's face on the *fumi-e'.*[6] This was a very shrewd observation. All the sadness Endo felt at having disappointed his mother (perhaps he even felt it a kind of betrayal), and the sad love she had continued to show toward him, found expression in his portrayal of Christ.

5 These statistics were given me by Fr Hubert Cieslik, SJ, an authority on the Christian period in Japan and the teacher to whom Endo went for information about the early Christians.
6 Quoted by Endo himself in his essay 'The Anguish of an Alien'. Cf. Vol. XI, No. 4 (Fall 1974) of the *Japan Christian Quarterly,* p. 181. Endo acknowledges there the truth of the critic's observation.

Further confirmation of this identification of Christ with mother is to be found in Endo's short story 'Mothers'. Visiting an island where there is a village of hidden Christians not yet reunited with the Church, the writer-narrator, who is never given a name, has a dream of his mother. He is surprised that twenty years after her death she should still appear so vividly in his dreams. He recalls how often he disappointed her, especially after he stopped going to church even on Sunday. One day after such a disappointment, 'she said not a word, but only looked at me. I watched her face slowly collapse and tears fall down her cheeks'. Until late that night, he could hear her sobbing in her room. He recalls with great sadness that even on the day of her death, at the very moment of her dying, he was engaged in an act that he is now heartily ashamed of.

When he meets the hidden Christians and is shown the ancient painting of Mary which they venerate, he recalls his mother's statue of the Sorrowful Mother. He had kept the statue with him in his hospital room. It has been greatly damaged in an air raid and 'the face looked sad and seemed to be staring at me ... The bombing and the passage of time had cracked the face and disfigured the nose so all that seemed to remain was the expression of sadness'. At some time or other he had come 'to associate the expression on my mother's face when she came to me in a dream with that of the statue'.

At the end of the story, the narrator feels that the hidden Christians, who had been able to hold on to their religion only by stepping each year on the *fumi-e,* are in the same condition of heart as he is. Near the end of the story is this telling paragraph:

> The missionaries long ago brought to this country the teaching of a Father God. But in the course of time, after the missionaries had been driven out and the churches destroyed, the hidden Christians gradually threw over all the elements of the religion that didn't suit them, replacing them with what is most essential in all Japanese religion, devotion to Mother. At that moment I thought of my own mother. She seemed to be standing beside me, a grey shadow. She was not playing the violin nor was she praying the rosary. She stood there hands folded, looking at me with sorrowful eyes.

Thus Christ, for Endo, in his tender, all-forgiving love for men is more mother than father. The weakest and most vicious dwellers in the mudswamp are ever looked upon by the loving eyes of Christ. He will never desert them, even while they are committing their crimes. It is the maternal love of Christ that makes it possible for even a Japanese to be a Christian, that rescues the Japanese from the mudswamp.

In a series of novels, Endo depicted characters who were Christ figures and showed how their great love effects changes in those around them, empowering them to take at least the first step out of the swamp. Typical of these novels is *Wonderful Fool,* in which Gaston, a kind of holy fool, rescues the killer Endo (*sic*) from death in an actual mudswamp and succeeds in turning him aside from his path of revenge.

Suguro in *Scandal,* as we have seen, considers his latest novel to be the culmination of everything he has tried to accomplish as a novelist. Here Endo is undoubtedly making reference to his own novel *Samurai,* a novel which does indeed represent a kind of culmination to Endo's career as a Catholic novelist.

In the early 17th century the Japanese feudal lord Masamune Date sent emissaries to Mexico to try to establish trade relations with that country. In return, Christian missionaries would be welcomed in the realm and given freedom to evangelize. The chief emissary was Rokuemon Hasekura, a low-ranking samurai, whose lands were literally swampland. (He hopes that if his mission is successful he will be given better land.) Accompanying the samurai are twenty or so Japanese and a Franciscan friar. Their mission carried them first to Mexico and then on to Spain and Rome. In Rome, the samurai received baptism. (In the novel the baptism is merely a political expedient; Hasekura never intended to become Christian). But the mission is unsuccessful. Moreover, when the samurai returns to Japan, he finds the political climate is completely changed. Masamune is no longer interested in trade with Mexico, and Christianity is now proscribed throughout the country. What finally became of the historical Hasekura is not known, though according to one account he died a martyr. In the novel, when it is learned that he received baptism, for whatever reason, he is apprehended and killed.

The point of view of the novel is equally distributed between the samurai and the Franciscan friar, so that here again we have the familiar dichotomy: the passionate Western priest fighting a furious battle against evil, and the apathetic mudswamp Japanese who wants nothing more than to enjoy an ordinary sort of contentment in life. In this novel both are victorious. In the words of Van G. Gessel, the translator of *Samurai:*

> Here Velasco (the friar), once he has cast off his pride, is allowed to worship and serve a glorified Christ with a rational and aggressive faith, and his martyr's death is an undiluted reflection of his dynamic Western beliefs. In contrast, Hasekura accepts the companionship of Jesus in an almost passive way. His faith is primarily non-rational and thoroughly internalized ... Endo in this novel grants both men a place in the eternal mansions of heaven.[7]

Endo himself says of his protagonists:

> Velasco and Hasekura are like two men climbing a mountain from dif-

---

7    Postscript to *Samurai* (New York, Harper & Row, 1982), pp.271-2.

ferent sides and reporting to each other all the time. At the top they realise it's the same mountain. They meet in the last chapter, which I didn't write.'[8]

Thus it can be seen that Shusaku Endo is well deserving of the epithet 'Catholic novelist'. From the beginning of his writing career until now, he has been literally obsessed with Christ. And through his life and work he has succeeded in interesting in Christianity many Japanese who would not otherwise have been reached. These include a number of intellectuals and fellow writers, several of whom have consequently received baptism.

All the same, it must also be said that the scope of Endo's Catholicism is very narrow. In Endo's religion there is no Church, no community, no sacraments other than baptism, no Vatican Council II, no empowering Spirit. In reaction to the sin-conscious, duty-oriented, Jansenist-tinged Church that he was introduced to in his childhood,[9] Endo has created a Christianity in no need of Church or, indeed, as is well illustrated in the case of the samurai, of any intermediary between God and man.

This is not to fault Endo as a novelist, but readers should be aware of the fact that in Endo they are getting not the whole symphony but only the solo flute.[10] As for the persistent claim that there is something in the Japanese sensibility that cannot receive Christ, thirty-four years of evangelizing in Japan have convinced me that this is false. The main obstacle I have encountered is the busyness of the Japanese, but once they can be led to inner silence, they very quickly hear the voice of the Holy Spirit and encounter Christ *and his Church*.

8   Quoted in *Asia Week* (October 21, 1983), p.63.
9   The Catholic Church in Japan today still suffers from the harsh, joyless, penitential, individualistic brand of Christianity that the new missionaries of the 19th century brought to Japan. The 17th century Church was far more joyful and had a far greater sense of community.
10  Endo uses this same image. In a magazine interview he once stated: 'It seems to me that Catholicism is not a solo, but a symphony. It fits, of course, man's sinless side, but unless a religion can find place for his sinful side in the ensemble, it is a false religion. If I have trust in Catholicism, it is because I find in it much more possibility than in any other religion for presenting the full symphony of humanity. The other religions have almost no fullness: they have but solo parts. Only Catholicism can present the full symphony. And unless there is in that symphony a part that corresponds to Japan's mudswamp, it cannot be a true religion.'

# On *The Violent Bear It Away*[1]

## FLANNERY O'CONNOR

I'm sorry the book [*The Violent Bear It Away*] didn't come off for you but I think it is no wonder it didn't since you see everything in terms of sex symbols, and in a way that would not enter my head – the lifted bough, the fork of the tree, the corkscrew. It doesn't seem to be conceivable to you that such things merely have a natural place in the story, a natural use. Your criticism sounds to me as if you have read too many critical books and are too smart in an artificial, destructive, and very limited way.

The lack of realism would be crucial if this were a realistic novel or if the novel demanded the kind of realism you demand. I don't believe it does. The old man is very obviously not a Southern Baptist, but an independent, a prophet in the true sense. The true prophet is inspired by the Holy Ghost, not necessarily by the dominant religion of his region. Further, the traditional Protestant bodies of the South are evaporating into secularism and respectability and are being replaced on the grass roots level by all sorts of strange sects that bear not much resemblance to traditional Protestantism – Jehovah's Witnesses, snake-handlers, Free Thinking Christians, Independent Prophets, the swindlers, the mad and sometimes the genuinely inspired. A character has to be true to his own nature and I think the old man is that. He was a prophet, not a church-member. As a prophet, he has to be a natural Catholic. Hawthorne said he didn't write novels, he wrote romances; I am one of his descendants.

In any case, your critique is too far from the spirit of the book to make me want to go into it with you in detail. I do hope, however, that you will get over the kind of thinking that sees in every door handle a phallic symbol and that ascribes such intentions to those who have other fish to fry. The Freudian technique can be applied to anything at all with equally ridiculous results. The fork of the tree! My Lord, Billy, recover your simplicity. You ain't in Manhattan. Don't inflict that stuff on the poor students there; they deserve better. [407]

What you ask about Rayber loving Bishop is interesting. He did love him, but throughout the book he was fighting his inherited tendency to mystical love. He had the idea that his love could be contained in Bishop but that if Bishop were gone, there would be nothing to contain it and he would then love everything and specifically Christ. The point where Tarwater is drowning Bishop is the point where he has to choose. He makes the Satanic choice, and the inability to feel the pain of his loss is the immediate result. His collapse

1 From *Letters of Flannery O'Connor: the habit of being,* selected and edited by Sally Fitzgerald, Farrar, Strauss, Giroux, New York, 1979. (Page references are given at the end of each extract.)

then may indicate that he is not going to be able to sustain his choice – but that is another book maybe. Rayber and Tarwater are really fighting the same current in themselves. Rayber wins out against it and Tarwater loses; Rayber achieves his own will, and Tarwater submits to his vocation. Here if you like are two interpretations. There is still an authority to say which interpretation is right. [484-485]

I think the strongest of Rayber's psychological pulls are in the direction that he does not ultimately choose, so I don't believe he exhibits in any sense a lack of free will. You might make out a case of sorts for Tarwater being determined since his great uncle has expressly trained him to be a prophet and to expect the Lord's call, but actually neither of them exhibits a lack of free will. An absence of free will in these characters would mean an absence of conflict in them, whereas they spend all their time fighting within themselves, drive against drive. Tarwater wrestles with the Lord and Rayber wins. Both examples of free will in action. [485]

My only criticism is in certain things you imply about *The Violent Bear etc.* I don't think old Tarwater can quite be compared to Johnson's grandfather because old T. was really a fanatic by your definition of it. He wasn't all belief without deeds; he was a man who could act. I think you need to make a distinction between what the world calls a fanatic (anybody who believes and acts literally on his belief) and your own definition of a fanatic in this essay.

On page 1, you sort of leave the impression old T. is Calvinist and sees people as dammed by God. He sees them as dammed by themselves.

On page 2, you probably ought to make it clear that Tarwater escapes the Devil by accepting his vocation to be a prophet.

One minor thing on page 4 – Sheppard didn't get that telescope until Johnson came. He wasn't interested in training his own child to reach the stars. Rufus was the incentive [506-507].

# D. H. Lawrence[1]

## SIGRID UNDSET

It may safely be said that the whole of Lawrence's production was autobiographical to an even greater extent than is the case with all imaginative writing. For one thing, his life from his very youth was a ceaseless struggle against the pulmonary complaint of which he died, at the early age of forty-five. Thus he was debarred more than most people from forgetting himself, were it only for a moment, in admiration or ecstasy over some person or thing. In the last years of his life, he produced a series of poems on animal and plant motives, some of them of rare beauty. They are a perfect expression of man's primeval instinct for picturing his own spiritual life through flowers and tortoises and mountains and heraldic figures – through anything non-human. Finally his poetical imagination carried him into chaos and cosmos. In mystical speculations Lawrence applied himself to ancient astrological ideas about the twelve signs of the zodiac, which were supposed to 'govern' the various parts and organs of the human body – of his body.

*Sons and Lovers,* however, is autobiographical in a more direct sense than the rest of Lawrence's writing. His sister, Ada Lawrence, has made superabundantly clear the exact correspondence between 'Paul Morel's' story and the life of David Herbert Lawrence in adolescence and youth. And she has illustrated her book with photographs of Lawrence's parents and family, of houses and places which under slightly disguised names are the scene of action in Lawrence's novels and tales. So that anyone may convince himself that, seen with the eyes of an outsider, it was an unspeakably dull and ordinary, but entirely respectable little world that Lawrence grew up in.

His mother and sisters called him Bert. – In English comic papers 'Bert' is the stock name for the Cockney youth, the amorous counter-jumper, the pale and skinny errand-boy who revels in wish-fulfilment dreams about ardent love and desperate deeds as he sits at the cinema gulping down pictures of shadowy film stars' adventures, or works himself up yelling with the crowd at a football match. And there have been some who would like to reduce Lawrence to a rebellious Bert, breaking windows to let air into the stuffy, taboo-ridden homes of the respectable lower middle class.

His sister tells us that as a little boy Lawrence actually was subject to fits of tears, and if his mother asked what he was crying for he only cried worse: 'I don't know.' Over-sensitive to changes of mood and ill humor on the part of those who surrounded him, the child felt, before he was conscious of it, that he was growing up on a battle-ground.

His mother, Lydia Beardsall, had been a school-teacher. She hungered and thirsted after all that in her young days was meant by intellectuality and idealism; she had a strongly developed sense of responsibility and a fanatical respect for herself. Then she fell in love with a miner, Arthur Lawrence, and married him. Later on she could never forgive him for this love-match, which shut her off from all she desired to get out of life. The husband seems on the whole to have been a happy, easy-going nature. His capacity for enjoying life had not been impaired by the hardships of his childhood – he had worked in the coalmines since the age of seven. He did not possess that kind of self-absorption which is a necessary component of all social advancement, but he was well supplied with another sort of self-confidence: he was proud of being strong and good-looking, a likeable fellow with a cheerful spirit which was not to be repressed by poverty and hard work. And then he was to find out that his charming, refined wife was not so well pleased with him as to be able to reconcile herself to the conditions to which he had introduced her. She never managed to feel at home among the miners and their wives, in the ugly, dirty little towns of the coal-mining district round Nottingham. And she never allowed the pressure of poverty and her surroundings to make her abandon the fight for her ideals. She fought for her children – they at any rate should have as much as possible of all that she had been deprived of; they should belong to her people, not to their father's. *He* was the enemy in their mother's eyes. Perplexed and humiliated, he had recourse to all kinds of deplorable shifts in order to assert himself. She was a rigid abstainer – so he sat at the public-house with his mates till late at night. When he came home, 'slightly fuddled and apologetic,' and his wife received him with freezing indignation, he turned brutal. Among the children's memories was that of being constantly waked up by the stormy disputes of their parents – they lay in the dark and heard the voices warring in the room below. – The tragic part of it was that the husband was really a home-loving man in his way. His daughter tells us how handy he was at fixing up anything that was broken in the house. He loved to have his children standing round him as he repaired the alarm-clock or patched their shoes; that was his way of playing with them. 'If, instead of wanting the impossible from him, we had tried to interest ourselves in the things for which he really cared, we should have been spared many unhappy and sordid scenes,' Ada Lawrence writes. But the children took their mother's part fanatically. This was natural – they had to thank her industry, her sense of order, both spiritual and material, for all they knew of well-being and home comfort. She backed their efforts to improve themselves, socially and intellectually. No doubt their father had intended from the first that the boys might start in the coal-mine, the daughters go out into the service, as soon as they were old enough. Later on he took great pride in his talented children. And it is singularly painful to read what his daughter writes of him after mother's death. He was asked why he did not marry again, and he replied: 'I've had one good woman – the finest woman in the world, and I don't want another.' But so long as she was alive the children excluded their father from their life with their mother. He had his revenge, unreflecting creature of instinct that he was, by doing all he could to pain this 'swell' family of his – adopting rude manners and undesirable habits, this man who had once been so proud of his fine healthy appearance. But it is certainly due in the first place to the boy's reaction to his father that Lawrence later on showed such a persistent tendency to romanticize manliness. In his books he constantly talks about 'the strong indomitable male.' With the shyness and pride and boldness of a wild animal he woos and wins and loves and withdraws into his silent and haughty isolation, as mysteriously manly as any figure to be found in the sloppiest of young ladies' novels. Lawrence had been brought up to look down on his father, but his father was the only person in the home over whom his mother did not hold sway – he both defied her openly and managed to evade her control.

In his flights of fancy on the subject of psychoanalysis and the subconscious, Lawrence wrote with unsparing bitterness of the husband who fails his wife and of the wife who in her disappointment bestows all her affection on her sons. She thus conquers the finest element of their personality, the flowering of the boys' spiritual eroticism. When the time comes for them to have actual erotic experience, they have nothing but remnants to give away to other women. – There is now available a whole literature about D. H. Lawrence's life, written for the most part by ladies who can boast of having known him more or less well. As Compton Mackenzie aptly remarks, the dead Lawrence has suffered the same fate as the living Orpheus: to be torn to pieces by his female followers. It was, by the way, a male 'friend' of Lawrence, Middleton Murry, who let loose the whole flood of personal reminiscences about the dead poet. In a somewhat nauseous and turgid book Murry tried to reduce the mysterious quality in Lawrence to so simple a supposition as his alleged impotence. The chorus of protesting women's voices makes it clear in any case that the enigmatic element in Lawrence's genius is not to be explained quite so easily. After all we have been told about him – by friends male and female and by Lawrence's widow – about the irresistible charm of his manner, about his terrible unsociableness, about his candour and his disingenuousness – there still remains something mystical about his person. But finally the girl who had been his companion and confidante during the years when he was feeling his way to his own individuality – Miriam he calls her in *Sons and Lovers* – wrote a little book about her relations with the lad Lawrence. Time after time Lawrence returns to this Miriam figure – a girl who detests the sexual element in love, but who wants to love a man spiritually and to possess his soul and his talent. Against these ideas, then, 'Miriam' herself finally protested. She was a perfectly normal and healthy young woman and had never thought or felt that there was any opposition between the physical and the spiritual in love. It was Lawrence who was uncertain, who dared not embark on a real love-affair with her, because his mother was jealous and he was dominated by her, and because his sisters did all they could to separate their brother and his girl friend. When at last the lad tried to transform their friendship into a love-affair, it was too late. The girl had *turned* cold, from long waiting and from humiliation.

Mrs Lawrence must have perceived at an early stage that 'Bert' possessed more than ordinary ability, though she can hardly have grasped either its nature or its extent. He did a little painting as a boy, he won a scholarship which qualified him for a higher school, he became a teacher, he began to write – and of course this was all to the good. Step by step her children were freeing themselves from the social surroundings in which she had been imprisoned. But if they were forced to marry, as the saying is, while still quite young, why, then their whole future would be ruined. And in that no doubt most sensible people would agree with her.

Her son was just able to place an advance copy of his first book, *The White Peacock,* in his mother's hands, but she died without having read it. And then he had to try to work his way out of the environment which had wrapped him round like a mother's womb. When some time later he gave up his position as teacher and left England with the lady he married a couple of years afterwards – that is, as soon as her divorce was made absolute – he thought he was born anew for a life under more spacious skies and was to breathe the air of other worlds. But so forcible had been the pressure of his home on the mind of the abnormally sensitive lad that D.H. Lawrence bore to his dying day the stamp of the influences that act upon young Paul Morel in *Sons and Lovers.*

The after-effects of the feud between his parents reverberate through all his writings. Lawrence, who made himself the prophet of an altogether mystical sexual religion – the 'regeneration by sex' of England and of the white race in general – describes the sexual relation as a war to the death between man and woman. This ground–motive recurs incessantly in his work, infinitely varied – the man in revolt, the man in flight from the woman who tries to tamper with him, to kill and devour him; woman is a fury who ranges against man for reducing her to subjection and who despises him when he fails to do so. The latent dread of the horrors of sexual warfare culminates with Lawrence in scenes of a savage, uncanny beauty, unlike anything else that has been written of the primitive dread of life – scenes like that of the final chapter of *The Rainbow,* where Ursula Brangwen meets with a mob of untethered horses in a field. The incomparably lifelike description of this troop of horses, galloping, halting, and circling again in a thundering trot round the terrified girl, becomes a symbol of all life's obscure and overpowering impulses; and Ursula's fear, that of everyone's sense of horror and impotence under the dominance of these impulses. This runs like a leading motive through all his poetry – culminating in the imagination and moving verses about the tortoises that he used as sacred symbols of life's crucifixion in the torment of sex. Lawrence is seldom convincing when he tries to force the creatures born of his fancy to realize his own gospel of a new and saving kind of abandonment – a dark and mystical communion of the blood which is just as much the expression of the human instinct of death and destruction as of the will to life. But Lawrence dreamed of a sexual act in which the individuals die from their old ego and are reborn to a new life, each as master of his own soul, but united with his mate in profound tenderness, saved from all lust of power involved in sexual feeling, cleansed of all the elements of petty vanity which are a part of all erotics, but with their manly or womanly self-consciousness intensified. It was something of this sort that he wished to believe in. But the people who live in his books are in everlasting revolt against his new religion – irreclaimably timid, bitter, and suspicious men and women who are incapable of abandoning themselves to another human being without regretting it and immediately trying to recover themselves. This is true in particular of his most discussed book, *Lady Chatterley's Lover.* This book gave great offence when it came out. The majority of those scandalized were undoubtedly in good faith in explaining that what scandalized them was that Lawrence had tendentiously put into print a number of expressions which can have a neutral value only in the minds of very dull or sexually exhausted individuals; to most people they are too highly charged with heterogeneous emotional values; they belong at the same time to the most intimate love-making and to the most elementary outbursts of range. Unconsciously the feeling of offence went far deeper, at any rate with many people. They felt how intolerably tragic were the naked descriptions of two human beings who in their embraces are trying to crush out of themselves their unbounded bitterness at their own erotic disappointments in the past and the immeasurable hatred they have gathered up in previous love-affairs. We may call the tendency of *Lady's Chatterley's Lover* immoral, just as we may say the same of any book whose object is to relate an untruth, however honestly the untruth may be expressed, or however it may be candied in the sugar of morality. But Lawrence simply could not be untrue to his vision; he could not allow Connie Chatterley and her lover to *be* reborn in any blood-communion. The novel does not end with their bringing any peace to each other. The most we can say is that they arrive at a sort of armistice – in the hope that this may end in peace.

He has a Balaam's ass inside him, Lawrence writes in another connection. 'When I try to turn my travelling nose westwards, *grazie!* he won't budge. So, after vainly shoving and prodding the ass of my unwilling spirit, I have given up.' In reality these words are typical of the relation between tendency and vision in Lawrence's writing.

For a visionary is what he was, and a poet of genius. But his own wish was to be a prophet, a saviour of the world, a Messiah. His passionately antichristian attitude was due above all to the fact that the figure of Jesus stood in his way. True, he and his brothers and sisters during the whole of their childhood and adolescence had been obliged every Sunday to attend three services besides Sunday school in the dissenting chapel to which his parents belonged. So it was natural enough that he should identify Christianity with the strict puritanism which dominated that place of worship. And he never got away from these impressions; he carried on the war against the maternal Bethel. But the new flesh-and-blood religion he sought to found bore the fundamental stamp of the unsmiling solemnity of his childhood's religion: when he strips men and women of their clothes and exposes the secret places of the body he is as serious as a priest at the sacrificial stone. In the end he fabled that Jesus Himself had been converted to his, Lawrence's religion – he makes the crucified and risen Saviour renounce His errors and acknowledge that not His but Lawrence's way of salvation is the right one.

And he makes the discovery that the Revelation of John is in reality a pre-Lawrencian prophecy, an ancient pagan evidence of his own cosmology – John, like some kind of early Christian sectarian preacher, had merely tampered with the texts and stuffed them full of his own sanctimonious phraseology.

But no matter what he wrote – novels, short stories, poetry, essays, letters, travels – in his hands the subjects became new and his own property in a curious way. Like ore that has been heated in the furnace and comes out gleaming with unsuspected colours, bright and dark, the English language is fused in this burning brain and leaves his forge resmelted, with new and wonderful values. Infinitely susceptible to all sensuous impressions, Lawrence had felt from his boyhood in the very marrow of his soul the opposition between life, organic matter, and dead inorganic masses. The country surrounding his home is charming – pretty-pretty perhaps some would call it. But Lawrence absorbed it and identified himself with the life of the little wild animals and the flowers and trees and the life of the river under its banks. Even the refuse of life – dead leaves and manure in the farmyard of Miriam's rustic home, straw and haycocks – belongs to life as distinguished from dead inorganic things – the cancerous sores of coalmines and railways on the green countryside, the eruption of work-men's dwellings, rows of houses built of ugly blackened brick. This opposition is lively even in his first book, *The White Peacock,* which deals more with a landscape and an old farm than with the people who live there. And in *Lady Chatterley's Lover,* which is in a way Lawrence's testament – or at any rate one of them – what is unforgettable is the description of the little copse where the lovers meet. A spot of nature besieged on every side by mines and slag-heaps, surrounded by railway lines – the night around it glowing with reflections from the works. The faun, Mellors, is forced into the defensive. He tries to defend his own and Connie Chatterley's lives against the mechanization of existence and against the cerebral activity of them both, which he fears, holding it to be the origin of all that is mechanical and bloodless and grey in the world and in human souls. Against the intellectual, Lawrence sets up the Panic in men; this is the source which sustains life in fear and in joy. Lawrence, who wished to be Messiah, wished also to be Pan.

He was egocentric like most sick people, but his ego was sufficiently elastic to absorb people he met and foreign countries and new skies – and yet he always carried with him the England that had been his native soil. It was this England that he saw slipping down into the melting-pot of the World War – and even today there is no-one who can say exactly how much of it was lost in the fiery ordeal and how much has survived, substantially the same though cast into new forms. Then he set out on journeys all over the world to find people and places which might represent the object of his dreams – the primitive, unworn, red-blooded. He found them nowhere – he was not at home among the dusky natives of Ceylon nor among Australian colonists, Polynesians, nor dancing Indians in Mexico. The contact with foreign conditions seems in itself always to have troubled Lawrence – except when he was living in Italy; but then Italy has been for centuries the home of the Englishman's longing and the land of his dreams. It is significant in this connection that in Italy he wrote a number of his most beautiful poems to the dead mother who has fostered his longing for travel and who herself had never been able to see the land of her desire. But with his own hypersensitive nerves he was revolted by the reptilian lack of sympathy he thought he could discern in the impenetrable dark eyes of really primitive peoples – though time after time he tries to accept and admire them, as he does in his tales from Mexico. It is true that he ended by attributing to the Mexicans a prophet and a revival of the local religion. In *The Plumed Serpent* a landowner founds a new faith which is composed of Lawrence's notions of ancient Mexican paganism, reinterpreted and improved according to his own mystical ideas. The book has an uncanny symptomatic interest in that it foreshadows the kind of religion-making which set it shortly after his death – the attempts to revive local pagan beliefs as they were apt to be popularized in accordance with the taste of a more or less cultured middle class for antiquarian romance and characterized by middle-class puritanical-materialistic idealism. – But by degrees, as he digested his impressions of the passing glories of this world, reliving in his mind what his eyes had told him, he fashioned from these impressions his incredibly hallucinatory art, which produces on the reader the effect of direct sensations of taste, vision, and feeling. With the same power of suggestion he makes the reader share his perception either of the landscape of his native district or of a single flower in a garden by the Mediterrranean, a bathe in the Pacific on the coast of Australia, a morning in Mexico, or a steamer trip in midwinter from Sicily to Sardinia. If he fairly and squarely shocked a great part of the English public with his descriptions of erotic situations – and delighted another section of the same public with them – it was not because they were more 'sensuous' than his pictures of flowers or animals or his travel scenes. His art acts directly upon the senses, whether it reproduces physical caresses or a night in a haycock or the motions of the berth one occupies on board a steamer in heavy weather. But it was natural that his art should give offence and alarm to a public accustomed to finding something literary or unlifelike and distant in the very tone of erotic descriptions, whether these were cynical or sentimental in treatment, tragic or pleasant or frivolous.

It was equally natural that Lawrence should feel himself wronged and finally persecuted: he was treated as a writer of immoral books, and perhaps no other author in the whole world had taken sex so desperately seriously as he! Lawrence the puritan saw red when anyone permitted himself to trifle frivolously or obscenely with the instincts which cause people to perform so many grotesque antics. In ages and among peoples which actually realized the freedom of speech that he believed would save humanity, Lawrence would have felt extremely ill at ease. In his berserk attacks on current English taboo-ideas he did not ask how such ideas arise. One explanation of them is the reaction against the guffaws of a period of free speech – even dogs and little children cannot bear to be laughed at; grown-up people hate it. And sometimes a taboo arises when people's imagination develops into compassion for the sufferings of others. Lawrences mind swung ceaselessly between intense compassion for others and attempts to rebel against this tormenting fellow-feeling. This is connected with a quality which is both the strength and the weakness of Lawrence as a novelist. Few of the figures in his books have achieved the right to exist and act according to their own natures – more often than not Lawrence forces them to be and to act as he wishes. In dealing with his own creations he was like a mother – his own mother – who wishes to direct her offspring in everything. His knowledge of humanity is boundless. His knowledge of other persons than D.H. Lawrence is a great deal less.

But so many-sided was Lawrence and so intensely did he live his life that he becomes a representative figure – the man of mystery who symbolises his civilisation at the moment when it has reached a crisis. It is among other things a crisis of population and an economic crisis. In the language of mythology it means the the Phallus has lost its old significance as a religious symbol. Since the days of Malthus the Europeans in any case had lost the ancient happy belief that fertility was unconditionally a good thing. When primitive races from time to time suspended the moral precepts of everyday life and celebrated orgies in order to make rain or assure a good harvest and a plentiful supply of game and domestic animals, it was because they confidently regarded their own life as a part of nature's economy. Crop failures and periods of famine were certainly not unknown to them, but it never occurred to them that some day mankind might be faced by the problem of the population exceeding its food supply to a possibly dangerous extent. The passionate attempts to emancipate sexuality from the service of propagation and to find its highest values under other aspects are first heard of precisely during the lifetime of Malthus. Not that they were influenced by his writing; this was rather the attempt of an intellectual to investigate the spectre that lurked behind the tendency of the poets. The romantics glorified love as the source of the loving souls' rapture – true love is that which makes the soul great and strong, causes the mind to soar, the heart to swell with noble feelings, gives wings to the imagination. This was the program – in reality most people probably contented themselves with pretending they were beautiful souls and loved in the correct romantic fashion. Poetry again reflected this sham romanticism – it came to concern itself with imitated emotions, sentimentality. Then the reaction set in – people were no longer willing to be told that they must please dress up and act a long charade before they could permit themselves sexual gratification. They were now to begin taking their sex naturally. – This reaction was no more disposed than the romantics had been to acknowledge that 'Nature,' so far as we humans can have any knowledge of the matter, has never had any object in driving individuals to the act of propagation except that they should propagate their species; after that the parent individuals can die, like the insects whose offspring do not require their care, or wear themselves out in bringing up their young, as among the higher animals. The desperate dilemma of the nineteenth century, which the twentieth has inherited, is precisely that with which Laurence wrestles. As he says in his painfully beautiful, ithyphallic *Virgin Youth*:

> Traveller, column of fire,
> It is vain.
> The glow of thy full desire
> Becomes pain.

He himself never had a child. From the letters he wrote to her whom he afterwards married it appears as though in the early days of their connection he had wished for a child by her. She herself had three by a former marriage, a fact which hurt him both in his self-esteem as a man and in his, as it were, filial attitude towards the woman with whom he was to live; he wished at the same time to dominate and to be dominated in their relations. Soon, however, he grew so ill that it would have been unnatural if he had continued to wish for a child. And so he had to seek for another and more mystical meaning in the play of instincts. Indeed, it is very general for childless men to become pronouncedly erotic and given to erotic theorizing.

In opposition to the naïveté which looks forward to a new age simply because it is new, he was a voice crying in the wilderness. When simple souls call themselves the children of steel and concrete it is time to remind them of the yawning gulf fixed between life, which can beget life – whether by splitting up or pollination or copulation – and the whole inorganic world, which cannot reproduce itself. Steel and concrete are useful enough in their way. Nor, we may be sure, could Lawrence seriously imagine that modern technics could be got rid of. But if men appoint lifelessness and sterility as their adoptive parents, there is a danger that technics, instead of serving life, will destroy it. The widespread fear of the results of the mechanization of existence – a slow death from loss of heat – finds voice with Lawrence in poems and descriptions which burst like spouting blood from a severed artery, in intensely animated pictures of struggling life. And sometimes in reflections so obscure that they seem to express a dread the depth of which no-one, not even Lawrence, dares to plumb. What can each individual human being make of himself, of his own life? – this is what will decide what the new age is to be like. Collectivism cannot in itself be the remedy for any distress, if the separate individuals are ciphers – for nought plus nought will never equal anything but nought, however many million ciphers we may add.

Lawrence's perpetual harping on the sexual act, which to his sensitive soul meant communion, holy matrimony, the blood-contact between man and woman – between the two rivers, Euphrates and Tigris, which encircle Paradise, he says somewhere in his speculations upon the future destiny of the human race – was quite naturally misunderstood by the great mass of his fellow-countrymen; it had not yet occurred to him that their world might be threatened with freezing to death. It is another matter that the poet Lawrence continually put the words of the prophet Lawrence to shame. The new phallus-cult he sought to found no more brings peace and warmth in reality than it does to the eternally restless persons of his novels.

But the idea that the human blood is such a mystical source of power and warmth, the saving fluid, occurs naturally to men who are fighting against the fear of an ice age and of anything that depresses vitality. 'For the blood is the substance of the soul, and of the deepest consciousness. It is by blood that we are: and it is by the heart and the liver that we live and move and have our being. In the blood, knowing and being, or feeling, are one and undivided: no serpent and no apple has caused a split.' This is not a quotation from some modern German racial theologian; it was written by Lawrence in his *A Propos of Lady Chatterley's Lover.* – Much of what is happening in Europe today and yet more that will doubtless happen in the future are the brutal reaction of mass humanity to the problems which the exceptional man, the genius D.H. Lawrence, perceived and faced and fought against in his own way: in his writings, a great part of which in any case will pass into the heritage which our age will hand on to future generations.

# Felix Culpa?[1]

## EVELYN WAUGH

Of Mr Graham Greene alone among contemporary writers one can say without affectation that his breaking silence with a new serious novel is a literary 'event'. It is eight years since the publication of *The Power and the Glory*. During that time he has remained inconspicuous and his reputation has grown huge. We have had leisure to re-read his earlier books and to appreciate the gravity and intensity which underlie their severe modern surface. More than this, the spirit of the time has begun to catch up with them.

1    From Donat Gallagher (ed.), *Evelyn Waugh: a selection from his journalism*, London, Eyre Methuen, 1977.

The artist, however aloof he holds himself, is always and specially the creature of the *zeitgeist;* however formally antique his tastes, he is in spite of himself in the advance guard. Men of affairs stumble far behind.

In the last twenty-five years the artist's interest has moved from sociology to eschatology. Out of hearing, out of sight, politicians and journalists and popular preachers exhort him to sing the splendours of high wages and sanitation. His eyes are on the Four Last Things, and so mountainous are the disappointments of recent history that there are already signs of a popular breakaway to join him, of a stampede to the heights.

I find the question most commonly asked by the agnostic is not: 'Do you believe in the authenticity of the Holy House at Loreto?' or 'Do you think an individual can justly inherit a right to the labour of another?' but 'Do you believe in Hell?'

Mr Greene has long shown an absorbing curiosity in the subject. In *Brighton Rock* he ingeniously gave life to a theological abstraction. We are often told: 'The Church does not teach that any man is damned. We only know that Hell exists for those who deserve it. Perhaps it is now empty and will remain so for all eternity.' This was not the sentiment of earlier and healthier ages. The Last Judgment above the medieval door showed the lost and the saved as fairly equally divided; the path to salvation as exceedingly narrow and beset with booby-traps; the reek of brimstone was everywhere. Mr Greene challenged the soft modern mood by creating a completely damnable youth. Pinkie of Brighton Rock is the ideal examinee for entry to Hell. He gets a pure alpha on every paper.

His story is a brilliant and appalling imaginative achievement but falls short of the real hell-fire sermon by its very completeness. We leave our seats edified but smug. However vile we are, we are better than Pinkie. The warning of the preacher was that one unrepented slip obliterated the accumulated merits of a lifetime's struggle to be good. *Brighton Rock* might be taken to mean that one has to be as wicked as Pinkie before one runs into serious danger.

Mr Greene's latest book, *The Heart of the Matter,* should be read as the complement of *Brighton Rock.* It poses a vastly more subtle problem. Its hero speaks of the Church as 'knowing all the answers', but his life and death comprise a problem to which the answer is in the mind of God alone, the reconciliation of perfect justice with perfect mercy. It is a book which only a Catholic could write and only a Catholic can understand. I mean that only a Catholic can understand the nature of the problem. Many Catholics, I am sure, will gravely misunderstand it, particularly in the United States of America, where its selection as the Book of the Month will bring it to a much larger public than can profitably read it. There are loyal Catholics here and in America who think it the function of the Catholic writer to produce only advertising brochures set-

1     From *Commonweal,* 14 August 1992.

ting out in attractive terms the advantages of Church membership. To them this profoundly reverent book will seem a scandal. For it not only portrays Catholics as unlikeable human beings but shows them as tortured by their Faith. It will be the object of controversy and perhaps even of condemnation. Thousands of heathen will read it with innocent excitement, quite unaware that they are intruding among the innermost mysteries of faith. There is a third class who will see what this book intends and yet be troubled by doubt of its theological propriety.

Mr Greene divides his fiction into 'Novels' and 'Entertainments'. Superficially there is no great difference between the two categories. There is no Ruth Draper switch from comic to pathetic. 'Novels' and 'Entertainments' are both written in the same grim style, both deal mainly with charmless characters, both have a structure of sound, exciting plot. You cannot tell from the skeleton whether the man was baptised or not. And that is the difference; the 'Novels' have been baptised, held deep under in the waters of life. The author has said: 'These characters are not my creation but God's. They have an eternal destiny. They are not merely playing a part for the reader's amusement. They are souls whom Christ died to save'. This, I think, explains his preoccupation with the charmless. The children of Adam are not a race of noble savages who need only a divine spark to perfect them. They are aboriginally corrupt. Their tiny relative advantages of intelligence and taste and good looks and good manners are quite insignificant. The compassion and condescension of the Word becoming flesh are glorified in the depths.

As I have said above, the style of writing is grim. It is not a specifically literary style at all. The words are functional, devoid of sensuous attraction, of ancestry and of independent life. Literary stylists regard language as intrinsically precious and its proper use as a worthy and pleasant task. A polyglot could read Mr Greene, lay him aside, retain a sharp memory of all he said and yet, I think, entirely forget what tongue he was using. The words are simply mathematical signs for his thought. Moreover, no relation is established between writer and reader. The reader has not had a conversation with a third party such as he enjoys with Sterne or Thackeray. Nor is there within the structure of the story an observer through whom the events are recorded and the emotions transmitted. It is as though out of an infinite length of film, sequences had been cut which, assembled, comprise an experience which is the reader's alone, without any correspondence to the experience of the protagonists. The writer has become director and producer. Indeed, the affinity to the film is everywhere apparent. It is the camera's eye which moves form the hotel balcony to the street below, picks out the policeman, follows him to his office, moves about the room from the handcuffs on the wall to the broken rosary in the drawer, recording significant detail. It is the modern way of telling a story. In Elizabethan drama one can usually discern an artistic sense formed on the dumb-show and the masque. In Henry James' novels scene after scene evolves as though on the stage of a drawing-room comedy. Now it is the cinema which has taught a new habit of narrative. Perhaps it is the only contribution the cinema is destined to make to the arts.

There is no technical trick about good story-telling in this or any other manner. All depends on the natural qualities of the narrator's mind, whether or no he sees events in a necessary sequence. Mr Greene is a story-teller of genius. Born in another age, he would still be spinning yarns. His particular habits are accidental. The plot of *The Heart of the Matter* might well have been used by M. Simenon or Mr Somerset Maugham.

The scene is a West African port in war time. It has affinities with the Brighton of *Brighton Rock*, parasitic, cosmopolitan, corrupt. The population are all strangers, British officials, detribalized natives, immigrant West Indian Negroes, Asiatics, Syrians. There are poisonous gossips at the club and voodoo bottles on the wharf, intrigues for administrative posts, intrigues to monopolize the illicit diamond trade. The hero, Scobie, is deputy-commissioner of police, one of the oldest inhabitants among the white officials; he has a compassionate liking for the place and the people. He is honest and unpopular and, when the story begins, he has been passed over for promotion. His wife Louise is also unpopular, for other reasons. She is neurotic and pretentious. Their only child died at school in England. Both are Catholic. His failure to get made commissioner is the final humiliation. She whines and nags to escape to South Africa. Two hundred pounds are needed to send her. Husband and wife are found together in the depths of distress.

The illegal export of diamonds is prevalent, both as industrial stones for the benefit of the enemy and gems for private investment. Scobie's police are entirely ineffective in stopping it, although it is notorious that two Syrians, Allit and Yusef, are competitors for the monopoly. A police-spy is sent from England to investigate. He falls in love with Louise. Scobie, in order to fulfil his promise to get Louise out of the country, borrows money from Yusef. As a result of this association he is involved in an attempt to 'frame' Tallit. The police-spy animated by hate and jealousy is on his heels. Meanwhile survivors from a torpedoed ship are brought across from French territory, among them an English bride widowed in the sinking. She and Scobie fall in love and she becomes his mistress. Yusef secures evidence of the intrigue and blackmails Scobie into definitely criminal participation in his trade. His association with Yusef culminates in the murder of Ali, Scobie's supposedly devoted native servant, whom he now suspects of giving information to the police-spy. Louise returns. Unable to abandon either woman, inextricably involved in crime, hunted by his enemy, Scobie takes poison; his women become listlessly acquiescent to other suitors.

These are the bare bones of the story, the ground plan on which almost any kind of building might be erected. The art of story-telling has little to do with the choice of plot. One can imagine the dreariest kind of film − (Miss Bacall's pretty head lolling on the stretcher) − accurately constructed to these specifications. Mr Greene, as his admirers would expect, makes of his material a precise and plausible drama. His technical mastery has never been better manifested than in his statement of the scene – the sweat and infection, the ill-built town, which is beautiful for a few minutes at sundown, the brothel where all men are equal, the vultures, the priest who, when he laughed 'swung his great empty-sounding bell to and fro, Ho, ho, ho, like a leper proclaiming his misery', the snobbery of the second-class public schools, the law which all can evade, the ever-present haunting underworld of gossip, spying, bribery, violence and betrayal. There are incidents of the highest imaginative power - Scobie at the bedside of a dying child, improvising his tale of the Bantus. It is so well done that one forgets the doer. The characters are real people whose moral and spiritual predicament is our own because they are part of our personal experience.

As I have suggested above, Scobie is the complement of Pinkie. Both believe in damnation and believe themselves damned. Both die in mortal sin as defined by moral theologians. The conclusion of the book is the reflection that no one knows the secrets of the human heart or the nature of God's mercy. It is improper to speculate on another's damnation. Nevertheless the reader is haunted by the question: Is Scobie damned? One does not really worry very much about whether Becky Sharp or Fagin is damned. It is the central question of *The Heart of the Matter*.[2] I believe that Mr Greene thinks him a saint. Perhaps I am wrong in this, but in any case Mr Greene's opinion on that matter is of no more value than the reader's. Scobie is not Mr Green's creature, devised to illustrate a thesis. He is a man of independent soul. Can one separate his moral from his spiritual state? Both are complex and ambiguous.

First, there is his professional delinquency. In the first pages he appears as an Aristides, disliked for his rectitude; by the end of the book he has become a criminal. There is nothing inevitable in his decline. He compromises himself first in order to get his wife's passage money. She is in a deplorable nervous condition; perhaps, even, her reason is in danger.

He is full of compassion. But she is making his own life intolerable; he wants here out of the way for his own peace. As things turn out the trip to South Africa was quite unnecessary. Providence had its own cure ready if he had only waited. He gets the commissionership in the end, which was ostensibly all that Louise wanted. But behind that again lies the deeper cause of her melancholy, that Scobie no longer loves her in the way that would gratify her vanity. And behind the betrayal of his official trust lies the futility of his official position. The law he administers has little connection with morals or justice. It is all a matter of regulations – a Portuguese sea-captain's right to correspond with his daughter in Germany, the right of a tenant to divide and sub-let her

2    In a letter dated 11 August 1948 about a French translation of this review, Waugh asked A.D. Peters to delete the passage: 'I believe that Mr Greene thinks him a saint...a man of independent soul.' Waugh continued: 'You might make a note of this correction in case anyone else ever wants to reprint the review – as I should very much like them to do.' A letter to the *Tablet,* 17 July 1948, p.41, also indicates the need for this correction. Ed.

hut, the right of a merchant to provide out of his own property for the securi-
ty of his family. He knows that his subordinates are corrupt and can do nothing about it. Whom or what has he in fact betrayed, except his own pride?

Secondly, there is his adultery. His affection for the waif cast up on the
beach is at first compassionate and protective; it becomes carnal. Why? He is
an elderly man long schooled in chastity. There is another suitor of Helen
Rolt, Bagster the Air Force philanderer. It is Bagster's prowling round the bun-
galow which precipitates the change of relationship. It is Bagster in the background who makes him persevere in adultery when his wife's return affords a
convenient occasion for parting. Bagster is a promiscuous cad. Helen must be
saved from Bagster. Why? Scobie arrogates to himself the prerogations of providence. He presumes that an illicit relation with himself is better than an illicit
relation with Bagster. But why, in fact, need it have been illicit? She might
marry Bagster.

Thirdly there is the murder of Ali. We do not know whether Ali was
betraying him. If he had not been a smuggler and an adulterer there would
have been nothing to betray. Ali dies to emphasize the culpability of these sins.

Fourthly there are the sacrilegious communions which Louise forces upon
him; and fifthly, his suicide, a re-statement of that blasphemy in other terms.
He dies believing himself damned but also in an obscure way – at least in a
way that is obscure to me – believing that he is offering his damnation as a
loving sacrifice for others.

We are told that he is actuated throughout by the love of God. A love, it is
true, that falls short of trust, but a love, we must suppose, which sanctifies his
sins. That is the heart of the matter. Is such a sacrifice feasible? To me the idea
is totally unintelligible, but it is not unfamiliar.

Did the Quietists not speak in something like these terms? I ask in all
humility whether nowadays logical rule-of-thumb Catholics are not a little
too humble towards the mystics. We are inclined to say: 'Ah, that is mysticism.
I'm quite out of my depth there,' as though the subject were higher mathe-
matics, while in fact our whole Faith is essentially mystical. We may well fight
shy of discussing ectastic states of prayer with which we have no acquaintance,
but sacrilege and suicide are acts of which we are perfectly capable. To me the
idea of willing my own damnation for the love of God is either a very loose
poetical expression or a mad blasphemy, for the God who accepted that sacrifice could be neither just nor lovable.

Mr Greene has put a quotation from Péguy at the beginning of the book
'*Le pécheur est au coeur même de chrétienté…Nul n'est aussi compétent que le pécheur
en matière de chrétienté. Nul, si ce n'est le saint,*' and it seems to me probable that
it was in his mind to illustrate the '*Nouveau Théologien*' from which it is taken,
just as in *Brighton Rock* he illustrates the Penny Catechism. The theme of that
remarkable essay is that Christianity is a city to which a bad citizen belongs
and the good stranger does not. Péguy describes the Church, very beautifully,
as a chain of saints and sinners with clasped fingers, pulling one another up to
Jesus. But there are also passages which, if read literally, are grossly exorbitant.

Péguy was not three years a convert when he wrote it, and he was not in communion with the Church. He daily saw men and women, who seemed to him lacking his own intense spirituality, trooping up to the altar rails while he was obliged to stay in his place excommunicate. The *'Nouveau Théologien'* is his meditation on his predicament. He feels there is a city of which he is a true citizen, but it is not the community of conventional Catholics, who are not, in his odd, often repeated phrase, *'compétent en matière de chrétienté.'* He feels a kinship with the saints that these conventional church-goers do not know and in his strange, narrow, brooding mind he makes the preposterous deduction that this very true and strong bond is made, not by his faith and love, but by his sins. *'Littéralement,'* he writes, *'celui qui est pécheur, celui qui commet un péché est déjà chrétien, est en cela même chrétien. On pourrait presque dire est un bon chrétien.'* *'Littéralement'*?: what is the precise force of that passage? Much depends on it. Does 'literally' mean that any and every sinner is by virtue of his sin a Christian? Was Yusef a sinner and therefore Christian? No, because Péguy has already stated that strangers outside the chain of clasped hands cannot commit sin at all. Is Yusef damned? Can a sinner by this definition never be damned? The argument works in a circle of undefined terms. And what of the *'presque'*? How does one 'almost' say something? Is one prevented by the fear of shocking others or the realization at the last moment that what one was going to say does not in fact make sense? In that case why record it? Why 'almost' say it? This is not a matter of quibbling. If Péguy is saying anything at all, he is saying something very startling and something which people seem to find increasingly important. Mr Greene has removed the argument from Péguy's mumbled version and restated it in brilliantly plain human terms; and it is there, at the heart of the matter, that the literary critic must resign his judgment to the theologian.

# Grammars of Assent and Dissent in Graham Greene and Brian Moore[1]

## J.C. WHITEHOUSE

Graham Greene's *Monsignor Quixote* and Brian Moore's *Catholics* are two powerful fables by major writers haunted by Catholicism in which the central theme is the religious experience of the main character. In both, his situation is lucidly and effectively presented as an epitome of one kind of general religious experience. In each case, a similar technique is used: the description of a

1    From *Renascence* 42.3, Spring 1990.

critical encounter with another man for whom faith, or a replacement for it, is important. Monsignor Quixote and the Abbot have their reconstructed Catholic counterparts. For the former, it is Zancas (Sancho) the Marxist ex-mayor and ex-seminarian clever enough, unlike his friend, to have studied at Salamanca and to have been influenced by the half-believing Unamuno. For the Abbot of Muck, it is 'James Kinsella, Catholic priest', the post-Vatican IV ecumenical cleric who understands his colleague's spiritual crisis but for whom the Church's mission is primarily to foster the necessary social revolution. Whether the reader sees them as mirror-images of the protagonists, as devil's advocates, or as independent entities is perhaps not of great significance, since their function, which is to suggest effectively compelling and alternative ways of seeing, understanding, and experiencing a human predicament and presenting a parallel but different and demystified vision of morality and ends, remains the same. In both books there is a strong sense of the subjectivity of human ways of making sense of the world.

Neither, however, offers a coercive conclusion. Their treatment of the theme is entirely phenomenological, in that all the reader sees is the subjectivity of the four men chiefly involved. There are no authorial asides or explanatory interventions, and any reflection apart from that engaged in by the characters is a direct result of the interplay between the intelligence and sensibility of a receiving mind and imagination and the account of certain physical and mental events. Such a reflection is nevertheless potentially very rich, and doubly so if both books are taken into consideration. Their differences are as interesting as their similarities, and the perceptions and reactions of the two protagonists are divergent enough to merit attention and comparison. At first sight, there is very little difference between the situation the Monsignor and the Abbot find themselves in. Both are old and old-fashioned priests in trouble with the Church they represent and faced with the discipline it imposes. The Abbot is ordered to give up the old Mass his community has insisted on retaining: the Monsignor is suspended *a divinis*. Neither has ever found faith (or indeed obedience) a particularly easy matter. Both are forced to face that faith again in particularly painful ways. Where they differ radically, however, is in their final attitude to it. Once this is seen and the reflections leading up to it are examined, it begins to seem that both the books and their protagonists are less alike than one might think. To see this clearly, we need to look carefully at the ideas about religion they suggest and, what is perhaps even more important, to distinguish various kinds of religious or irreligious concepts.

As a first step in that direction, we should look briefly at words that are often used as interchangeable synonyms. Are there any significant differences between *belief and faith?* For the purposes of this essay, belief means the mental assent to or acceptance of a statement or proposition on the basis of reasonably intellectual evidence, whereas faith means specifically the acceptance of the truth of the Christian religion as contained in scripture and the teachings of the Church and, more generally, the spiritual apprehension of divine truths. Although brief, these definitions clash with neither the formulations of lexicographers nor those of Catholicism, which is the 'faith' in the loose and general sense of the word (i.e., the system of suppositions, attitudes, and practices) reflected in both novels. It is as well to keep its stricter sense in mind, because that is the one in which both authors use the word. The Epistle to the Hebrews (XI:i) says that faith 'makes us certain of realities we do not see' (*New English Bible*) or is 'the evidence of things not seen' (*Authorized Version*) or 'the evidence of things that appear not' (*Douay Bible*). In Catholic theology, it is 'a firm persuasion whereby a person assents to truths that are not seen and cannot be proved' (*New Catholic Encyclopaedia*), a 'virtue.... by which we believe...all that God has revealed and, through his Church, proposes for our belief' and means 'believing the truths of Religion because God, who is Truth itself, and who cannot deceive us, has revealed them to us' (*The Student's Catholic Doctrine*). In other words, it is a gift and a revelation, something that cannot be attained, although the way to it may be cleared by normal intellectual processes.

These distinctions are important, since a number of the reflections in *Monsignor Quixote* and *Catholics* have to do with one or both of the slightly different concepts they illustrate, and it is always helpful to establish common terms of reference. When Sancho or Kinsella has something to say about the Church or the Monsignor or the Abbot about doubt or disbelief, we have to make some assumption as to what precise sense their remarks should be taken in. More fundamentally, we might need to ask whether in the final analysis the books are about belief or faith.

In Greene's book the range of shades from disbelief to faith is wide and subtle. Indeed, it is often hard to decide which of Quixote's various utterances reflects which particular possibility or even whether it appears to suggest several apparently mutually contradictory ideas at the same time. To some extent the reader is tempted to suspect that there is some truth in the frequently-made criticism that Greene's writing relies too heavily on paradox. That observation is not entirely valid in this particular case, however, since the states of mind or orientations of the will suggested in *Monsignor Quixote* are both complex and fully comprehensible only when their opposites are perceived. In short, belief, disbelief, doubt, and faith are so interlinked and complementary in his work in general and in this book in particular that any attempt to keep them in watertight compartments is a self-defeating exercise. They are as simultaneous, interwoven, and conflicting as they are in the mind of any conscious Christian. There is nothing new or specifically contemporary in this. The conflicts and contradictions the Monsignor expresses are those found equally often in the Gospels ('Lord, I believe: help thou mine unbelief') and twentieth-century fiction.

It is clear that the account of Quixote's last weeks provides a terse but lucid presentation of his understanding of life and the concluding stages of what we could perhaps call his religious *peripeteia*. Greene's enigmatic introductory quotation from *Hamlet* ('There is nothing either good or bad,/but thinking makes it so') sets a tone and background for much of the priest's thought. Are we in a world where there are no values, but only value-judgments? Is truth any better than delusion or falsehood? Sanctity any better than sin? Life any better than death? The (mistaken?) idea of God any better than a (probable?) no-God? Does it matter that, as we learn on the first page of the book, so many of Quixote's prayers have remained unanswered, or that he hopes that his prayer that his little Seat ('Rocinante') might survive him 'had lodged all the time like wax in the Eternal ear?' The fact that he celebrates his morning mass in an empty church (*Monsignor Quixote* 16) may reflect on his parishioners' faith (or religious practice) rather than his own. On the other hand, the thought that it is difficult to reconcile the idea of a merciful and loving God with that of Hell, which sometimes disturbs his sleepless nights (51), is an indication of what passes through his own mind. The half-serious, half-facetious remarks of the clerical dignitary he helps when his car runs out of petrol (the Bishop of Mopoto, in *partibus infidelium*, of course) also strengthen the interrogatory tone: 'Perhaps we are all fictions, Father, in the mind of God'. [22]

Doubt (or at very least the serious difficulties associated with religious faith) is constantly suggested, even if intermittently and with no apparent great anxiety. When Quixote talks about *belief,* however, a thread of negations runs through his thinking, and the real theme of his reflection is the obstacles to belief or the undesirable consequences it entails.

At the beginning of their travels, Sancho tells Quixote that (or more accurately implicitly asks whether ) the old priest still believes '...all that nonsense. God, the Trinity, the Immaculate Conception'. [29] Quixote, who has been talking about the permanently incomplete nature of any conversion, replies that he *wants* to believe and *wants* others to believe. In the face of life 'at its dirty work,' Sancho goes on, 'belief dies away like desire for a woman.' A little later, answering Sancho's questions about his own doubts, the good father expresses the hope that his friend also has them, since it is human to do so. Each assures the other that he tries to avoid them. What is more interesting, however, is Quixote's further thought immediately after this exchange:

> It's odd, he thought, as he steered Rocinante with undue caution round a curve, how sharing a sense of doubt can bring men together perhaps even more than sharing a faith. The believer will fight another believer over a shade of difference: the doubter fights only with himself. [52]

The uncomfortable articles of his faith seem to be accepted at a single level, namely that of obedience to authority. He believes in Hell, he says, 'from obedience but not from the heart. Like a full stop it was the end of the conversation' (66). This more or less permanent way of seeing things is similar to, without perhaps being the same as, that recalled by Sancho, describing his student days at Salamanca when he heard Unamuno talking of 'a muffled voice, a voice of uncertainty which whispers in the ear of the believer. Who knows?

Without this uncertainty how could we live?' (97-98). Quixote himself expresses the same idea just after he has made his final farewells to his house-keeper, Teresa:

> 'No, no, Teresa, for a Christian there's no such thing as goodbye for ever.'
> He raised his hand from habit to make the sign of the cross in blessing, but he didn't complete it.
>
> I believe what I told her, he told himself as he went to find the Mayor, I believe it of course, but how is it that when I speak of belief, I become aware always of a shadow, the shadow of disbelief haunting my belief? [171-72]

Such reflections, prompted by reactions to ordinary and even banal incidents, could appear to suggest that he is about to become another in the long line of fictional priests who have lost their faith, another figure like Father William Callifer in Greene's *The Potting Shed* or the subtle and lucid Canon Cénabre in Bernanos's *L'Imposture*. That does not happen, and a distinction he himself makes explains why. Future generations (epitomized in Sancho's great-great-grandson) may, he says, have nothing to hope for but death. To Sancho's statement that by then death itself may have been conquered by transplants, he replies that a happy death, by which he means the hope of something further, would be preferable. Sancho then asks whether he means 'the beatific vision and all that nonsense. Believing in eternal life?' Quixote's answer to the sarcastic question is important: 'No. Not necessarily believing. We can't always believe. Just having faith' [70-71]. In other words, belief and faith are *different things,* in the Monsignor's eyes at least.

As they leave the familiar world of La Mancha, Quixote observes to Sancho that nothing seems safe any more. Not even your faith? asks the latter. It was, we learn, a question which the priest did not bother to answer. Why he remained silent subsequently becomes more apparent, when we begin to see the complex interplay of doubt, belief, and faith in his mind. Later in the same day, we have the first intimation of the dream that is weighing on him, which 'stayed with him like a cheap tune in the head'. [67] It is worth recalling:

> He had dreamt that Christ had been saved from the Cross by the legion of angels to which on an earlier occasion the Devil had told Him that he could appeal. So there was no final agony, no heavy stone which had to be rolled away, no discovery of an empty tomb. Father Quixote stood there watching on Golgotha as Christ stepped down from the Cross triumphant and acclaimed. The Roman soldiers, even the Centurion, knelt in His honour and the people of Jerusalem poured up the hill to worship Him. The disciples clustered happily around. His mother smiled through her tears of joy. There was no ambiguity, no room for doubt and no faith at all. The whole world knew with certainty that Christ was the Son of God. [67].

One might have expected him to be haunted by the horror of doubt or disbelief, but the fact of the matter is that he is deeply disturbed by that of the *abolition of faith*: 'no room for doubt and no room for faith at all'. Doubt and faith are complementary and inseparable, and not synonymous with disbelief and belief. The latter both depend on the acceptability and credibility of some kind of evidence, whereas faith is beyond reason although it can include it, and for the person possessing it, it is of the nature of a gift. It is possible to understand why Quixote talks of the shadow of disbelief behind his belief, accepts his doubts, and prays that Sancho, too, may be saved from belief.

Despite the shadows, Quixote never loses that gift. Whatever absurdities Sancho might manage to dig out of his works of theology, he tells him that he will still have faith in the historic fact that Christ died on the Cross and rose again (75). He knows what Sancho thinks: that his God is an illusion like the windmills in the book about his fictional ancestor. His retort is lively: 'He exists, I tell you, I don't just believe in Him. I touch Him'. [139] In response to the mayor's observation that he *knows* that Marx and Lenin existed, but that the priest only *believes,* Quixote repeats what he has already said: 'I tell you it's not a question of belief. I touch Him'. [140] For him, consecration and communion in the Eucharist are where God and man meet. His ultimate *suspensio a divinis,* which means that he is no longer allowed to say mass, is 'the sentence of death'. [180]

He is only to say it once more, in fact. The truncated, concentrated, sleep-walking version of it he offers in the Osera monastery, injured and sedated, brings together all the threads of the book. What happens during it? The visiting American Hispanist, Pilbeam, a 'rather nominal' Catholic, simply asks as he witnesses it, 'Sleep? Delirium? Madness?'. [215] That suggests one end of the range of possible explanations. The other would be some kind of real but mystical experience. Between them, a number of reasonably plausible accounts might be offered. At the phenomenological level, it is presumably fact for Quixote, who as far as he knows is consecrating bread and wine. For the others, it is presumably probably fiction, if only because there is no bread and wine for him to consecrate. In the end, we are in a realm where neither the reader nor characters know what is fact and what is fiction, an idea contained in the whole book and strengthened by the conversation between Pilbeam and the Trappist monk, Father Leopoldo. The latter's observations perhaps suggest the ultimate nature of religious faith: 'Faith and fiction – in the end you can't distinguish between them – you just have to choose ... I think, you know, professor, that when one has to jump, it's so much safer to jump into deep water'.[206] In Greene's writing, here as elsewhere, those who have made that jump are still surrounded and sometimes submerged by deep water and cannot always keep the world above and around them clearly in sight.

In *Catholics,* the situation is rather different. There, only the protagonist himself seems susceptible to any radical doubt. Whatever their weaknesses, however 'simple' their faith may seem, to whatever extent we may judge it to be based on a shared and mutually-supported way of understanding life, the monks he rules never look for more than a degree of reassurance. What they need to feel certain of is not the existence of God, for that they never seem to question, but that it is indubitably His will that they preserve the old mass, said in the old way. They do not feel the need to be told that there is a Trinity, or that Christ died to redeem a fallen humanity, or that the sacraments are efficacious.

Their Abbot's need is greater than theirs. Intermittently in the past, and henceforth perhaps continually, the 'null' is with him. Like Iris Murdoch's Carel Fisher, the rector of St Eustace Watergate in *The Time of the Angels*, who said 'my vocation is to be a priest. If there is no God it is my vocation to be the priest of no God' [82], he presumably considers the role of the priest to be even more essential if the mysteries he celebrates have no objective correlative. That is presumably why, although he obeys the orders he receives from Rome (since to refuse to do so would mean his removal), he stays on the island to lead the community in its new kind of spiritual life.

His lack of faith is briefly indicated at one of two points in the book. The most important occasion follows the scene in which he has observed the brethren at their midnight vigil and told Father Walter to dismiss them, taxing him with disobedience and folly. Genuflecting 'from habit' as he faces the chancel, he recalls his first visit to Lourdes, 'that sad and dreadful place' which, Kinsella has told him, 'is no longer in operation':

> The Abbot thought of his own visit to Lourdes, remembering the thousands on thousands of banked candles in the grotto where the Virgin was supposed to have appeared to an illiterate French girl. With four other priests he had arrived on a pilgrimage excursion and, on the first morning, visited the shrine to see the myriad crutches and trusses hung on the grotto walls, the medical bureau with its certifications of 'miraculous' cures, the tawdry religious supermarkets, crammed with rosaries and statuettes, the long lines of stretchers and wheelchairs on which lay the desperate and the ill, the stinking waters of the 'miraculous' bathing pool. At noon, the Abbot fled to his hotel room, where, pleading dysentery, he shut himself up, seeing no one, until it was time for the excursion train to leave. Two days in that room, trying not to think of what he had seen, trying to say his prayers. [77-78].

Lourdes was not the first time such things had happened. There had been other, earlier, briefer occasions on Muck and the mainland when 'the bad time had come upon him, that time when, staring at the altar, he knew the hell of the metaphysician: the hell of those deprived of God'. [78] The sequence of symptoms seems well established: an inability to pray, and then a fit of trembling:

> Then his trembling began, that fear and trembling which was a sort of purgatory presaging the true hell to come, the hell of no feeling, that

null, that void. A man wearing the habit of a religious, sitting in a building, staring at a table called an altar on which there is a box called a ciborium, and inside the ciborium are twelve round wafers of unleavened bread made by the Sisters of Knock Convent, Knock, County Mayo. That is all there is in the tabernacle in this building which is said to be the house of God. And the man who sits facing the tabernacle is a man with the apt title of *prelatus nullius*, nobody's prelate, belonging to nobody. Not God's Abbot, though he sometimes tries to say the words, 'Our Father Who Art in Heaven', but there is no Father in Heaven, His name is not hallowed by these words, His kingdom will not come to he (sic) who sits and stares at the tabernacle; who, when he tries to pray, enters null; who, when in it, must remain, from day to day, weeks becoming months, and, sometimes, as after Lourdes, a year. [78–79]

As a consequence of such experiences of the cold heaven and the empty tabernacle, he has avoided prayer, pretending a preference for private devotions, for saying his mass alone, no longer reading his daily office, avoiding public prayer and allowing others to lead it. Sometimes, we learn, he had to say grace, uttering the words but not praying. [79]. His strategy has been to hold back, to avoid whenever possible even going through the motions of his prescribed life of prayer, and to be content to act as far as possible as an efficient leader and manager: 'If one did not risk invoking God, one did not risk one's peace of mind. He was needed here. He did his work. He did his best. But did not pray. He had not prayed now for, well, he did not want to think. A long time, yes. Some years'. [79]

After sitting in the church 'as a man sits in a empty waiting-room' and reprimanding the real ringleader of the secret vigils and prayers, the enormous, impressive and powerful Father Matthew, he does not genuflect as he leaves. [84] At the end of the book, however, as Kinsella departs, he consciously and deliberately leads the community in the Our Father. Prayer, he has told them, is the only miracle. We pray. If our words become prayer, God will come.[101] As he begins the ancient prayer, 'His trembling increased. He would never come back. In null'. [101]

That is certainly the end of one kind of evasion, since his leadership is renewed and confirmed, and he now accepts those aspects of it that in the past he has avoided because of the distress they cause him. Whether it is a return to a kind of faith ('Lord, I believe; help thou mine unbelief') is impossible to say. But he is forced to face up to his faith, or to the emptiness its disappearance has left in him and around him.

In the book, faith is pictured and presented in terms of the old faith, the old attitudes and assumptions, the old practices and language which, as we learn from the Father General's letter to the Abbot, have to be abandoned 'in view of the *apertura,* possibly the most significant historical event of our century. When interpenetration between Christian and Buddhist faith is on the verge of reali-

ty'. [44] Just after his first meeting with Kinsella on the rainswept beach, Father
Manus tells him vigorously what those old ways mean:

> offering up the daily sacrifice of the Mass *to God*. Changing bread and
> wine into the body and blood of Jesus Christ the way Jesus told his disci-
> ples to do it at the Last Supper ... And the Mass was said in Latin because
> Latin was the language of the Church and the Church was one and uni-
> versal...the Mass was not talking to your neighbour, it was talking to
> God...if you saw those people, their heads bare, the rain pelting off their
> faces, when they see the Host raised up, that piece of unleavened bread
> that, through the mystery of the Mass, is now the body and blood of
> Jesus Christ ... you would be ashamed to sweep all that away and put in
> its place what you have put there – singing and guitars and turning to
> touch your neighbour, playacting and nonsense ... [46-48]

When Kinsella explains to the Abbot why he has come to the island and enumerates and explains the nature of the abuses he has come to eradicate, it is
clear that they are all associated with a certain conception and practice of
Catholic faith that disturbs the wider world of ecumenical politics. What must
be prevented at all costs is 'the first stirrings of a Catholic counterrevolution'.
[85] When Father Matthew is told by the Abbot that the Mass is now merely
symbolic, he gives the only answer he can: 'That is heresy, pure and simple,'
and describes the Mass in the same words as those already used by Father
Manus.

When that faith is presented in other contexts – as in Kinsella's reflection
in Hern's Hotel [12-13] or in the Abbot's thoughts about the Brazilian political priest, Father Hartmann, there is always a stress on the difference between
the old and new patterns of thought. Kinsella recalls the words of his friend
Visher, a behaviourist, summing up his study of Catholic attitudes towards
their clergy: 'They want those old parish priests and those old family doctors.
Sheep need authoritarian sheepdogs nipping at their heels from birth to
funeral. They don't want this ecumenical tolerance. They want certainties'.
[12-13] The Abbot's question about Hartmann and Kinsella's reply are equally
illuminating: 'Does he talk much about God?...Is it souls he's after? Or is it the
good of mankind?' 'I would say the latter'. [40-41] When he explains to
Kinsella why the community has kept the old mass, he is careful to stress that
it was for positive reasons: because the people wanted and needed it. [61] The
latter learns that he has been referred to as 'the inquisitor', and is furious,
retorting that 'this is the end of the twentieth century, not the beginning of
the thirteenth. How can we even define what heresy is today'. [60]

However, an old orthodoxy is about to be replaced by a new one in the
interests of discipline and unity. The mass is to be, in Father Manus' words, no
longer 'talking to God' but 'talking to your neighbour'. [48] There is a new
role for the church, which will become 'a more generalized community concept, a group gathered in a meeting to celebrate God-in-others' [68]. Both

orthodoxies highlight each other by antithesis, and the two opposing concepts become apparent as Kinsella expresses his own beliefs, derived from the teaching of Hartmann, in which 'the Church ... despite its history and its dependence on myth and miracle, exists as the quintessential structure through which social revolution can be brought to certain areas of the globe'. [20-21].

We know that the locals, the monastic community, and the pilgrims see faith and its expression in human life in one way, and that Kinsella, the World Ecumenical Council, the Father General of the Albanesian Order, and the Abbot's immediate superior understand them in quite another. We also know that what the Abbot has lost is the first of those two ways, and that the second can never fill 'the null' that the loss has left. Beliefs, which in this case are rational, humane, and well-intentioned views about progress and the transformation of the structures of society, cannot replace faith, the acceptance of a reality, and an order that transcend the human and the social. In the state which he finds himself, belief in that sense is almost an irrelevance, separate and independent, having nothing to do with the empty tabernacle in which the no-God lives. The only link between the two perspectives is an essentially negative situation in which the man with at least a concept of what faith, hope, and charity mean can see the new horizontalism for the poor substitute that it is, and the new zealot can picture the earlier virtues enshrined in the vertical image of the relationship between man and God and outdated and naive symbols of the desire to create the just and decent earthly city.

Thus the Abbot is in a double null, since his faith has gone and what the new ecumenical religious sociology can offer him is not what he needs. If we accept that understanding of his position, what are we to make of the closing lines of the book when, having been told that 'prayer is the only miracle' and that 'with prayer God will come,' we see him stiff, trembling, and entering the void with no hope of return as he leads the community in the Our Father? A skilful deception, maintained for the sake of others at the cost of the painful sacrifice of his equilibrium, achieved with such difficulty? A conscious attempt to will God into existence? Self-abnegation before the overwhelming silence of God, in the desperate hope that the silence may in some way be construed as speech? Those and other answers are all possible. All the reader can know is that the Abbot is a man who needs the transcendent, that at a time of acute perception of its absence he enters a state of metaphysical shock, and that the crisis he undergoes as Kinsella leaves will, whatever its outcome, probably be the last of its kind in his life. What he can imagine is another matter, and here, as in *Cold Heaven*, Moore leaves him to his own devices.

In these two contemporary religious parables, therefore, there is a constant interplay of doubt, belief and faith. All are present in both, but arise in different ways and take different forms. Each author seems to see doubt as inevitable and belief as different from faith, with the latter implying a positive receptivity that has to go beyond the reasonable. Quixote has it, whatever his doubts and disbelief, and the need for it seems to him to be an essential feature of the inscrutable way in which God has chosen to work. The Abbot lacks it, but is appalled by its absence, and in the end is willing to act as if he had it. The two books, which might appear to present models of Catholic agnosticism and Catholic atheism respectively, are not as similar as they may seem. The major problem with the Monsignor's faith is not whether he has it, but whether it relates to fact or fiction, to a transcendent reality or a subjective state, to something 'out there' or to something 'in here'. With the Abbot, the crucial question is a different one: can the overwhelming sense of the empty tabernacle and the non-existence of God co-exist with a hidden faith? The Abbott certainly seems to have experienced a more radical kind of awareness of no-God than the Monsignor, since he 'knows' that there is nothing in the tabernacle but unleavened bread as profoundly as Quixote 'knows' that he touches God. It is hard to believe that when he prays at the end of the book he is engaging in the kind of farewell described in Don Cupitt's *Taking Leave of God*, seeing him as the best and greatest creation of the human mind. Perhaps his state of mind is more like that of Petru Dumitriu in his *To the Unknown God,* calling to the God in whom he cannot believe. He could perhaps reverse the Monsignor's statement that behind his belief there is always the shadow of disbelief, since he is obsessed by the faith he has lost. The phenomenological approach adopted by both authors obviously precludes any definite answer, but it also allows of intelligent and imaginative surmises.

There may be no authorial intervention in either *Monsignor Quixote* or *Catholics,* but it is perhaps possible to detect, or at least suspect, the shadowy existence of something like an authorial stance. The Monsignor and the Abbot can only think the thoughts, feel the emotions, and make the judgments at some time actually or potentially present in the minds and sensibilities of their creators. In other words, if Greene and Moore show different ways of reacting to Catholic faith, it is because their own reactions differ.

Without that faith, Quixote would probably feel much the same kind of anguish as the Abbot. Both have their 'bad times', even if such spells of misery are rather different in nature. In fact, the Monsignor's problem is marginal rather than central: despite all his doubts, disbelief, and sense of his own inadequacy, he clings to his faith, even though most of those around him see it as very probably an illusion, a view which the reader, and possibly even the author, may share. No judgement is possible, since we are in the realm of subjective mental phenomena not susceptible to empirical or intersubjective verification. All we can say is that he seems to remain simple, human, unshocked and, given a certain minimal tolerance, quite orthodox. In the Sartrean sense, his actions and choices determine his nature, and he dies a believing and practising Catholic priest.

The Abbot's case is more complicated. Although he can no longer accept the dogma of his religion (or at least the older form of it he has always insisted on adhering to), the reasons for this situation, or rather the mental states proving it, are totally convincing only if we see them primarily as a collection of neurotic symptoms. There may also be some doubt, as we have seen, about the general plausibility of the suppositions about Catholic doctrine and practices

Moore weaves into his reflections and memories. It might be as well to reca-
pitulate the most important of those elements.

The reactions described in his memories of Lourdes seem rather more like
those a skeptic appalled by a rather gamey new religious experience than
those of a dyed-in-the-wool Catholic who has seen all the moral and aesthetic
*grandeurs et misères* his religion might thrust upon him. Given his background,
experience, inherited and cultivated mentality and judgement of men, they are
only really credible if we posit a kind of exasperated hypersensitivity. Since the
Catholic Church is presumably by definition and institution for all human
beings, in all places and at all times, culture shocks are to be expected within
it, even for a much-travelled member. Catholic life in Lima, Nagasaki, or
Manila is not quite the same as Catholic life in Nijmegen, San Francisco, or
Dublin. The sight of crutches and trusses hanging on grotto walls, the religious
supermarkets, the desperate and ill, the smell of the bathing pool do not seem
enough to shatter the faith of anyone in a rude state of Catholic health, even if
they might offer the occasion for an unsympathetic outsider to write wittily
dismissive accounts of one kind of piety. We know that he had experienced
shorter spells of anguish before his visit to Lourdes. Was some kind of break-
down in that 'sad and dreadful place' merely the final blow to a shaky faith?

Other aspects of the way Moore presents his protagonist also grate a little.
In the passage describing the symptoms of his spiritual state (77-78) quoted
above, there is something even more striking than the grammatical mistake.
His use of language, or at least the language Moore uses to indicate his
thoughts, is unconvincing. As we have seen, he describes his fear and trembling
as 'a sort of purgatory preceding the true hell to come'. For an ecclesiastic in
high office, with a doctorate, presumably in some branch of theology, that is a
very odd image indeed, since in Catholic dogma as in good logic purgatory, a
place of purification, not punishment, can lead only to heaven. It is not a mistake than even the relatively unlearned Quixote would make. Similarly, the
private devotional practices he pretends to engage in to avoid participating in
the mass and community prayer seem, surprisingly, to arouse no comment,
speculation, protest, rebuke, comment, or indeed any reaction on the part of
his fellow monks. The Albanesians were an ancient order with a rule and way
of life presumably based on the kind of practices he seeks to avoid, and we
know that his Abbey was no hotbed of unavowed hankerings after some kind
of 'progressive' religious experience. Even if elsewhere the order in general was
not what it used to be, Muck is still set in its ways. Or we could take the ren-
dering of the ecclesiastical title *prelatus nullius* the Abbot (or Moore) offers us:
'nobody's prelate, belonging to nobody.' Understood even in that wrong sense,
it is not an altogether apt description of the Abbot's position, since he is very
much the leader of his community and has shown his independence of other
authority. Taken in the right sense, it is even less appropriate. Such a dignitary
has in fact considerable power and numerous responsibilities and is seen as
sharing the authority of the Pope. He is outside the jurisdiction of the local
bishop, and is *subject* to none, rather than belonging to none. If Moore's mis-

translation is deliberate, it is not particularly felicitous, since the irony fails to some extent. If, as is probably the case, it is unconscious, it is simply mildly irritating.

Superficial and carping as such observations may seem, they are important because cumulatively they are indicative. They suggest a new way of seeing the book, providing a kind of internal evidence to go hand-in-hand with the external knowledge that we often cannot help bringing to our reading. In the end, they perhaps help to contribute to a sharper sense of the difference between the two books, a difference all the more remarkable for their many similarities. On the one hand, both represent an interestingly parallel investigation into the nature of the religious mentality, into faith, and into the poverty of a horizontal rather than a vertical conception of the relationship between man and God, whatever He may be. Behind similarities of approach and subject-matter, however, there is a difference in the central characters arising from a difference between their creators. For all its doubts and disbelief, *Monsignor Quixote* still seems to be written from an insider's point of view. The real nature of a church and its faith are suggested by someone to whom, for all his quixotic relationship with them, they are still familiar. The attitudes and practices of a region of human reflection and hope are known and in principle interiorized. *Catholics* is a book by a former inmate of what used to be called 'the household of the faith' who knows, remembers, and understands quite a lot, but not everything, about the place he has left.

*Works cited*

Greene, Graham, *Monsignor Quixote*, London and New York, Simon and Schuster, 1982.

Hart, Charles, *The Student's Catholic Doctrine,* London, 1916, reprinted 1943.

Moore, Brian, *Catholics.* London and Toronto, McClelland and Stewart, 1972.

Murdoch, Iris, *The Time of the Angels.* London and New York, Viking Press, 1966.

*New Catholic Encyclopaedia,* ed. William J. McDonald (prepared by Catholic Universty of America), New York, McGraw-Hill, 1967.

*On Literature, and Catholic Literature*

# A Catholic View of Reality[1]

## GEORGE BERNANOS

No doubt there is something rather audacious and simplistic about suggesting that novelists should pay attention to the problem of evil at a time when so many of my young confrères are offering scandals for sale that supply may well soon exceed demand, and so much so that one day you will see the most outstanding pupils from the Gide or Proust conservatoires, all with their little diplomas in immoralism, vainly hawking their awful memoirs of their youth or adolescence around from door to door, all of them reading as if they had been produced in prisons but drearily impudent enough to wear down even the sense of decency of vergers and lady chair attendants. In times gone by, a writer would receive us at the threshold of his conscience and, like a suspicious host, prudently point out the general layout of his dwelling and the whereabouts of his most secret rooms, from afar. Nowadays, he gives us his key-ring, taps us encouragingly on the shoulder, and tells us to get on with it.

Well, that's how things are. We hardly go there now, and if we do, only unwillingly. Many things, often highly shameful, go on in such minds, discharging monotonously in an indeterminate and silent flow of muddy waters. There is nothing that holds out, no dam, no eddies, no foam. Evil passes through them as if through a sieve. Is it really evil, or rather the hallucinated pursuit of it, since acts are unimportant? All we can know in such works is intentions, which merely lead to a further proliferation of intentions that also founder in the void. Thus Proust's extraordinary work seems to me to be a graveyard of intentions, a cemetery shrouded in sea-mists, where still-born babies are buried.

Such literature is both frantic and dreary. The pallid heroes of the colourless world it portrays may well be restless, but they seem to work to order, and with repugnance. Their strange gymnastics disconcert me, and I feel like telling these hard-working acrobats who push themselves so cruelly to inspire terror or pity in us that enough is enough, to take a rest, or they will fall ill.

How is it that they produce such a sensation of boredom? Because they do evil without believing in it. They are quite capable of simulating passions, but not of feeling them in their hearts. What benefit is there in such deceptive creatures for a novelist? They have never found, or even sought, their conscience. They have never found, or even sought, their conscience. They passively live through circumstances and situations, have the same index of refraction as they do, and are no longer even distinguishable from them. What they have the great audacity to call their lives – 'I have lived', they proudly say to dazzled young women – is no more than a dreary, random succession of states of unbridled sensuality. What a boring list it is! And, of course, we are

---

1    From *Le Crépuscule des Vieux,* Paris, Gallimard, 1956.

unwilling to be convinced that if such people take very great care to hide nothing from us, it is perhaps because they have nothing much to say.

In literature, curiosity alone leads nowhere. Watching the restless agitation of human life may be satisfactory for a time, but all we ultimately obtain from it (unless we are completely taken in by the spectacle) is a bitter joy that in the end may well lead to a voluptuous, fatal and convulsive contempt. Knowledge of others, or ourselves, is not achieved through a precise and meticulous detailing of their stream of consciousness, all their actions, or even all their intentions. For the sum of all these is their lives, and few men resemble their lives.

Immoralism – by which I mean an indifference with regard to good and evil – scarcely disposes us to take human beings seriously. And if we don't take them seriously, how in heaven's name can we pity them? The wretched little adventure we call life will simply be a series of anecdotes linked by nothing more than a continually frustrated search for pleasure. The world of the curious psychologist is like the moral world in the same way as a globe covered with signs and figures is like our quivering planet flying through the black void of space towards Centaurus and a more mysterious destiny than any other star in the infinity of the heavens. What is the psychological world to me, if I have no access to the moral world? Life may be logical in the former, but only in the latter is it alive.

# On the Novel with a Purpose [1]

## G.K. CHESTERTON

I see that Mr. Patrick Braybrooke and others, writing to the *Catholic Times,* have raised the question of Catholic propaganda in novels written by Catholics. The very phrase, which we are all compelled to use, is awkward and even false. A Catholic putting Catholicism into a novel, or a song, or a sonnet, or anything else, is not being a propagandist; he is simply being a Catholic. Everybody understands this about every other enthusiasm in the world. When we say that a poet's landscape and atmosphere are full of the spirit of England, we do not mean that he is necessarily conducting an Anti-German propaganda during the Great War. We mean that if he is really an English poet, his poetry cannot be anything but English. When we say that songs are full of the spirit of the sea, we do not mean that the poet is recruiting for the Navy or even trying to collect men for the merchant service. We mean that he loves the sea; and for that reason

---

1    From *The Thing,* London, Sheed and Ward, 1939.

would like other men to love it. Personally, I am all for propaganda; and a great deal of what I write is deliberately propagandist. But even when it is not in the least propagandist, it will probably be full of the implications of my religion; because that is what is meant by having a religion. So the jokes of a Buddhist, if there were any, would be Buddhist jokes. So the love-songs of a Calvinistic Methodist, should they burst from him, would be Calvinistic Methodist love-songs. Catholics have produced more jokes and love-songs than Calvinists and Buddhists. That is because, saving their holy presence, Calvinists and Buddhists have not got so large or human a religion. But anything they did express would be steeped in any convictions that they do hold; and that is a piece of common sense which would seem to be quite self-evident; yet I foresee a vast amount of difficulty about it in the one isolated case of the Catholic Church.

To begin with, what I have said would be true of any other real religion; but so much of the modern world is full of a religiosity that is rather a sort of unconscious prejudice. Buddhism is a real religion, or at any rate, a very real philosophy. Calvinism was a real religion, with a real theology. But the mind of the modern man is a curious mixture of decayed Calvinism and diluted Buddhism; and he expresses his philosophy without knowing that he holds it. We say what is natural to us to say; but we know what we are saying; there-fore it is assumed that we are saying it for effect. He says what is natural to him to say; but he does not know what he is saying, still less why he is saying it. So he is not accused of uttering his dogma with the purpose of revealing it to the world; for he has not really revealed it to himself. He is just as partisan; he is just as particularist; he is just as much depending on one doctrinal sys-tem as distinct from another. But he has taken it for granted so often that he has forgotten what it is. So his literature does not seem to him partisan, even when it is. But our literature does seem to him propagandist, even when it isn't.

Suppose I write a story, let us hope a short story, say, about a wood that is haunted by evil spirits. Let us give ourselves the pleasure of supposing that at night all the branches have the appearance of being hung with hundreds of corpses, like the orchard of Louis the Eleventh, the spirits of travellers who have hanged themselves when they came to that sport; or anything bright and cheery like that. Suppose I make my hero, Gorlias Fitzgorgon (that noble character) make the sign of the cross as he passes this spot; or the friend who represents wisdom and experience advise him to consult a priest with a view to exorcism. Making the sign of the cross seems to me not only religiously right, but artistically appropriate and psychologically probable. It is what I should do; it is what I conceive that my friend Fitzgorgon would do; it is also aesthetically apt, or, as they say, 'in the picture'. I rather fancy it might be effec-tive if the traveller saw with the mystical eye, as he saw the forest of dead men, a sort of shining pattern or silver tangle of crosses hovering in the dark, where so many human fingers had made that sign upon the empty air. But though I am writing what seems to me natural and appropriate and artistic, I know that the moment I have written it, a great roar and bellow will go up with the word 'Propaganda' coming from a thousand throats; and that every other critic, even if he is kind enough to commend the story, will certainly add: 'But why does Mr. Chesterton drag in his Roman Catholicism?'

Now let us suppose that Mr. Chesterton has not this disgusting habit. Let us suppose that I write the same story, or the same sort of story, informed with a philosophy which is familiar and therefore unobserved. Let us suppose that I accept the ready-made assumptions of the hour, without examining them any more than the others do. Suppose I get into the smooth rut of newspaper routine and political catchwords; and make the man in my story act exactly like the man in the average magazine story. I know exactly what the man in the average magazine story would do. I can almost give you his exact words. In that case Fitzgorgon, on first catching a glimpse of the crowds of swaying spectres in the moon, will almost inevitably say: 'But this is the twentieth century!'

In itself, of course, the remark is simply meaningless. It is far more meaningless than making the sign of the cross could ever be; for to that even its enemies attach some sort of meaning. But to answer a ghost by saying, 'This is the twentieth century,' is in itself quite unmeaning; like seeing somebody commit a murder and then saying, 'But this is the second Tuesday in August!' Nevertheless, the magazine writer who for the thousandth time puts these words into the magazine story, has an intention in this illogical phrase. He is really depending upon two dogmas; neither of which he dares to question and neither of which he is able to state. The dogmas are: first, that humanity is perpetually and permanently improving through the process of time; and second, that improvement consists in a greater and greater indifference or incredulity about the miraculous. Neither of these two statements can be proved. And it goes without saying that the man who uses them cannot prove them, for he cannot even state them. In so far as they are at all in the order of things that can be proved, they are things that can be disproved. For certainly there have been historical periods of relapse and retrogression; and there certainly are highly organised and scientific civilizations very much excited about the supernatural; as people are about Spiritualism to-day. But anyhow, the two dogmas must be accepted on authority as absolutely true before there is any sense whatever in Gorlias Fitzgorgon saying, 'But this is the twentieth century.' The phrase depends on the philosophy; and the philosophy is put into the story.

Yet nobody says the magazine story is propagandist. Nobody says it is preaching that philosophy because it contains that phrase. We do not say that the writer has dragged in his progressive party politics. We do not say that he is going out of his way to turn the story into a novel with a purpose. He does not feel as if he were going out of his way; his way lies straight through the haunted wood, as does the other; and he only makes Gorlias say what seems to him a sensible thing to say; and I make him do what seems to be a sensible thing to do. We are both artists in the same sense; we are both propagandists in the same sense and non-propagandists in the same sense. The only difference is that I can defend my dogma and he cannot even define his.

In other words, this world of to-day does not know that all the novels and newspapers that it reads or writes are in fact full of certain assumptions, that are just as dogmatic as dogmas. With some of those assumptions I agree, such as the ideal of human equality implied in all romantic stories from *Cinderella to Oliver Twist;* that the rich are insulting God in despising poverty. With some of them I totally disagree; as in the curious idea of human inequality, which is permitted about races though not about classes. 'Nordic' people are so much superior to 'Dagoes', that a score of Spanish desperados armed to the teeth are certain to flee in terror from the fist of any solitary gentleman who has earned all the military and heroic virtues in Wall Street or the Stock Exchange.

But the point about these assumptions, true or false, is that they are felt as being assumed, or alluded to or taken naturally as they come. They are not felt as being preached; and therefore they are not called propaganda. Yet they have in practice all the double character of propaganda; they involve certain views with which everyone does not agree; and they do in fact spread those views by means of fiction and popular literature. What they do not do is to state them clearly so that they can be criticised. I do not blame the writers for putting their philosophy into their stories. I should not blame them even if they used their stories to spread their philosophy. But they do blame us; and the real reason is that they have not yet realised that we have a philosophy at all.

The truth is, I think, that they are caught in a sort of argument in a circle. Their vague philosophy says to them: 'All religion is dead; Roman Catholicism is a religious sect which must be particularly dead, since it consists of mere external acts and attitudes, crossings, genuflections and the rest; which these sectarians suppose they have to perform in a particular place at a particular time'. Then some Catholic will write a romance or a tragedy about the love of a man and woman, or the rivalry of two men, or any other general human affair; and they will be astonished to find that he cannot preach these things in an 'unsectarian' way. They say, 'Why does he drag in his religion?' They mean, 'Why does he drag in his religion, which consisted entirely of crossings, genuflections and external acts belonging to a particular place and time, when he is talking about the wide world and the beauty of woman and the anger and ambition of man?' In other words, they say, 'When we have assumed that his creed is a small and dead thing, how dare he apply it as a universal and living thing? It has no right to be so broad, when we all know it is so narrow.'

I conclude therefore that, while Mr. Braybrooke was quite right in suggesting that a novelist with a creed ought not to be ashamed of having a cause, the more immediate necessity is to find some way of popularising our whole philosophy of life, by putting it more plainly than it can be put in the symbol of a story. The difficulty with a story is in its very simplicity and especially in its swiftness. Men do things and do not define or defend them. Gorlias Fitzgorgon makes the sign of the cross; he does not stop in the middle of the demon wood to explain why it is at once an invocation of the Trinity and a memorial of the Crucifixion. What is wanted is a popular outline of the way in which ordinary affairs are affected by our view of life, and how it is also a view of death, a view of sex, a view of social decencies, and so on. When people understand the light that shines for us upon all these facts, they would no longer be surprised to find it shining in our fictions.

# On Two Allegories[1]

## G.K. CHESTERTON

Perhaps it is only fair that the modern iconoclasm should be applied also to the ancient iconoclasts; and especially to the great Puritans, those idol-breakers who have long been idols. Mr. Belloc was recently tapping the Parliamentary statue of Cromwell with a highly scientific hammer; and Mr. Noyes has suddenly assailed the image of Bunyan with something more like a sledgehammer. In the latter case I confess to thinking the reaction excessive; I should say nothing worse of Bunyan than of many old writers; that he is best known by his best passages, and that many, who fondly believe they have read him, would be mildly surprised at some of his worst passages. But that is not peculiar to Bunyan; and I for one should be content with saying what I said some years ago. A fair and balanced view of the culture and creeds involved can best be reached by comparing the Pilgrimage of Christian with the Pilgrimage of Piers Plowman. The Puritan allegory is much neater (even if it be not always neat) than the rather bewildering mediaeval medley. The Puritan allegory is more national, in the sense that the language and style have obviously become clearer and more fixed. But the Puritan allegory is certainly much narrower than the mediaeval allegory. Piers Plowman deals with the death or resurrection of a whole human society, where men are members of each other. In the later work schism has 'isolated the soul'; and it is certainly mere individualism, when it is not mere terrorism. But I will only say now what I said then; I do not want to damage the statute of John Bunyan at Bedford, where it stands facing (symbolically in more ways than one) the site of his own prison. But I do wish there were a statute of John Langland, uplifted on a natural height into a more native air, and looking across all England from the Malvern hills.

1    From *The Thing,* London, Sheed & Ward, 1939.

But there is one intellectual side issue of the debate that does interest me very much. Mr. James Douglas, who once presented himself to me as a representative of Protestant truth, and who is certainly a representative of Protestant tradition, answered Mr. Alfred Noyes in terms very typical of the present state of that tradition. He said that we should salute Bunyan's living literary genius, and not bother our heads about Bunyan's obsolete theology. Then he added the comparison which seems to me so thought-provoking: that this is after all what we do, when we admire Dante's genius and not his obsolete theology. Now there is a distinction to be made here; if the whole modern mind is to realize at all where it stands. If I say that Bunyan's theology is obsolete, but Dante's theology is not obsolete – then I know the features of my friend Mr. Douglas will be wreathed in a refined smile of superiority and scorn. He will say that I am a Papist and therefore of course I think the Papist dogmatism living. But the point is that he is a Protestant and he thinks the Protestant dogmatism dead. I do at least defend the Catholic theory because it can be defended. The Puritans would presumably be defending the Puritan theory – if it could be defended. The point is that it is dead for them as much as for us. It is not merely that Mr. Noyes demands the disappearance of a disfigurement; it is that Mr. Douglas says it cannot be a disfigurement because it has already disappeared. Now the Thomist philosophy, on which Dante based his poetry, has not disappeared. It is not a question of faith but of fact; anybody who knows Paris or Oxford, or the worlds where such things are discussed, will tell you that it has not disappeared. All sorts of people, including those who do not believe in it, refer to it and argue against it on equal terms.

I do not believe, for a fact, that modern men so discuss the seventeenth century sectarianism. Had I the privilege of passing a few days with Mr. Douglas and his young lions of the *Daily Express*, I doubt now that we should discuss and differ about many things. But I do rather doubt whether Mr. Douglas would every now and again cry out, as with a crow of pure delight, 'Oh, I must read you this charming little bit from Calvin'. I do rather doubt whether his young journalists are joyously capping each other's quotations from Toplady's sermons on Calvinism. But eager young men do still quote Aquinas, just as they still quote Aristotle. I have heard them at it. And certain ideas are flying about, even in the original prose of St Thomas, as well as in the poetry of Dante – or, for that matter, of Donne.

The case of Bunyan is really the opposite of the case of Dante. In Dante the abstract theory still illuminates the poetry; the ideas enlighten even where the images are dark. In Bunyan it is the human facts and figures that are bright; while the spiritual background is not only dark in spirit, but blackened by time and change. Of course it is true enough that in Dante the mere images are immensely imaginative. It is also true that in one sense some of them are obsolete; in the sense that the incidents are obsolete and the personal judgment merely personal. Nobody will ever forget how there came through the infernal twilight the figure of that insolent Troubadour, carrying his own head aloft in his hand, like a lantern to light his way. Everybody knows that such an image is poetically true to certain terrible truths about the unnatural violence of intellectual pride. But as to whether anybody has any business to say that Bertrand de Born is damned, the obvious answer is No. Dante knew no more about it than I do: only he cared more about it; and his personal quarrel is an obsolete quarrel. But that sort of thing is not Dante's theology, let alone Catholic theology.

In a word; so far from his theology being obsolete, it would be much truer to say that everything is obsolete except his theology. That he did not happen to like a particular Southern gentleman is obsolete; but that was at most a private fancy, in demonology rather than theology. We come to theology when we come to theism. And if anybody will read the passage in which Dante grapples with the gigantic problem of describing the Beatific Vision, he will find it is uplifted into another world of ideas from the successful entry to the Golden City at the end of the *Pilgrim's Progress.* It is a Thought; which a thinker, especially a genuine freethinker, is always free to go on thinking. The images of Dante are not to be worshipped, any more than any other images. But there is an idea behind all images; and it is before that, in the last lines of the Paradiso, that the spirit of the poet seems first to soar like an eagle and then to fall like a stone.

There is nothing in this comparison that reflects on the genius and genuineness of Bunyan in his own line or class; but it does serve to put him in his own class. I think there was something to be said for the vigorous denunciation of Mr. Noyes; but no such denunciation is involved in this distinction. On the contrary, it would be easy to draw the same distinction between two men both at the very top of all literary achievement. It would be true to say, I think, that those who most enjoy reading Homer care more about an eternal humanity than an ephemeral mythology. The reader of Homer cares more about men than about gods. So, as far as one can guess, does Homer. It is true that if those curious and capricious Olympians did between them make up a religion, it is now a dead religion. It is the human Hector who so died that he will never die. But we should remonstrate with a critic who, after successfully proving this about Homer, should go on to prove it about Plato. We should protest if he said that the only interest of the Platonic Dialogues to-day is in their playful asides and very lively local colour, in the gay and graceful picture of Greek life; but that nobody troubles nowadays about the obsolete philosophy of Plato. We should point out that there is not truth in the comparison; and that if anything the case is all the other way. Plato's philosophy will be important as long as there is philosophy; and Dante's religion will be important as long as there is religion. Above all, it will be important as long as there is that lucid and serene sort of religion that is most in touch with philosophy. Nobody will say that the theology of the Baptist tinker is in that sense serene or even lucid; on many points it necessarily remains obscure. The reason is that such religion does not do what philosophy does; it does not begin at the beginning. In the matter of mere chronological order, it is true that the pilgrimage of Dante and that of Bunyan both end in the Celestial City. But it is in a very different sense that the pilgrimage of Bunyan begins in the City of Destruction. The mind of Dante, like that of his master St Thomas, really begins as well as ends in the City of Creation. It begins as well as ends in the burning focus in which all things began. He sees his series from the right end, though he then begins it at the wrong end. But it is the whole point of a personal work like *The Pilgrim's Progress* that it does begin with a man's own private sins and private panic about them. This intense individualism gives it great force; but it cannot in the nature of things give it great breadth and range. Heaven is haven; but the wanderer has not many other thoughts about it except that it is haven. It is typical of the two methods, each of them very real in its way, that Dante could write a whole volume, one-third of his gigantic epic, describing the things of Heaven; whereas in the case of Bunyan, as the gates of Heaven open the book itself closes.

I think it worth while to write this note on the critical remark of Mr. James Douglas, because it is a remark that would be made as readily by many other intelligent men today. But it is founded on a fallacy; on the idea that the choice between living philosophies and dead philosophies is the same as the choice between old philosophies and new. It is not true of Plato and it is not true of Dante; and, apart from whatever is our own philosophy, we should realise that some of the most ancient are the most alive.

# Modern Novelists: A Catholic Viewpoint[1]

## PATRICIA CORR

### FIRST PRINCIPLES

The average good-living Irish Catholic tends to view the modern literary novel with distaste. This negative attitude must sooner or later be examined critically, for the novel form has become the most common medium of literary expression in this century. For the vast majority of people the novel is their only contact with literature. The Catholic reader is then, through prejudice,

---

1  From a reprint of her booklet published by the *Irish Messenger*, Dublin, 1966.

virtually cut off from one of man's most pleasurable and profitable entertainments. This can hardly be described as a desirable state of affairs.

Any writer attempting to introduce the modern novel suffers from two natural limitations. His criticism is confined to those books which he himself has read and the only thing he knows with any degree of certainty is how far he himself can go with profit and without danger in the matter of reading. The usefulness of his work will depend on his power to help others to reach a new level of maturity where they can judge for themselves.

FUNCTION

The function of the novel is to mirror life, to show man his own face in an objective way. The great novelist deals with man in all his fundamental relationships - his relationship to God, to his fellowmen, to himself. With his artistic breadth of vision he can see more fully the human face divine; consequently he can make his reader more aware of God and of man. Christian living is a question of loving God and his neighbour and this loving presupposes knowledge of God and of men. The knowledge of God is accumulated systematically by most Catholics but too often his knowledge of man is confined to a limited experience of individuals in the family and the society in which he moves. Generally he knows individuals but he can hardly be said to know mankind. Proper reading of the modern literary novel will help to rectify the position.

ALTERNATIVE

What, for the Irish Catholic, is the alternative to reading the modern novel? He may choose from a motley collection ranging from comics to cowboy and detective stories. The common denominator of these types is the happy wonderland into which the reader is brought, a kind of cloud cuckoo land in which reality is submerged, a world, it must be admitted, in which God is to a very great extent eliminated, and in which moral values are suspect. It might be argued that this type of reading has a real value, that the vicarious experience which it makes possible and the escape from reality which it provides can make an ordinary humdrum existence more tolerable. There is some point in this argument although the value of escaping from reality is debatable. Escape is often associated with cowardice and where reading is concerned it may mean a fear of facing and accepting reality. The mature man does not run from reality, he makes the most of it. Certainly a reading diet based exclusively on this type of literature can only retard maturity and deaden the critical faculty.

## ADVANTAGES

Reading the modern literary novel can, on the contrary, be an invigorating, stimulating and maturing experience. In the world of the modern novelist we are invited to take a plunge into reality, sometimes an icy plunge. Here man is depicted in all his beauty and ugliness. For the whole man must be exposed. We are confronted often brutally with the mental and moral climates of the times we live in; we are shaken out of our complacency by the horrifying knowledge of how other people live; we can be stimulated to action and prayer as we realise the suffering and empty Godless lives of so many of our contemporaries. In a word, here is a refreshing, beneficial experience and we should not refuse it. Instead we must consider how we can best profit from the literature available to us and how we can avoid the dangers involved in this kind of reading.

## DANGERS

Obviously there are pitfalls for the unprepared and immature reader who approaches the modern novel. Every sane person will agree that there must be some limits to our reading but where to draw the line is something which may cause concern to the conscientious reader. If censorship were to exclude all the novels which could be harmful to the unprepared reader many noteworthy and formative books would have to be withdrawn from libraries. From this fact emerges an important point. Apart from any official censorship, there must be another censorship rooted in each individual's conscience. A book which benefits one reader may harm another. How then is the individual to determine what can be read and what must be avoided? It is largely a question of enlightenment, of preparedness, of growing maturity. The idea might be inserted here that it is important for all Catholics to include some solid religious reading in their literary diet so that their knowledge of Christian doctrine may not be outstripped by their secular knowledge.

## TOPICS

The main sources of difficulty might be listed as sex, blasphemy, false idealogy and falsehood. Since sex is the main trouble spot for Irish Catholics, attention will be focused on this point. Almost every modern novel treats of sex. There are many good Catholics who panic at the mention of sex, jumping immediately to the usually erroneous conclusions that the book in question is evil, that they have committed sin by reading it. Two statements might be of help to such readers. Firstly, a serious work of literature is seldom evil; it is often considered to be so by people with immature minds and unhealthy imaginations. Secondly, panic and disgust are not sins. There are many Irish Catholics, and I repeat, they are good-living and conscientious, who view sex as a rather sordid affair not to be discussed or considered in polite society. They are really ashamed of the whole idea of sex as if it were a degrading thing. This attitude to a God-given gift is obviously wrong and it is the root of the objection to the serious modern novel. The modern novelist exposes the whole man and since sex is a basic fact of life then it must be treated. Consequently sex (and indeed the abuse of sex) figures frequently in novels. Cardinal Newman once wrote 'It is a contradiction in terms to attempt a sinless Literature of sinful man'. If a man is to be presented fully through the novelist's eye then we must be prepared to see his vices as well as his virtues. A glimpse of hell can be salutary.

## TREATMENT OF SEX

The matter doesn't end there however. The manner in which sex is treated by the writer is important. An author may view sex through reverent eyes, through the eyes of the moralist, the scientist, the psychologist, the poet or the artist. When he does, there is no danger to the mature reader. If, on the other hand, he sees sex through lecherous eyes, knowing nothing of the pathos and gentleness of sex, blinded by passion to its real beauty, then his writing is evil because he has deformed what is noble in human nature. For the mature reader there is no difficulty in assessing the writer's attitude to sex. The young reader might do well to consider whether the author's treatment of sex encourages in him an appreciation, a reverence for sex, or whether it stimulates his imagination and his passions. If his reaction to a scene in which sex is described is one of unhealthy excitement, as is likely, since lack of control of the imagination and emotions is characteristic of immaturity, then he must decide that for the moment this book is not for him.

Aware that passages are unduly stimulating, he quietly decides not to return to or linger over them. Reading a serious work of modern literature under the guidance of an enlightened teacher can be one of the greatest helps towards maturity.

## BLASPHEMY

Finally, a word about blasphemy, or rather what the Irish Catholic reader often mistakes for blasphemy. Morris West's and Graham Greene's treatment of the priest is often erroneously considered blasphemy. To attack a priest because he is unworthy of his office is not blasphemy; to attack his priesthood is. The Oils of Holy Orders do not make the priest a perfect man. He must still struggle towards perfection, he is still a weak human being and it is unrealistic to expect absolute virtue from him. Indeed it is good for us to realise that our priests are not perfect men, that they need our prayers. If the reading of *The Devil's Advocate or The Power and the Glory* can bring us to this understanding then they must be considered desirable reading.

These remarks are an introduction to short studies of works of some controversial modern novelists. Their aim is to help the serious reader to maturity of judgment, to a critical appraisal of contemporary literature. The serious reader is a great asset to the society in which he moves in guiding the thought of others and directing their minds towards helpful reading.

# Foreword to *L'Evidence et le Mystere*[1]

## JOSEPH MAJAULT

In the first half of the twentieth century, and for some time thereafter, the phrase 'Catholic literature' was in current use [*in France*]. Under that heading in histories of literature and anthologies were listed writers from Leon Bloy, J.K. Huysmans and Barbey d'Aurevilly to Bernanos and Mauriac, via Péguy and Claudel (to name only those most frequently mentioned) who has openly declared their twofold vocation as writers and Catholics. Some of them unambiguously declared that they were Catholic writers, others preferred to describe themselves as Catholics who wrote, but both groups played a large part in the intellectual debates of their time. Their reputation was based both on talent or genius and their active, important and influential role in social and political life. In particular, there is no doubt that the (successive) positions taken up by a Bernanos or a Mauriac before, during and after the second world war in the light of events in Spain, France or elsewhere forcefully affected pubic opinion and helped to change the judgement of a great number of people.

Now that they have gone, many feel that the last generation of those who brilliantly represented the alliance of literature and religion has disappeared with them. None of their successors has acquired either their authority or their readership, and what was called Catholic literature now seems no more than a remnant from a distant past. A century seems to have been the lifespan of an age

1    From *L'Evidence et le mystère,* Paris, Le Centurion, 1978.

when writers who were sons of the Church of Rome held the limelight and at one and the same time defended the interest of faith and established religion. The repercussions sometimes produced by their boldness or their bias have left behind enough of a ferment to arouse curiosity and interest and to endow with prestige and force of attraction a truth illustrated by such illustrious spokesmen. Their line has come to an end, and Catholic literature, after a hundred years, is no more. Or so it is generally said.

But those who say so forget that Christianity as it is now lived is part of and expressed in a very different framework of reflection and sensibility from that which established the norms at the close of the last century and up to the first half of this. The changes, of course, have not affected essentials, for the Truth is still intangible. But ways of understanding the Word, of translating it into terms adapted to the present day, and the consequent attempts to be faithful to sources and spiritual regeneration, are effacing an age when the law of numbers, the tradition of established practices and the store set by order were so many bases on which religious life was to a large extent founded. If we go further, we can also see a shift in certain ideas in theology and morality in the light of a renewed way of seeing the mystery and the love of God.

So there is nothing strange in the fact that representative works from the past, even though they still provide witness, arouse scarcely any echo in the writers of our own time, who are concerned to express, in language appropriate to the way in which literature has moved, the new kinds of resonance they detect, extend and diversify in accordance with their temperament and their own aspirations. They are not merely interpreters, but also protagonists, in the sense that in their writing their personal search is furthering current developments. They have no interest in the more or less official responsibility accepted by the prophets of a preceding generation, but in their desire to beat a path to knowledge and intelligence they are taking on, with both modesty and privilege, a unique task of relating being and Godhead through a way of writing which, in certain cases, goes hand in hand with a new and original creation. The last page of the chapter on Catholic literature may have been turned, but a further chapter on a literature of Christian inspiration has begun, with contents, features and perspectives that it is not too soon to describe.

# Freedom, Altitude, Realism[1]

## JACQUES MARITAIN

As for the freedom of the artist with regard to the subjects he is to represent, the problem seems to be as a rule badly stated, because it is forgotten
that the subject is merely the matter of the work of art. The essential question is not to know whether a novelist can or cannot depict such-and-such
an aspect of evil. The essential question is *from what altitude* he depicts it and
whether his art and mind are pure enough and strong enough to depict it
without connivance. The more deeply the modern novel probes human
misery, the more does it require superhuman virtues in the novelist. To write
Proust's work as it asked to be written would have required the inner light
of a St Augustine. Alas! It is the opposite which happens, and we see the
observer and the thing observed, the novelist and his subject, rivals in a
competition to degrade. From this point of view the influence of André
Gide on French literature must be considered as very characteristic. The way
in which he has surpassed himself in his latest books confirms the judgement passed on him by Massis.

I have mentioned the novel. The novel differs from other forms of literature in having for object not the manufacture of something with its own special beauty in the world of *artefacta,* deriving only its elements from human
life, but the conduct of human life itself in fiction, like providential art in reality. The object it has to create is human life itself; it has to mould, scrutinise and
govern humanity. Such seems to me to be the distinctive characteristic of the
art of the novel.[2] (I mean the modern novel of which Balzac is the father. Its
fundamental difference from the novel of antiquity has been rightly pointed
out by Ernest Hello in an essay which in other respects is rhetorical : the novel
of the Ancients was above all a voyage into the marvellous and the ideal, a
deliverance of the imagination.)

It may therefore be understood how honest, authentic and universal the
novelist's realism ought to be : only a Christian, nay a mystic, because he has
some idea of *what there is in man*, can be a complete novelist. 'There is not,'
said Georges Bernanos with reference to Balzac, 'a single feature to add to
any one of his frightful characters, but he has not been down to the secret
spring, the innermost recesses of conscience, where evil organises from
within, against God and for the love of death, that part of us the harmony of
which has been destroyed by original sin....' And again : 'Take the characters
of Dostoievsky, those whom he himself calls *The Possessed*. We know the

1    From *Art and Scholasticism,* London, Sheed and Ward, 1930.
2    Cf. Henri Massis, *Reflexions sur l'art du roman* (Paris, Plon, 1926); Frederic Lefèvre,
     *Georges Bernanos* (Paris, La Tour d'Ivoire, 1926).

diagnosis of the great Russian in regard to them. But what would have been the diagnosis of a Curé d'Ars, for instance? What would he have seen in those obscure souls?'

# Is Christian Literature a Contradiction in Terms?[1]

## JOHN J. MULLOY

Some critics, who conceive of the idea of Christian culture in terms of full conformity to a moral ideal, have denied that there is any possibility of a culture's being Christian. I think the answer to that negative claim is found in the view of cultural anthropology on the significance of values for a culture. A.L. Kroeber, outstanding American anthropologist of a generation ago, has written:

> Of course, no society is ideal in its behaviour. The society aims to conform to the value standards, but we are all more or less lazy, mean, self-centered, cowardly, spiteful, motivated by personal interest. There is thus an unavoidable gap between the 'pure' picture of the culture and the actuality of how this ideal is lived out by the average adherent of the culture ... This is a difference to be aware of without worrying too much about it. He who is really interested in the phenomena of culture knows that their ideal values always suffer in the actual human living of them. But, at the same time, he knows that in apprehending cultures the most essential thing to apprehend is their values, because without these he will now know either toward what the cultures are slanted or around what they are organized. [*The Nature of Culture,* 1953, p.131.]

Or as Dawson has written, taking note of this gap between ideals and behaviour: 'Nevertheless, this does not mean that moral and spiritual values are socially negligible. They influence culture in all sorts of ways – through institutions and symbols and literature and art, as well as through personal behaviour ... A Christian civilization is certainly not a perfect civilization, but it is a civilization that accepts the Christian way of life as normal and frames its institutions as the organs of a Christian order' (*The Historic Reality of Christian Culture,* p.36).

In this article I wish to deal with a somewhat related question, that is, whether it is possible to have a Christian literature. Certainly if we use the principle which Etienne Gilson employed in *The Spirit of Medieval Philosophy* to determine whether a Christianization of Hellenic philosophy had occurred,

1    From *The Dawson Newsletter,* 1984, II, 1.

the case for a Christian literature would seem fairly conclusive. That principle is to discover whether there are ideas and values in philosophic thought, as a result of Christians having become philosophers, which were not there when philosophy was practised by men who were pagan.

NEWMAN ON A CHRISTIAN LITERATURE

As against that expectation, however, we have the sharp denial by John Henry Newman of any possibility of a Christian literature, in a work that is regarded as a classic on the meaning of education and culture. That is, Newman's *The Idea of a University.* If so dedicated a Catholic intellectual as Newman holds to such a negative judgment, then it would seem difficult to controvert it. Apparently we have to accept the fact that, whatever may have been the case in philosophy, as shown by Gilson and Maritain and numerous others, quite another state of affairs obtains when it comes to literature. In this area of culture, closest of all to man in his emotions and imagination, Christianity, it would seem, has had no real influence. But let us consider the precise form of Newman's denial of a Christian literature.

> Moreover, he (i.e. man) is this sentient, intelligent, creative, and operative being, quite independent of any extraordinary aid from Heaven, or any definite religious belief; and *as such*, as he is in himself, does Literature represent him; it is the Life and Remains of the natural man, innocent or guilt ... Circumstances, such as locality, period, language, seem to make little or no difference in the character of Literature, as such; on the whole, all Literatures are one; they are the voices of the natural man ... I am speaking of University Education, which implies an extended range of reading, which has to deal with standard works of genius, or what are called the *classics* of a language; and I say, from the nature of the case, if Literature is to be made a study of human nature, you cannot have a Christian literature. It is a contradiction in terms to attempt a sinless Literature of sinful man (pp. 227-9).

The first fact to remember about the whole of this section on Literature (Discourse IX, sections 6,7 and 8) is that it was written in reply to the proposal made by a certain Abbé Gaume in France for restricting the use of the Greek and Latin classics in the curriculum, on the ground of their danger to the morals of Christian youth. Such a proposal, if heeded by the Bishops of Ireland who were establishing the Catholic university which Newman was to head, would have undermined the program of liberal education which he planned for the institution. This was a program which Newman himself inherited from his own Oxford University formation. Consequently, the rejection of 'a

---

1    From the *Dawson Newsletter,* 1984, II, 1.

Christian literature' by Newman was at the same time a defense of the right of the pagan classics to be included in the curriculum of a Catholic university.

Second, one should note in this passage the difference between Nature and Grace which Newman, for the purposes of contrast, so frequently sharpened in his writings. Thus, when he makes his famous comparison between the gentleman and the Christian in the eighth discourse of *The Idea of a University*, the gentleman becomes self-sufficient human nature, outwardly fair and attractive, but without any real substance of virtue within. The same method is used in a number of Newman's sermons. For purposes of definition and distinction, as well as for pastoral warning, this emphasis upon the difference between Nature and Grace is no doubt of great importance.

## CRITICISM OF NEWMAN'S VIEW

But is it true that human nature, as we find it in reality, is simply untouched by Grace, so that we can confidently say of its various manifestations in literature that they are merely the products of an unregenerate heart? Could it be truly said of such writers as Plato and Marcus Aurelius, to cite but two classical authors, that their work is only the expression of sinful human nature, and is not in some way the result of the workings of Grace upon that Nature? Did not St Paul himself find in Hellenistic literature an implicit preparation for the coming of Christianity, when he spoke to the men of Athens of the testimony which their own poets had given concerning the Unknown God? And do not St Augustine and the Church Fathers look upon the work of Plato as a preparation of the Greeks for the acceptance of the Gospel?

Third, it is striking to observe the implications of Newman's thought in this Discourse, as though literature represented the voice of universal human nature, and was not in any way affected by the conditions of history and society which formed the environment for the writer who produced it. The coming of Christianity, for example, is a particular historical event, with important consequence for both history and culture. But if in fact we follow Newman in his rejection of the influence of history and culture upon human nature (the latter here seen under its aspect of universal subjection to Original Sin), then we must necessarily reject the idea that Christianity has had an influence, not only upon literature, but also upon human nature. Newman's polemical purposes and skills would seem to have got the better of him when he wrote: 'If Literature is to be made a study of human nature, you cannot have a Christian Literature. It is a contradiction in terms to attempt a sinless Literature of sinful man.'

For who indeed ever defined Christian literature as 'a sinless Literature'? One might just as well define a Christian as one who does not commit sin, and then look for Christians only in Heaven. Could either the Old Testament or the New for one moment be thought of as a sinless literature? Or would this objection have any meaning when applied to such recognized Christian classics as St Augustine's *Confessions* or *The City of God*, Dante's *Divine Comedy*, or Langland's *Piers Plowman?* Or in the twentieth century, the work of such writers as Eliot, Undset, Mauriac, and Bernanos?

Now this non-historical approach to literature which Newman makes use of to defend the classics, is not one which especially recommends itself to classical scholarship today. The greater knowledge which the present century has gained of the nature of the Graeco-Roman culture, as well as of the literature of other cultures, has made it clear that, for a true understanding of any literature, there must be an awareness of the historical soil from which it has grown. Werner Jaeger, one of the foremost classical scholars of the twentieth century, in his justly famous *Paideia,* points out the need for this historical approach in relation to Greek literature:

> The 'ideals of Greek culture' are not to be set up separately in the empty space of sociological abstraction, and treated as universal types. Every form of arete, every new moral standard produced by the Greek spirit must be studied in the time and place where it originated — surrounded by the historical forces which called it forth and conflicted with it, and embodied in the work of the great creative writer who gave it its representative form' [*Paideia,* Introduction to Vol. 11].

### SOCIAL TRADITION

Nor is this conception of culture and literature really foreign to Newman's thought, when it is taken in its full range, rather than being narrowed to serve a particular polemical purpose. In the second half of *The Idea of a University,* Newman presents us with a conception of literature which involves a cultural tradition and a social inheritance. In the first three chapters of this section of the volume, although Newman stresses the contributions made to a nation's literature by its classical authors, he also points out the mutual relationship which exists between the tradition and the individual writers, and he illustrates the different ways in which the writer is dependent upon the tradition of which he is a part.

In a number of passages from these chapters Newman seems to anticipate the more technically stated conclusions of cultural anthropology today. For he is here speaking of a people's whole way of life, and of literature as one of the means by which the values of that way of life find expression. For example, he points out that 'every people has a character of its own, which it manifests and perpetuates in a variety of ways,' and he then enumerates the different ways in which this character is shown, which extend over a wide range of social institutions and material artifacts, and include the national language and literature. In conclusion Newman observes: 'If a literature be, as I have said, the voice of a particular nation, it requires a territory and a period, as large as the nation's extent and history, to mature in

... at least in the case of great writers, the history of their works is the history of their fortunes of their times. Each is, in his turn, the man of his age, the type of a generation, or the interpreter of a crisis. He is made for his day, for his day for him' (*op. cit.*, pp.308; 311).

Christopher Dawson expresses this same idea of the intimate relationship between the writer and his society, but puts it in terms of the culture rather than the nation:

> A great culture sets its seal on a man, on all that he is, and all that he does, from his speech and gesture to his vision of reality and his ideals of conduct; and the more living it is, the deeper is the imprint, and the more highly developed is the element of form in society. Hence every culture develops its own types of man, and norms of existence and conduct, and we can trace the curve of the growth and decline of cultural life by the vitality of these characteristic types and institutions as well as by the art and literature in which the soul of the culture finds expression' [*Dynamics of World History*, 57].

Obviously, from this viewpoint, one does not study literature as though 'all literatures are one literature.' Instead, we examine the cultural tradition and historical circumstances in which each particular literature, and indeed each particular literary work, has had its origin. No doubt there are universal human elements present in all literature, but these are counterbalanced by the variety of national character and cultural difference to which literature also gives expression. To attempt to emphasize the universal element, without at the same time giving attention to the particular language and individual history by which that element has been enabled to find a voice, is to condemn literature to what Werner Jaeger rightly calls 'the empty space of sociological abstraction.'

CHRISTIAN LITERATURE AND THE CHRISTIAN TRADITION

And the same thing is true of Christian literature, which is not only Christian, but is also a reflection of the different national cultures and different historical periods in which it has been created. Moreover, each individual person who is the creative source of Christian literature exemplifies the same twofold relationship. For, on the one hand, he uses the product of the common culture which is language and is inspired by the common spiritual tradition of Christianity. And, on the other, he makes his own individual use of the language and expresses the universal truths of Christianity through his own particular experience of life and through the understanding of the Faith which this has provided him. And therefore the work of a St Augustine will differ from that of a William Langland, or the work of a St Francis of Assisi from that of a Blaise Pascal.

Without these differences of national character and personal experience and temperament, Christian literature and culture would be immeasurably poorer. They would lack that richness and vitality which in fact characterize their manifold historical development through the ages.

Thus we may conclude that Christian literature is indeed a reality, and that it can give us a better understanding of the influence which Christianity has had upon both human nature and culture. And that in fact Newman's own principles and more balanced judgment, when seen in their proper perspective, give support to that conclusion.

## PART II

Let us now consider another conception of Newman in *The Idea of a University* which runs quite counter to his statement that 'You cannot have a Christian literature.' This is his view that 'English literature will ever have been Protestant,' despite what may be achieved may happen in the future by Catholic writers in the English language. If a Christian literature is impossible, how can English literature be designated as Protestant?

It is only when we recognize the polemical purpose of his claim that a Christian literature is a contradiction in terms, and we rely instead on Newman's more balanced view that each literature expresses the tradition of a people and its special character, that we understand how Newman can speak of the Protestant nature of English literature. But is Newman's judgment in fact an accurate one?

First, let us hear Newman's statement of his case for the predominant Protestant influence on English literature. He writes:

> Certain masters of composition, as Shakespeare, Milton, and Pope, the writers of the Protestant Bible and Prayer Book, Hooker and Addison, Swift, Hume, and Goldsmith have been the making of the English language; ... and we Catholics, without consciousness and without offence, are ever repeating the half sentences of dissolute playwrights and heretical partisans and preachers. So tyrannous is the literature of a nation; it is too much for us. We cannot destroy or reverse it; we may confront and encounter it, but we cannot make it over again...anyhow we cannot undo the past. English literature will ever have been Protestant' [*The Idea of a University*, pp. 321/314].

What Newman apparently means here by Protestantism, is a kind of catch-all category which can include indiscriminately the Anglicanism of the Book of Common Prayer and of the thought of Hooker, each with its strong Catholic influence, the Puritanism of Milton, the Deism of Pope, and the Enlightened ideas of David Hume. Consequently, if we use the term Protestant to cover the outlook of all these writers, we rely upon a merely superficial classification which has little to do with the actual content of their work.

Moreover, it seems significant that Newman, writing this lecture as late as 1858, gives no attention whatever to the great literary figures of the nineteenth century. For the work of these writers reflected in many ways the growing interest in Catholicism, especially in its medieval cultural form, which was characteristic of the Romantic movement.

Let us now consider just how accurate is Newman's judgment concerning the 'Protestant' character of English literature in its formative period. Was earlier English literature so moulded by Protestant influences that it possesses an indelible Protestant stamp? Or did a process of Catholic Christianization take place in earlier English culture which is reflected in the literature of the formative period?

First, let us note what Thomas Carlyle, Victorian prose writer who was contemporary with Newman, had to say concerning Shakespeare's worldview. In Heroes and Hero-Worship he stated:

> In some sense it may be said that this glorious Elizabethan era with its Shakespeare, as the outcome and flowerage of all which had preceded it, is itself attributable to the Catholicism of the Middle Ages ... And remark here, as rather curious, that Middle-Age Catholicism was abolished, so far as acts of parliament could abolish it, before Shakespeare, the noblest product of it, made his appearance. He did make his appearance nevertheless. [pp. 120-1]

This was in 1841, some seventeen years before Newman's lecture was delivered. And note its view that not only Shakespeare, but the whole of Elizabethan literature was 'the outcome and flowerage of ... the Catholicism of the Middle Ages.' Consequently, even writers like Spenser and Marlowe, with their obvious Protestant bias, are in fact drawing upon the medieval Catholic heritage.

The twentieth century has provided impressive scholarly support for Carlyle's intuitive judgment concerning the essentially Catholic character of Shakespeare's thought and work. As one example, two German scholars — Mutschmann and Wentersdorf — have brought together a great deal of evidence to show how thoroughly Shakespeare knew the teachings of the Catholic faith and how often he presented them in his plays. This, despite the dangers which such sympathy might encounter from the Protestant authorities who ruled Great Britain at that time. These German scholars write:

> Firstly, Shakespeare reveals a most comprehensive knowledge of the Roman Catholic Church, its teachings and its practices. Secondly, his knowledge is correct, and it is always aptly applied. Raich hits the mark when he points out: 'Shakespeare is never guilty of errors such as are of common occurrence in the works of even the very best non-Catholic writers.' Shakespeare's reference, in fact, cover almost all aspects of the

Catholic doctrines on the subject of grace, ethics and eschatology. [*Shakespeare and Catholicism* (Sheed and Ward, 1952), p. 213]

One of the Catholic teachings most strongly controverted by Protestants was the Sacrament of Confession. On this point the German scholars state:

The Catholic doctrine of auricular confession and the remission of sins by the confessor was most decisively rejected by the Protestant…(there was) violent opposition from the Puritan element to what was regarded as 'Romish' superstition. It is, therefore, significant that it is precisely this sacrament which is referred to by Shakespeare most frequently of all, and in the greatest detail. On numerous occasions, Shakespeare makes the characters in his dramas talk about going to confession, and always in the most natural manner imaginable. [ibid., pp. 218-19]

Also significant is the analysis which the authors provide of the comparative frequency of the references to Catholic teaching and practice which occur during the different periods into which Shakespeare's play are customarily divided. The third period, that of the great tragedies and the 'bitter comedies,' lasting from 1601 to 1607, has been seen by some critics as the time when Shakespeare gave way to pessimism and relapsed into an unbelieving paganism. Yet these scholars show that it is precisely in this period that references to Catholic teaching are most frequent, being almost 50 percent greater than in his earliest period (see pp. 366-68.)

The overall conclusion of the authors, at the end of their extended survey of the background and plays of Shakespeare, is as follows: 'It may be said without fear of contradiction that there is much more evidence in support of Shakespeare's Catholicism than there is for any other assumption: his birth into a Catholic family, his education and upbringing in Catholic surroundings, … and above all, the Catholic spirit which permeates his works' (ibid., p.379).

If 'English literature will ever have been Protestant,' apparently it will have achieved this character without the aid of Shakespeare, its greatest poet and its greatest dramatist.

Now, let us go back somewhat farther into the formative period of English literature. One of the characteristics of literary criticism in the twentieth century has been the greatly increased attention it has paid to the poetic achievement of the Catholic Middle Ages, and its identification of not one, but three outstanding poets in the age of Chaucer. In addition to Chaucer himself, there are also William Langland, author of *Piers Plowman*, and the Pearl-Poet, so called after one of his works because his identity is not known.

Of Langland, Christopher Dawson wrote almost fifty years ago in terms that sound the keynote for much literary evaluation of the poet since that time. He said, in contrasting Langland with Dante:

Langland, on the other hand, had the scanty learning of a poor clerk, a knowledge of the liturgy and the Bible and the common faith of Christendom. His way was the muddy highroad of common life, and he found his guide and saviour in the common man, Piers Plowman, who is, the type of Labour and Christian charity and at last of Christ himself. And Dawson speaks of Langland's poem, *Piers Plowman,* as 'this great classic, which is one of the landmarks of English literature and English religion.' [*Medieval Essays,* pp. 250/239]

And J.R.R. Tolkien, an outstanding authority on Middle English Literature as well as the author of the Ring trilogy, speaks in similar terms of the literary genius of the Pearl-Poet and his Catholic moral purposes.

It is unlikely that Newman would have been aware of the Catholic character of either of these poets, for their work had not yet become widely known. But it does seem significant of the limitations of Newman's view that he does not even mention Geoffrey Chaucer in speaking of the outstanding names in English literature. He thereby closes off any recognition of the medieval Catholic achievements, and need not take it into account in his judgment of the basically Protestant character of English literature.

Matthew Arnold had not yet made his well-known criticism of Chaucer which twentieth-century criticism has done so much to correct: 'Something is wanting (i.e.,in Chaucer's poetry) which poetry must have before it can be placed in the glorious class of the best. What is lacking is the high and excellent seriousness, which Aristotle assigns as one of the grand virtues of poetry.' But it is possible that the same kind of view may have been responsible for Newman's own neglect of Chaucer.

Now, how do twentieth-century critics regard the significance of Chaucer? Let us first take an estimate of his merits from an anthology for colleges published in the first half of this century, which, in its introduction to Chaucer, summarizes the contemporary estimate of his achievement. Under the heading. 'The Four Great Writers of Medieval England' (Thomas Malory is also included), Chaucer's characteristics are thus presented:

> Keen, witty, shrewd, kindly, the trained observer of men, and the penetrating reporter of what he saw about him. Chaucer shows in addition a narrative skill which for directness and sustained interest has not been matched by any other English narrative poet. He is, in addition, a talented portrait-painter, the broad telling sweeps of his brush in the *Prologue to the Canterbury Tales* are at once impressionistic and unforgettable ... The gallery of portraits in the Prologue to this varied collection of stories both popular and artistic would have been sufficient to assure its author a high place, and the sweep and versatility of the stories themselves are a further tribute to his genius.' [From *The Literature of England* (1936), by Woods, Watt and Anderson]

In another college anthology published a generation later, with an impressive cast of literary critics as its joint editors (e.g., Basil Willey, Walter J. Bate, C.S. Lewis, Lionel Trilling, Douglas Bush, L.A. Richards, etc.), Chaucer's concern with Catholic belief and practice is given in these terms by Charles W. Dunn, author of the volume's introduction to Chaucer:

> The deeply religious undercurrent of medieval life is clearly apparent in Chaucer's Canterbury pilgrimage. It springs to birth in a common meeting place at the cross roads of England under the inspiration of a worldly innkeeper and commences with a courtly romance told by a knight. But the pilgrims worldly and unworldly alike, regardless of rank or of wealth, are all directed toward a holy shrine in a solemn cathedral. The last tale they hear is a sermon by a godly parson who points their thoughts towards 'the perfect glorious pilgrimage called heavenly Jerusalem', and this tale is concluded by Chaucer with a repudiation of all that is sinful in his writing and a prayer that he 'may be one of them at the Day of Judgment that shall be saved'.

Dunn then presents this overall estimate of Chaucer's place in English literature:

> In his lifetime Chaucer was hailed as the greatest poet of his age. And today, after more than five and a half centuries, during which the warmth, color, humor, and humanity of his poetry have endeared him to his readers, his name stands in the annals of English literature second only to Shakespeare.' [*Major British Writers* (1959), vol·1, pp. 5-6,7]

When Newman was writing in the mid-19th century, Milton was probably assigned this position of second only to Shakespeare. So if Chaucer is a faithful reflection of the spirit and idea of medieval English Catholicism, as Milton is to a large degree a reflection of the Puritanism of his own age, we can see how this provides a further reason for revision of Newman's view of the character of English literature. That is, that 'English Literature will ever have been Protestant', having received an imprint which no future achievements by Catholic writers can ever possibly efface. But what if the imprint which was actually given is far more Catholic than Newman realized. Certainly if the two greatest poets in the English language are both Catholic and both present a Catholic view of the world and of mankind, and both made their contribution during the formative period of English literature, then it would seem that Newman's judgment might almost have to be reversed. That is, that considering Chaucer and Shakespeare, and Langland and the Pearl-Poet, and a strong Catholic influence upon the Elizabethan age, 'we cannot destroy or reverse it ... we cannot undo the past. English Literature will ever have been' Catholic.

Under any circumstances, the twentieth century revival of Catholic thought and writing – whether taking place under Roman Catholic or Anglo-Catholic auspices — has a long and honorable tradition behind it in English literature. Newman himself, when he inspired and led the Oxford Movement, and later the movement of Anglican conversion to Rome, was supported not only by the earlier centuries of English Catholic literature. It is a pity he did not realize that fact when he was presenting his program for liberal education for Catholics in his *Idea of a University.*

# Literature[1]

## JOHN HENRY, CARDINAL NEWMAN

Literature, then is of a personal character; it consists in the enunciations and teachings of those who have a right to speak as representatives of their kind, and in whose words their brethren find an interpretation of their own sentiments, a record of their own experience, and a suggestion for their own judgments. A great author, Gentlemen, is not one who merely has a *copia verborum*, whether in prose or verse, and can, as it were, turn on at his will any number of splendid phrases and swelling sentences; but he is one who has something to say and knows how to say it. I do not claim for him, as such, any great depth of thought, or breadth of view, or philosophy, or sagacity, or knowledge of human nature, or experience of human life, though these additional gifts he may have, and the more he has of them the greater he is; but I ascribe to him as his characteristic gift, in a large sense the faculty of Expression. He is master of the two-fold Logos, the thought and the word, distinct, but inseparable from each other. He may, if so be, elaborate his compositions, or he may pour out his improvisations, but in either case he has but one aim, which he keeps steadily before him, and is conscientious and single-minded in fulfilling. That aim is to give forth what he has within him; and from his very earnestness it comes to pass that, whatever be the splendour of his diction or the harmony of his periods, he has within him the charm of an incommunicable simplicity. Whatever be his subject, high or low, he treats it suitably and for its own sake. If he is a poet, 'nil molitur *inepte*.' If he is an orator, then too he speaks, not only 'distinctè' and 'splendidè,' but also 'aptè.' His page is the lucid mirror of his mind and life —

> Quo fit, ut omnis
> Votia pateat veluti descripta tabella
> Vita senis.

1    From a lecture given at the Catholic University, Dublin, in 1852, reprinted in Martin Svaglic (ed), *The Idea of a University*, New York, Rinehart, 1960.

He writes passionately, because he feels keenly; forcibly, because he conceives vividly; he sees too clearly to be vague; he is too serious to be otiose; he can analyse his subject, and therefore he is rich; he embraces it as a whole and in its parts, and therefore he is consistent; he has a firm hold of it, and therefore he is luminous. When his imagination wells up, it overflows in ornament; when his heart is touched, it thrills along his verse. He always has the right word for the right idea, and never a word too much. If he is brief, it is because few words suffice, when he is lavish of them, still each word has its mark and aids, not embarrasses, the vigorous march of his elocution. He expresses what all feel, but all cannot say; and his sayings pass into proverbs among his people, and his phrases become household words and idioms of their daily speech, which is tesselated with the rich fragments of his language, as we see in foreign lands the marbles of Roman grandeur worked into the walls and pavements of modern palaces.

Such pre-eminently is Shakespeare among ourselves; such pre-eminently Virgil among the Latins; such in their degree are all those writers who in every nation go by the name of Classics. To particular nations they are necessarily attached from the circumstance of the variety of tongues, and the peculiarities of each, but so far they have a catholic and ecumenical character, that what they express is common to the whole race of man, and they alone are able to express it ...

If then the power of speech is a gift as great as any that can be named, – if the origin of language is by many philosophers even considered to be nothing short of divine, – if by means of words the secrets of the heart are brought to light, pain of soul is relieved, hidden grief is carried off, sympathy conveyed, counsel imparted, experience recorded, and wisdom perpetuated, – if by great authors the many are drawn up in unity, national character is fixed, a people speaks, the past and the future, the East and the West are brought into communication with each other, – if such men are, in a word, the spokesmen and prophets of the human family, – it will not answer to make light of Literature or to neglect its study; rather we may be sure that, in proportion as we master it in whatever language, and imbibe its spirit, we shall ourselves become in our own measure the ministers of like benefits to others, be they many or few, be they in the obscurer or the more distinguished walks of life – who are united to us by social ties and are within the sphere of our personal influence.

# English Catholic Literature[1]

## JOHN HENRY, CARDINAL NEWMAN

The past cannot be undone. That our English Classical Literature is not Catholic is a plain fact, which we cannot deny, to which we must reconcile ourselves as best we may, and which, as I have shown above, has after all its compensations. When, then, I speak of the desirableness of forming a Catholic Literature, I am contemplating no such vain enterprise as that of reversing history; no, nor of redeeming the past by the future. I have no dream of Catholic Classics as still reserved for the English language. In truth, classical authors not only are national, but belong to a particular age of a nation's life; and I should not wonder if, as regards ourselves, that age is passing away. Moreover, they perform a particular office towards its language, which is not likely to be called for beyond a definite time. And further, though analogies or parallels cannot be taken to decide a question of this nature, such is the fact, that the series of our classical writers has already extended through a longer period than was granted to the Classical Literature either of Greece or of Rome; and thus the English language also may have a long course of literature still to come through many centuries, without that Literature being classical.

Latin, for instance, was a living language for many hundred years after the date of the writers, who brought it to its perfection; and then it continued for a second long period to be the medium of European correspondence. Greek was a living language to a date not very far short of that of the taking of Constantinople, ten centuries after the date of St Basil, and seventeen hundred years after the period commonly called classical. And thus, as the year has its spring and summer, so even for those celebrated languages there was but a season of splendour, and, compared with the whole course of their duration, but a brief season. Since, then, English has had its great writers for a term of about three hundred years – as long, that is, as the period form Sappho to Demosthenes, or from Pisistratus to Arcesilas, or from Aeschyllus and Pindar to Carneades, or from Ennius to Pliny – we should have no right to be disappointed if the classical period be close upon its termination ...

Such as I consider, being the fortunes of Classical Literature, viewed generally, I should never be surprised to find that, as regards this hemisphere, for I can prophesy nothing of America, we have well nigh seen the end of English Classics. Certainly, it is in no expectation of Catholics continuing the series here that I speak of the duty and necessity of their cultivating English literature. When I speak of the formation of a Catholic school of writers, I have respect principally to the matter of what it written, and to composition only so far forth as style is necessary to convey and to recommend the matter. I

---

1    From a lecture given at the Catholic University, Dublin, in 1852, reprinted in Martin Svaglic (ed), *The Idea of a University*, New York, Rinehart, 1960.

mean a literature which resembles the literature of the day. This is not a day for great writers, but for good writing, and a great deal of it. There never was a time when men wrote so much and so well, and that, without being of any great account themselves. While our literature in this day, especially the periodical, is rich and various, its language is elaborated to a perfection far beyond that of our Classics, by the jealous rivalry, the incessant practice, the mutual influence, of its many writers. In point of mere style, I suppose, many an article in the *Times* newspaper, or Edinburgh Review, is superior to a preface of Dryden's, or a pamphlet of Swift's, or one of South's sermons.

Our writers write so well that there is little to choose between them. What they lack is that individuality, that earnestness most personal yet most unconscious of self, which is the greatest charm of an author. The very form of the compositions of the day suggests to us their main deficiency. They are anonymous. So was it not in the literature of those nations which we consider the special standard of classical writing, so is it not with our own classics. The Epic was sung by the voice of the living, present poet. The drama, in its very idea, is poetry in persons. Historians begin, 'Herodotus, of Halicarnassus, publishes his researches,' or, 'Thucydides, the Athenian, has composed an account of the war.' Pindar is all through his odes a speaker. Plato, Xenophon, and Cicero, throw their philosophical dissertations into the form of a dialogue. Orators and preachers are by their very profession known persons, and the personal is laid down by the Philosopher of antiquity as the source of their greatest persuasiveness. Virgil and Horace are ever bringing into their poetry their own characters and tastes. Dante's poems furnish a series of events for the chronology of his times. Milton is frequent in allusions to his own history and circumstances. Even when Addison writes anonymously, he writes under a professed character, and that in a great measure his own; he writes in the first person. The 'I' of the Spectator, and the 'we' of the modern Review or Newspaper, are the respective symbols of the two ages in our literature. Catholics must do as their neighbours; they must be content to serve their generation, to promote the interests of religion, to recommend truth, and to edify their brethren today, though their names are to have little weight, and their works are not to last much beyond themselves.

# On the Moral Basis of Writing[1]

## FLANNERY O'CONNOR

I suppose when I say that the moral basis of Poetry is the accurate naming of the things of God, I mean about the same thing that Conrad meant when he said that his aim as an artist was to render the highest possible justice to the visible universe. For me the visible universe is a reflection of the invisible universe. Somewhere St Augustine says that the things of the world poured forth from God in a double way: intellectually into the minds of the angels and physically into the world of things. (I am sure that an angelic world is no part of your belief but of course it is very much a part of mine.) Since you believe that the world itself is God, that all is God, this can hardly meet with your sympathy. No more than [Father Walter] Ong. About him, let me say that his position would be the same if Freud had never been alive and that it is certainly no part of his concern whether the male or female is the superior sex ain't going to ruffle his orthodoxy any; or mine. You may be right that a man is an incomplete woman. It don't change anybody's external destination however, or the observable facts of the sex's uses (a nice phrase) ...

To get back to the accurate naming of the things of God, I am wondering if what worries you about that, what may seem THE contradiction for me to say such a thing is the fact that I write about good men being hard to find. The only way I can explain that is by repeating that I think evil is the defective use of good. Perhaps you do too ... [128-9].

But to go back to determinism. I don't think literature would be possible in a determined world. We might go through the motions but the heart would be out of it. Nobody then could 'smile darkly and ignore the howls.' Even if there were no Church to teach me this, writing two novels would do it. I think the more you write, the less inclined you will be to rely on theories like determinism. Mystery isn't something that is gradually evaporating. It grows along with knowledge. [489]

About scandalizing the 'little ones.' When I first began to write I was much worried about this thing of scandalizing people, as I fancied that what I wrote was highly inflammatory. I was wrong – it wouldn't even have kept anybody awake, but anyway, thinking this was my problem, I talked to a priest about it. The first thing he said to me was, 'You don't have to write for fifteen- year-old girls.' Of course, the mind of a fifteen-year-old girl lurks in many a head that is seventy-five and people are every day being scandalized not only by what is

1   From *Letters of Flannery O'Connor: the habit of being,* selected and edited by Sally Fitzgerald, Farrar, Strauss, Giroux, New York, 1979. (Page references are given at the end of each extract.

scandalous of its nature but by what is not. If a novelist wrote a book about Abraham passing his wife Sarah off as his sister – which he did – and allowing her to be taken over by those who wanted her for their lustful purposes – which he did to save his skin – how many Catholics would not be scandalized at the behaviour of Abraham? The fact is that in order not to be scandalized, one has to have a whole view of things, which not many of us have.

This is a problem that has concerned Mauriac very much and he wrote a book about it called *God and Mammon*. His conclusion was that all the novelist could do was 'purify the source' – his mind. A young man had written Mauriac a letter saying that as a result of reading one of his novels, he had almost committed suicide. It almost paralyzed Mauriac. At the same time, he was not responsible for the lack of maturity in the boy's mind and there were doubtless other souls who were profiting from his books. When you write a novel, if you have been honest about it and if your conscience is clear, then it seems to me that you have to leave the rest in God's hands. When the book leaves your hands, it belongs to God. He may use it to save a few souls or to try a few others, but I think that for the writer to worry about this is to take over God's business.

I'm not one to pit myself against St Paul but when he said, 'Let it not so much as be named among you,' I presume he was talking about society and what goes on there and not about art. Art is not anything that goes on "among" people, not the art of the novel anyway. It is something that one experiences alone and for the purpose of realizing in a fresh way, through the senses, the mystery of existence. Part of the mystery of existence is sin. When we think about the Crucifixion, we miss the point of it if we don't think about sin.

About bad taste, I don't know, because taste is a relative matter. There are some who will find almost everything in bad taste, from spitting in the street to Christ's association with Mary Magdalen. Fiction is supposed to represent life, and the fiction writer has to use as many aspects of life as are necessary to make his total picture convincing. The fiction writer doesn't state, he shows, renders. It's the nature of fiction and it can't be helped. If you're writing about the vulgar, you have to prove they're vulgar by showing them at it. The two worst sins of bad taste in fiction are pornography and sentimentality. One is too much sex and the other too much sentiment. You have to have enough of either to prove your point but no more. Of course there are some fiction writers who feel they have to retire to the bathroom or the bed with every character every time he takes himself to either place. Unless such a trip is used to further the story, I feel it is in bad taste. In the second chapter of my novel, I have such a scene but I felt it was vital to the meaning. I don't think you have to worry much about bad taste with a competent writer, because he uses everything for a reason. The reader may not always see the reason. But it's when sex or scurrility are used for their own sakes that they are in bad taste.

What offends my taste in fiction is when right is held up as wrong, or wrong as right. Fiction is the concrete expression of mystery – mystery that is lived. Catholics believe that all creation is good and that evil is the wrong use of good and that without Grace we use it wrong most of the time. It's almost impossible to write about supernatural Grace in fiction. We almost have to approach it negatively. As to natural Grace, we have to take that the way it comes – through nature. In any case, it operates surrounded by evil.

I haven't so much been asked these questions as I have asked them of myself. People don't often even have the courtesy to ask them – they merely tell you where you have failed. I don't take the questions lightly and my answers are certainly not complete, but they're the best I can do to date. [142-4]

# The Changing Accent of Catholic Literature[1]

## KARL G. SCHMUDE

An intriguing development since the 1960s is the quantity of popular literature that has been published by authors with a Catholic background. The phenomenon is intriguing because it has occurred in countries such as the United States, Britain and Australia, where the Church is not culturally dominant – where, indeed, Catholicism is a minority religion.

The evidence of this phenomenon is readily observable. In England, for example, there have been novels like Piers Paul Read's *A Married Man* (1979), David Lodge's *How Far Can You Go?* (1980), and Anthony Burgess's *Earthly Powers* (1980), as well as plays by Mary O'Malley and Ted Whitehead. Mary O'Malley's play, *Once a Catholic* (1977), won large audiences in London and was subsequently staged in a number of Australian cities.

In America, Colleen McCullough achieved prodigious success with her novel, *The Thorn Birds* (1977), while a multitude of other authors attracted widespread notice – such as Wilfrid Sheed (the son of Frank Sheed) with *Transatlantic Blues* (1978), James Carroll with *Mortal Friends* (1978) and *Fault Lines* (1980), John Gregory Dunne with *True Confessions* (1978), and Mary Gordon with *Final Payments* (1978) and *The Company of Women* (1981).

In Australia, the past decade and a half have yielded an abundance of literature which draws its main interest and energy from the life of Catholics. There have been novels like Thomas Keneally's *Three Cheers for the Paraclete* (1968), Desmond O'Grady's *Deschooling Kevin Carew* (1974); plays like Peter Kenna's *A Hard God* (1973), Ron Blair's *The Christian Brothers* (1976), and John O'Donoghue's *A Happy and Holy Occasion* (1982); short stories like Barry Oakley's *Walking through Tigerland* (1977); and poetry like Les Murray's *The Boys Who Stole the Funeral* (1980).

1   From *Quadrant* 28, 1-2, 1984.

What does this phenomenon mean? Can it simply be seen as a coincidence of individual efforts, and the process of differentiating Catholics an outmoded exercise in head-counting? Or does it signify the movements of an important cultural process – a series of changes beneath the surface, as it were, which Catholics as a people have undergone in modern times? What does the appearance of this writing tell us about the Catholic sensibility today?

I believe that this burgeoning of literature is more than a coincidence. Literature, after all, is not only the communication of a personal vision. It is also the expression of a communal experience. It is the dramatisation of a culture – a means of revealing and exploring the beliefs and values, the myths and symbols, the customs and institutions which make up the life of a people. A valuable approach to social history has always been to read the literature of the time – to discern what authors have taken for granted or, in a period of turmoil, how they have responded to changes in the fabric of cultural life. It is difficult for conventional histories to convey this richness of perception, for they tend to be concerned with externals or to deal in abstract issues of which ordinary people are often enough unaware.

In my judgment, the kind of literature cited sheds light on the cultural world which present-day Catholics inhabit: The changing accent of Catholic literature provides some clues to the changed workings of the Catholic imagination.

Already problems of definition are emerging. What precisely *is* Catholic literature? Is it simply literature written by Catholics? Do the main themes or characters need to be explicitly Catholic? Must there be a depiction of spiritual drama or experience, an illumination of the mystery of faith? The title of 'Catholic' novelist – has generally been rejected by those to whom it has been applied. Graham Greene has frequently protested that he is simply a novelist who happens to be a Catholic, and his fear of being mistaken for a propagandist is not unusual.

Yet it is remarkable how persistent the idea of a 'Catholic' literature is; how readily even non-Catholics seem to see the Church as the source of focus of a special kind of writing. It says something about the cultural power of Catholicism, its incarnational penetration of society, even in our time when that power and penetration might appear to have declined markedly. When the thirteen-hour adaptation of Evelyn Waugh's *Brideshead Revisited* was shown on British television in late 1981, The London *Observer* declared: 'Never, on TV at least, has Catholicism seemed so desirably *special.*' The Catholic identity has continued to manifest a richness and an energy far greater than other traditions in our culture. In the words of the American film director, Brian De Palma, who was reared as a Presbyterian despite an Italian Catholic heritage: 'When you reach back for mysterious or terrifying images, you're going to dredge up many more Catholic memories than Presbyterian ones.'

In the 1930s, the French critic Jacques Rivière argues that Christianity gives the novelist a special power of insight, a particular profundity, because the characters he creates are not only individuals. They are also *creatures.* The characters, for example, in Dostoievsky are not merely exciting and clear-cut personalities. They are more than the sum of their passions. They possess that extra dimension – an image of God which is never quite effaced. They have in them what Rivière called 'that little crack which enables a human being to escape from himself,' to establish communion with his neighbour. As creatures they have souls which may be saved or lost. They stand in need of mercy and forgiveness. We can be moved to pray for them.

Another Frenchman, Georges Bernanos, observed that his characters undergo *temptations* – a word that suggests a universe of ultimate meaning within which one acts. A purpose exists from which one can be deflected, a destiny of glory which one can forfeit. 'The Catholic novel,' argued Bernanos, 'is not the novel which only nourishes us with nice sentiments; it is the novel where the life of faith is at grips with the passions. Everything possible must be done to make the reader feel the tragic mystery of salvation.'

In terms of such criteria, various critics have pronounced unfavourably on the current output. Gerard Windsor, for example, commented in the *Australasian Catholic Record* (April 1981):

> Catholicism is not given credit for anything more than quaintness and a traumatic emotional power. There is no interest in it as a vehicle of religious experience, no advertence to any of its central doctrines. There is no sense in which we can describe our 'Catholic' writers as religious writers. There is plenty of guilt in their work, but no sense of sin nor of grace, nor of conversion nor redemption nor revelation nor any of the range of concepts that make up the notion of religion.

This is not the first time in the present century that such discussions have taken place. In the 1930s and 1940s, Graham Greene provoked debate on the subject of the 'Catholic' novel by his publication of works like *Brighton Rock* (1938) and *The Power and the Glory* (1940). In Australia at that time, as novels by Greene and his fellow Englishmen, Evelyn Waugh, Bruce Marshall and other, succeeded one another, the literary pages of the Melbourne *Advocate* were alive with controversy. The debate turned mainly on John Henry Newman's argument, that it is a 'contradiction in terms to attempt a sinless literature of sinful man.' Some argued, in the words of the American authoress, Flannery O'Connor, that the writer has to make moral corruption believable before the infusion of divine grace can become meaningful. Others declared that the 'Catholic' novel cannot depict evil without conniving at it. Perhaps the climax of these discussions occurred in the London *Tablet* of June 5, 1948, when Evelyn Waugh reviewed Graham Greene's novel *The Heart of the Matter.* He queried the theology embodied in the book, commenting that the idea which Scobie, the main character, had of willing his damnation for the love of God is 'either a very loose poetical expression or a mad blasphemy, for the God who accepted that sacrifice could be neither just nor lovable.'

Reviewing the course of that debate more than three decades later, one is struck by the intensity of theological interest which was demonstrated. The various contributors – ranging from literary critics and priest-journalists to interested laypeople writing 'Letters to the Editor' – were concerned to focus upon questions of sin and grace and redemption. A conscious interest was shown in questions of Catholic doctrine, especially as these affected the fate of souls.

The major reasons for this pattern of response suggest themselves, and both are important as marks of comparison with the new 'Catholic' literature. The first is that the popular authors of the time, who set the agenda of debate, were, in overwhelming numbers, converts to Catholicism. This characteristic, of course, applied not only to the novelists but to virtually all the leading figures of the Catholic intellectual revival in Britain in the opening decades of the century to historians (like Christopher Dawson), artists (like Eric Gill), philosophers (like E.I. Watkin and T.S. Gregory), and popular apologists (like G.K. Chesterton and Sir Arnold Lunn). When the publisher and author Frank Sheed visited my home town of Armidale several years ago, he told me that, without the converts there would have been no revivial in the century in the English-speaking world. When Sheed edited in 1954 an anthology called *Born Catholics,* as a counterpoise to the many 'Road to Damascus' books produced by converts, it served to illustrate his point, for it contained only one cradle Catholic of undoubted literary stature – Hilaire Belloc.

Humanly speaking, the converts were brought to Catholicism largely by intellectual means. They often spoke of the thinness of their emotional commitment to the Church. Even Graham Greene, who has admitted that his conversion was prompted by a desire to share the faith of his Catholic fiancée, and whose theological ideas have often been criticised as peculiar if not heterodox, has stated that he entered the Church with intellectual conviction but with no emotional or aesthetic feeling.

The convert is most often drawn to the Church in adult life, and thus is conscious of the element of free will and choice in the act of conversion. Being convinced of the truth of Catholicism, he is apt to be interested in knowledge about God – in learning what God has revealed about human nature and destiny. Hence the influx of converts at that time – in countries where the Catholic Church was not pre-eminent and Catholics themselves felt isolated – became an occasion for communicating the Catholic experience, in a way few born Catholics had the imaginative readiness or the cultural confidence to do. The converts felt no inhibitions about presenting the Church to the world. They did not feel besieged. They were God's spies who had come in from the cold. Within the household of the Church, in Belloc's famous metaphor, they found the human spirit had roof and hearth. Outside it was the Night. To the misery of that metaphysical darkness the Church appeared as the only authentic answer – and the converts felt a profound calling to give witness to that fact.

The second major reason for the kind of Catholic literature produced is that the Catholic identity at that time was clear and coherent. The popular culture of the Church, which mediated the beliefs that the converts found so powerful and appealing, was still intact. It was a community which imposed considerable demands on its members but provided a vestment of meanings that made the sacrifices endurable. As the chief character in Mary Gordon's novel, *Final Payments* (1978), recalls about the Church:

> I always lived in a world where people asked the impossible. Anything else has always seemed mediocre.

Both these features have been reversed among the new 'Catholic' writers. Unlike Evelyn Waugh and Graham Greene, the new writers are, almost entirely, cradle Catholics. There is only the occasional convert – for example, the poets Les Murray and Kevin Hart. The television scriptwriter Tony Morphett has remarked that, if a dinner were organised for contemporary Australian writers, a significant number of the guests would be ex-Christian Brothers' boys; whether of the older generations (like Morris West, who actually trained to be a Christian Brother) or of the newer (like Ron Blair, Barry Oakley, Peter Kenna and Christopher Koch). Those now writing were reared at a critical moment in modern history. One might say they were born between two religious cultures, one dying, the other struggling to be born, and they received their formation in the matrix of a Church on the threshold of transformation. They were brought up believing in a way of life which was ceasing to believe in itself. Thus the literature produced by contemporary Catholics tends to have been preoccupied with Catholic subjects and scenes – seminaries and churches and religious schools. It has revealed a fascination with guilt. A special importance has been attached to a Catholic childhood. In books like Gerald Murnane's *Tamarisk Row,* the treatment of childhood affords a means by which authors seek to come to terms with the traditions which shaped them. The promises and celebrations of the Catholic upbringing, the burdens and sacrifices, the haunting mysteries, the unutterable sentiments – all these experiences were part of a distinctive way of life beneath the conformities of a mass secular culture. They furnish the means of explaining what one is – or, more often, obliterating what one used to be. Thomas Keneally has suggested, in a Melbourne *Age* interview (February 2, 1980), that authors do not write problems or preoccupations out of their systems: they write them in; absorb them into the blood stream, as it were; then move on to other themes. Presently I want to examine whether the writing of the new Catholics has ceased to be affected by the images and perspectives of a distinctive past. For the moment, however, it can be noted that the features of that past have been used as symbols of change – ways of dramatising the cultural distance which has been travelled in the recent passage of the Catholic people.

For the most part, traditional Catholic culture has been portrayed in the new literature with a mingling of astonishment and scorn – that a religious climate now judged to be tenuous and unworthy should have exacted the psychic costs it did. Much of the writing is laced with vindictiveness and self-hatred, and is almost entirely produced by embittered 'lapsed' Catholics. Had it been the work of non-Catholics, it might have provoked old-fashioned charges of Protestant bigotry. A recent example is the American play *Sister Mary Ignatius Explains It All for You*. Written by Christopher Durang, it enjoyed a triumphant reception when it opened in New York in 1981 and has since played in other American cities, with the exception of St Louis where it was cancelled in response to criticism that it was like 'a racist minstrel show or an anti-Semitic spoof of the holocaust.' Some readers may have seen it recently in Sydney.

In trying to recreate the world of traditional faith, the new writers face a formidable problem. Simply to stigmatise that world, to satirise its inhibitions and apparent puerilities, is not tolerable from either an artistic or a historical standpoint. This approach has of course been widely evident in recent times, but it represents a rupture in the Catholic imagination, for it serves only to render the devotion and faith of earlier generations unbelievable. From very little of the contemporary literature can one derive a sense of the profound meaning and appeal which the Church held for vast multitudes. The power of the traditional Catholic culture has not been conveyed – its capacity to hold all kinds of people, to draw them back, to inspire and change them. With a few exceptions, there has been a failure to evoke what it *felt* like, at that time, to believe in and practise the Catholic faith, particularly at the popular level in Australia.

This problem is strikingly reflected in Edmund Campion's book, *Rock-choppers,* which forms a non-fictional counterpart to the recent literary exorcisms of a traditional Catholic identity. Campion articulates the attitudes and longings of a new Catholic élite, which came to prominence in the years leading up to the Second Vatican Council and executed the changes which they thought were demanded by a sanctified modernity. *Rockchoppers* seems to have been widely received as the definitive account of 'growing up Catholic in Australia', and Edmund Campion's story as *the* story of the Australian Catholic people. Yet, despite some evocative passages, the book is curiously lacking in affection for the religious culture that makes Campion's story historically so gripping; as if a Church that has been 'depopularised' will have anything like the organic richness of traditional Catholicism. If the Church whose emergence is celebrated in *Rockchoppers,* and foreshadowed in much recent Catholic literature, is destined to be the Church of the twenty-first century, it will hardly yield the fascinated explorations of a future Edmund Campion.

Only with the passage of time might it prove practicable to penetrate the spiritual quality of popular Catholic culture in Australia, and to present it in fiction with imaginative sympathy. Few novels by modern Catholic authors can rival, for example, Sigrid Undset's great saga published in the 1920s, *Kristin Lavransdatter.* The book is set in fourteenth-century Norway – Undset herself was born in Norway and became a Catholic in 1924 – and it offers a living picture of popular medieval culture. Its power flows in part from its reanimation of a world that is distant enough not to stir repressed grievances on the part of the modern reader, but sufficiently vivid and true-to-life to kindle the attention of anyone interested in the nature and destiny of human beings. We are permitted to enter into the minds and hearts of ordinary people of that time, as the farmers till the earth, the priests tend their flocks, and the nobles struggle with affairs of state. However remote such circumstances may be from our present-day experience, we can identify instantly with the truth of Undset's vision. Her characters are real people, neither romanticised nor reviled by their fictional creator. Graham Greene has argued, in his recently published interview with Marie-Françoise Allain (*The Other Man*), that 'all writers, even the worst, are led into assuming a role vaguely comparable to God's, for they create characters over whom they exercise total control.' Undset's control of her characters is tempered by the freedom she grants them to embrace good or evil. She knows and loves them deeply: she knows their pride, their impiety, their less-than-heroic virtue – but she loves them all as possible vessels of grace.

That outlook informs Undset's novels, as it inspires those of a contemporary Catholic writer, James Carroll. Speaking of his novel, *Fault Lines,* in the American weekly, *Our Sunday Visitor* (November 2, 1980), Carroll noted that:

> all three main characters are flawed people, but as the author I love all three of them absolutely. My commitment as a writer is to communicate somehow that this love of the novelist for his characters is an authentic image of how the Author of Life loves all His people, always.

Probably we will have to wait several generations before the world of popular Catholicism which has recently passed can be retrieved in all its spiritual and cultural intensity – to be seen as neither a tormenting oppression nor a quaint memory, but as a lived experience of faith that possesses supernatural value and significance and links the people of recent centuries with those of our own time.

If it is true that authors eventually write out of their system – or, as Keneally suggests, write *into* their system – the particular ideas that have seized their imagination, then we might expect that the recent burst of literature by and about Catholics will abate as the flames of bitterness die out. Certainly a distinct mellowing of outlook is discernible among some of the writers who grew alienated from the Church in the 1960s. They are apt to exhibit a deep ambivalence – an attitude of regret as well as relief. They are poignantly conscious of the diminished power of the Catholic tradition. Their imaginations appear to throb at times with the knowledge that they can no longer embody in their lives what they still feel, intensely if reluctantly, is an unalterable identity. Thus, Thomas Keneally recently questioned what he calls 'the new style of jiving Catholicism', which he believes has emptied the Church of much of its mystery and menacing fascination:

> Maybe religion should put people on the edge, where it used to put them. Whatever the truth is, I feel that a lot of the ceremonies have

been debased. It's much cosier now, with the failed pop songs that they sing. The central mystery of the Mass is still there (though quite well concealed). The rites are now on the level of those for the opening of a supermarket. I am simply bemused – and have been, in several stages. First, by the old, shut-in attitudes, then by disillusion, when I struggled to get out, then I was very very bitter, and followed this by indifference. I am now coming back to a period in which I am absolutely open to it, but still confused.

Or again, the English writer, Anthony Burgess, describing the longings of the 'lapsed' Catholic:

I avoid envying the believer, but it is with no indifferent eye that I view the flood of worshippers pouring into the Catholic church at the corner of my street. I want to be one of them, but wanting is not enough. The position of standing on the periphery is one that I share with many men of good will; the state of being a lapsed Catholic is so painful that it sometimes seems to generate a positive charge, as though it had in itself a certain religious validity. Perhaps some of the prayers that go for the souls in purgatory might occasionally be used for us. Those souls at least know where they are. We don't. I don't.

Two kinds of response now seem to be occurring among writers of a Catholic background. One is what might be seen as a traditional approach, consisting of the depiction of Catholic characters and the analysis of Catholic themes. This approach shares a ready affinity with the self-consciously Catholic literature produced in an earlier generation by authors like Graham Greene. An impressive contemporary example is the novelist Mary Gordon. Raised as an only child in New York City during the 1960s, she experienced an intensely religious upbringing. She recalls that, as a child, she read the lives of the saints over and over. She wrote religious treatises and poetry for her own edification. 'The metaphors of Catholicism,' she has said in an interview in *Publishers Weekly* (February 6, 1981), 'the Catholic way of looking at the world, these are in my bones. It is my framework of language.'

Gordon's first novel, *Final Payments,* bears the impress of that childhood ardour. It is remarkable that a book whose main themes are self-sacrifice, death, old people, and the enduring vitality of the Catholic faith should prove such a bestseller. Her most recent work is *The Company of Women,* which is also emphatically Catholic in its subject matter and the characterisations. I would surmise that this kind of literature will gradually diminish as the years lengthen; for the writers producing it belong to the last generation formed in the crucible of a traditional Catholic culture. They were shaped by the idea that Catholicism is not only a faith but a Church – a living body of people, made up of the weak and the unspiritually minded as well as the committed, which expresses its beliefs and values in a certain way of life. They believed that a sharp tension existed between the Church and the world, and that this reflected deeper dichotomies in life – between good and evil, sin and sanctity, heaven and hell.

The conspicuously Catholic novel in the English-speaking world, whether of Graham Greene or Mary Gordon, is essentially the product of a certain religious culture – one that was still intact and accepted in the 1940s and imaginatively accessible only to the convert, but one which has now largely gone, opening up a cultural void which only the cradle Catholic is able to plumb.

Yet as this form of novel fades, Catholicism will not, I believe, suddenly cease to generate a literature. A different kind of novel is now making a vital impact on the literary scene. It is 'Catholic' in a less striking sense than the earlier *genre*. While it commonly contains Catholic characters, it is not so interested in, or dependent upon, specifically Catholic subjects or themes. One might claim that it does not impress the general reader as the literature of a sect or a denomination. It does not treat of sacrilegious communions or rubrical niceties or childhood singularities or ecclesiastical conflicts – themes that were fairly characteristic before the Catholic identity began to dissolve. In sum, it no longer depicts the struggles of a religious people within a definite context of belief and habit, for such a context no longer obtains.

Mary Gordon, in an interview in 1981 in the *Chicago Tribune*, has recognised the effect on literature of recent shifts in the secular culture and the Catholic identity:

> In general I think the religious experience is a less and less formative experience in a communal sense, because people's communities are less and less religiously defined. So any kind of religious life becomes less prevalent a subject of novels... I think that people in my generation are coming back to religion, having been away from it in their youth. But it hasn't reached fiction yet, I don't think.

What *has* reached fiction is the attempt of Catholic novelists to bring their spiritual traditions to bear on a new cultural situation. This means exploring themes that may have been previously addressed by non-Catholic writers, treating them in a new secular ambience, and yet raising the basic issues of human existence from a distinctively Catholic perspective. The sorts of issues being dramatised are those of the contest between good and evil, the sacramental character of human life, the universal scope of divine love.

The dissolution of the traditional religious culture is prompting the Catholic novelist to search out other traditions with which to probe eternal realities; to resort even to symbol systems other than Christianity. Writers like Christopher Koch and Blanch d'Alpuget have recently turned to Asia and been drawing on symbols from non-Christian religions. Koch's highly successful novel, *The Year of Living Dangerously* (1978), now translated by Peter Weir to the screen, is built on the structure of a Javanese puppet show, which represents the shadows on the screen as human souls and allows the novelist to dramatise the conflict between good and evil, between the forces of light and the forces of darkness. The novelty of this metaphor, combined with the quality of Koch's writing, generates an atmosphere of inexhaustible mystery.

The element of mystery is central to any work that seeks to portray spiritual conflict, and yet it is forbiddingly difficult to evoke in the midst of a modern secularist culture. As the Melbourne literary critic, Terry Monagle, has observed, several contemporary authors have been pushing, largely in vain, the form of the novel to see if it can bear the depiction of the supernatural without disintegrating. Insofar as the task admits of success, it finds a powerful exemplar in the fiction of Flannery O'Connor (1925-64). This American novelist and short-story writer is proving to be more relevant to the 1980s than to the period in which she wrote. She produced only a handful of books, having been weakened and finally killed by a rare disease at the age of thirty-nine. But these works provide an extraordinary foreshadowing of the form of Catholic novel that is now likely to be effective.

Flannery O'Connor was born and spent most of her life in the American State of Georgia. Her writings do not use Catholic characters and settings. They are concerned with the region where she lived and the people she knew: fundamentalist Protestants in the American South. For all its intensity, the religion of the South is not sacramental in character. It is not an incarnational faith in the way Catholicism is. It does not take root, visibly and tangibly, in the surrounding culture, touching all aspects of popular life – the mundane as well as the momentous. The challenge which Flannery O'Connor had to meet in the 1950s, however, is similar to that confronting the Catholic novelist in the 1980s: how to depict spiritual action and change to an audience which receives few intimations of the supernatural from its own culture. Where Christianity becomes relegated to the private sphere, as it tends to in the American South and increasingly throughout Western society, it ceases to find social channels for the transmission of religious truth. Flannery O'Connor's way of coping imaginatively with these conditions was to use natural phenomena – like water and fire – as symbols of the supernatural. And she peopled her work with strange and overpowering characters. Her fiction abounds with raging prophets and fanatical preachers.

All of these elements are memorably combined in what is perhaps her finest novel, *The Violent Bear It Away* (1960). It is a taut and compelling story of an adolescent boy in rural Tennessee, who is raised by his great-uncle to be a Christian prophet. When the old man dies, the boy repudiates this vocation, refuses to honour his great-uncle's request for Christian burial and leaves for the city. The novel traces the consequent struggle for his soul.

The vital centre of the book is supplied by a remarkably potent metaphor – that of hunger. The boy had been told by the old man that 'Jesus is the Bread of Life'. From the time he leaves his dead great-uncle, the boy feels famished. yet he cannot bear to eat; the thought of ordinary food nauseates him. When he returns to the site of his great-uncle's death, he has an overwhelming sense of his own unfaithfulness. 'As he looked,' writes Flannery O'Connor, 'his dry lips parted. They seemed to be forced open by a hunger too great to be contained inside him.' Presently, the boy has a vision of the Sermon on the Mount. He sees his great-uncle before him and he realises at last the true object of his hunger. He is 'aware that it was the same as the old man's and that nothing on earth would fill him. His hunger was so great that he could have eaten all the loaves and fishes after they were multiplied.'

Such a summary gives barely a hint of the power of this novel. Yet as a study of the workings of grace in a culture without obvious religious supports, *The Violent Bear It Away* points a path forward for the Catholic novel. It fulfils the key criterion of that novel – namely, the portrayal of the human person in a spiritual universe. It reveals a being who is never simply secular in his needs; who seeks to remain self-sufficient and earthbound but is finally prized open by the levering of a divine love. Thus the modern reader is given some insight into the transcendent importance of human life. He sees the human soul engaged in an adventure with eternity. And he feels moved by the experience which lies at the heart of Catholic literature – the experience of spiritual struggle which Georges Bernanos once described so graphically:

> I am between the Angel of light and the Angel of darkness, looking at them each in turn with the same enraged hunger for the absolute.

# Literary Style in England and America[1]

## EVELYN WAUGH

From the middle of the eighteenth century until the middle of the nineteenth there was published in England a series of architectural designs for the use of provincial builders and private patrons. The plates display buildings of varying sizes, from gate-lodges to mansions, decorated in various 'styles,' Palladian, Greek, Gothic, even Chinese. The ground plans are identical, the 'style' consists of surface enrichment. At the end of this period it was even possible for very important works such as the Houses of Parliament in London to be the work of two hands, Barry designing the structure, Pugin overlaying it with medieval ornament. And the result is not to be despised. In the present half century we have seen architects abandon all attempt at 'style' and our eyes are everywhere sickened with boredom at the blank, unlovely, unlovable facades which have

---

1    From Donat Gallagher (ed.), *Evelyn Waugh: a selection from his journalism*, London, Eyre Methuen, 1977.

arisen from Constantinople to Los Angeles. But this use of style is literally superficial. Properly understood style is not a seductive decoration added to a functional structure; it is of the essence of a work of art.

This is unconsciously recognized by popular usage. When anyone speaks of 'Literary style' the probability is that he is thinking of prose. A poem is dimly recognized as existing in its form. There are no poetic ideas; only poetic utterances and, as Wordsworth pointed out, the true antithesis is not between prose and poetry, but between prose and metre. Now that poets have largely abandoned metre, the distinction has become so vague as to be hardly recognizable. Instead of two separate bodies of writing, we must see a series of innumerable gradations from the melodious and mystical to the scientific.

Literature is the right use of language irrespective of the subject or reason of the utterance. A political speech may be, and sometimes is, literature: a sonnet to the moon may be, and often is, trash. Style is what distinguishes literature from trash. Nevertheless in certain quarters the appellation 'stylist' bears a prejorative sense. Logan Pearsall Smith, that splendid American, is dismissed fretfully while D.H. Lawrence, who wrote squalidly, is accepted as an artist because his themes were of wider and deeper interest. This is a paradox which academic critics, to whom one would look to correct popular misconceptions, do little to resolve. Many indeed aggravate it, for there is a lurking puritanism at Cambridge (England) and in many parts of the New World, which is ever ready to condemn pleasure even in its purest form. If this seems doubtful consider the case of James Joyce. There was a writer possessed by style. His later work lost almost all faculty of communication, so intimate, allusive and idiosyncratic did it become, so obsessed by euphony and nuance. But because he was obscure and can only be read with intense intellectual effort – and therefore without easy pleasure – he is admitted into the academic canon. But it is just in this task of communication that Joyce's style fails, for the necessary elements of style are lucidity, elegance, individuality; these three qualities combine to form a preservative which ensures the nearest approximation to permanence in the fugitive art of letters.

Lucidity does not imply universal intelligibility. Henry James is the most lucid of writers, but not the simplest. The simplest statements in law or philosophy are usually those which, in application, require the greatest weight of commentary and provoke the longest debate. A great deal of what is most worth saying must always remain unintelligible to most readers. The test of lucidity is whether the statement can be read as meaning anything other than what it intends. Military orders should be, and often are, models of lucidity. The correspondence of businessmen abound in ambiguities.

Elegance is the quality in a work of art which imparts direct pleasure; again not universal pleasure. There is a huge, envious world to whom elegance is positively offensive. English is incomparably the richest of languages, dead or living. One can devote one's life to learning it and die without achieving mastery. No two words are identical in meaning, sound and connotation. The majority of

English speakers muddle through with a minute vocabulary. To them any words not in vulgar use, are 'fancy' and it is, perhaps, in ignoble deference to their susceptibilities that there has been a notable flight from magnificence in English writing. Sixty years ago, when 'jewelled prose' was all the rage, there were some pretentious efforts at fine writing which excited great ridicule. There was an inevitable reaction, but surveying the bleak prospect today, one can recognize that those absurdities are a small price to pay for the magnificence of the preceding masters. When I hear the word 'tawdry', I suspect the puritan. The man who can enjoy the flimsy and fantastic decorations of Naples is much more likely to appreciate the grandeur of Roman baroque, than the prig who demands Michelangelo or nothing. It is a matter for thankfulness that the modern school of critics are unable or unwilling to compose a pleasurable sentence. It greatly limits the harm they do.

Individuality needs little explanation. It is the hand-writing, the tone of voice, that makes a work recognizable as being by a particular artist (or in rare decades of highly homogeneous culture, by one of a particular set).

Permanence is the result of the foregoing. Style is what makes a work memorable and unmistakable. We remember the false judgments of Voltaire and Gibbon and Lytton Strachey long after they have been corrected, because of their sharp, polished form and because of the sensual pleasure of dwelling on them. They come to one, not merely as printed words, but as a lively experience, with the full force of another human being personally encountered – that is to say because they are lucid, elegant and individual.

Among living writers of English prose there are few who attempt magnificence. Sir Osbert Sitwell's great five volume autobiography and Sir Winston Churchill's historical studies stand almost alone and the latter, though highly creditable for a man with so much else to occupy him, do not really survive close attention. He can seldom offer the keen, unmistakable aesthetic pleasure of the genuine artist. Elegance in the present century tends to be modest. We have no organ voice to rival Sir Thomas Browne's but we have a volume of exquisite and haunting music. Sir Max Beerbohm and Msgr Ronald Knox; each stands at the summit of his own art. They differ in scope. Where they attempt the same tasks, in parody, they are equal and supreme over all competitors. Sir Max has confined himself to the arts; Msgr. Knox goes higher, to the loftiest regions of the human spirit. His *Enthusiasm* should be recognized as the greatest work of literary art of the century. Below these two masters there is an honourable company of very fine craftsmen, none it must be admitted, in their first youth. Mr. E.M.Forster, particularly in the first half of *Pharos and Pharillon*, set a model of lucidity and individuality in which the elegance is so unobtrusive as to pass some readers unnoticed. Curiously enough it is not in the Universities that one finds fine writing; Sir Maurice Bowra is learned and lucid, but dull; Lord David Cecil has grace but no grammar; Mr. Isiah Berlin is diffuse and voluble; Mr. Trevor-Roper vulgar. Among critics in the press the standard is higher. Mr. Raymond Mortimer never fails. Mr. Cyril Connolly has fitfully achieved some lovely effects. Among novelists Mr. Anthony Powell, Mr.

Graham Greene, Miss Compton-Burnett, Mr. Henry Green all have intensely personal and beautiful styles. One could never mistake a page of their writing for anyone else's.

It will be noticed that all these examples are drawn from England. Logan Pearsall Smith wrote:

> And America, the land of my birth, America! ...Youth has its dreams, its longings for distinction; among all the eager young men and women of that vast county....in not one of those resounding cities or multitudinous universities, does the thought never come to anyone, I ask myself, that the instrument of speech which they make use of all day long has resonances within it of unimaginable beauty?...The golden sceptre of style gilds everything it touches, and can make immortal those who grasp it : to not one of those aspiring youths does the thought ever suggest itself that it might be an adventure among adventures to try to wield that wand? ... From the point of view of Style that whole Continent could sink beneath the sea and never leave a ripple.

That was written in 1934. Can we today qualify the severe judgment? There is Mr. Hemingway. He is lucid and individual and euphonious. He has imposed limits on his powers which only a master can survive. He has won mastery, but at the cost of a sad brood of imitators. Mr. Faulkner has individuality but nothing else. Perhaps the languages of the two continents have grown so separate that it is impossible for an Englishman to catch the nuances of American diction. From this great distance it seems that there are editorial styles only, – a rather good, dry style in the *New Yorker*, a very poor style in *Time* – and one sometimes suspects that austerity has been imposed on the contributors so that they shall not distract attention from the more luxurious wording of the advertisements. American critics, I believe, are impatient of the airs and graces of English writers. It is one of the great gulfs between our two civilizations that each finds the other effeminate. To the American, English writers are like prim spinsters fidgeting with the china, punctilious about good taste, and inwardly full of thwarted, tepid and perverse passions. We see the Americans as gushing adolescents, repetitive and slangy, rather nasty sometimes in their zest for violence and bad language. The difference, I think, is this. All English boys, of the kind who are now writers, learned Latin from the age of nine. Very few girls did. The boys did not become ripe scholars, but they acquired a basic sense of the structure of language which never left them, they learned to scan quite elaborate metres; they learned to compose Latin verse of a kind themselves. Little girls learned French and were praised for idiomatic volubility. When they grew up they wrote as though they were babbling down the telephone – often very prettily, like Miss Nancy Mitford. We regard this sort of writing as womanly and that is the quality we find in American male writers, who, I believe, learn Latin late and thoroughly in a few cases but often not at all. But in the Protestant schools in England, Latin is no longer universally taught. It may be that in the next generation only the boys from Jesuit and Benedictine schools will carry on the tradition of English prose. That is by the way.

One thing I hold as certain, that a writer, if he is to develop, must concern himself more and more with Style. He cannot hope to interest the majority of his readers in his progress. It is his own interest that is at stake. Style alone can keep him from being bored with his own work. In youth high spirits carry one over a book or two. The world is full of discoveries that demand expression. Later a writer must face the choice of becoming an artist or a prophet. He can shut himself up at his desk and selfishly seek pleasure in the perfecting of his own skill or he can pace about, dictating dooms and exhortations on the topics of the day. The recluse at the desk has a bare chance of giving abiding pleasure to others; the publicist has none at all.

# Catholic Writing: Some Basic Notions, Some Criticisms, and a Tentative Reply[1]

## J.C. WHITEHOUSE

Although many Catholic writers often seem anxious to avoid the label, presumably in an attempt to disclaim any possible polemical or ideological role which might be thrust upon them by the critic or the reader, it is clear that there are such things as Catholic writing and Catholic writers. We should perhaps try to define these terms.

Most Catholic writing seems to derive from two kinds of thinking. The first, which we might describe as practical and calculating, is aimed ultimately at influence and control, and the second, which we could call meditative and reflective, is receptive rather than dominating. Thus, on one hand, we have a body of work which has fundamentally a non-literary purpose and is produced to illustrate, expound, explain and justify the beliefs and doctrines explicitly contained in Catholic faith. Examples of this kind of writing would include all kinds of theology from St John the Evangelist to Rosemary Haughton or Teilhard de Chardin, liturgical and devotional works, apologetics and polemics. Chesterton, Bernanos, Undset and Mauriac, to name but a few modern Catholic writers, have all produced work which could be classified

1    From *Modern Language Review,* 73,2,1978.

under one or more of these headings. There is an ancient tradition of such writing, and its purpose is apparent: the defence, illustration, exploration of the Catholic view of God and Man and their relationship. The method adopted may be that of reasoned argument or of emotional appeal, but the end product is essentially explanatory, justificatory or didactic in tone.

On the other hand we have a second kind of writing which is as easy to recognize but rather more difficult to define, and could more properly be called Catholic *literature*. Its *raison d'être* is artistic rather than apologetic or didactic, and it is basically the expression of a personal reaction to human life and a personal vision of it. It is produced by an imagination and a sensibility formed and influenced by a specific faith, which contains concepts of man's nature and destiny. Such writing arises not primarily, necessarily, or even probably, from an attempt to convert the reader to a view, having its origin rather in the portrayal of the imaginative universe of a particular human being. In this, it comes closer to the work of an imaginative writer who is an atheist or an agnostic than it does to Aquinas's philosophical texts, Bossuet's sermon's or Newman's essays. The writer who produces work of this kind, in fact, is very likely to be the kind of Catholic writer who is ill at ease with such a label, perhaps feeling that although he may legitimately show a Catholic view of the world and of human life, he should be seen as unwilling to provide special pleading for their objective truth. To what extent a Catholic writer is or is not an apologist, either consciously or unconsciously, is highly debatable. That some, on occasion, exercise this function seems clear, and one could cite Bloy or Claudel as examples. Perhaps the best Catholic writers are those in whose case it is difficult or impossible to form a judgement. Bernanos's faith, for example, seems to me so enormously powerful an imaginative influence in his novels that one could scarcely begin to separate the persuasive from the more strictly imaginative or creative aspect of them, and Alrik Gustafson's observation on Sigrid Undset's novels ('...the thorough-going consistency with which she develops Catholic dogma') is an extremely simplistic remark.[2] It is easy for a slightly obtuse or unsympathetic critic to misunderstand the nature of the writing and, by seizing upon certain features of it, to distort the whole mental climate of a given author. It cannot be argued that Catholic writers of powerful imagination are never, even implicitly, apologists, but neither can it be justly argued that they almost always are.

Clearly, too, as a given writer may simultaneously produce both the kinds of writing mentioned above, the differences between the two modes are not always clear-cut. Despite the fine literary qualities of Newman's essays, he remains in them essentially an explanatory writer and an apologist. But what of the *Dream of Gerontius?* Are the *Confessions* of St Augustine works of piety or imaginative psychological exploration? Are Chesterton's 'novels of ideas' polemical or imaginative works? It is obvious that in certain cases it might be difficult to decide which kind of writing we are examining. The danger is that

2   Alrik Gustafson, *Six Scandinavian Novelists* (Minneapolis, 1960), p. 360.

it is often tempting to see modern Catholic literature as basically an ideological literature, setting out to convert, to influence, and almost, in extreme cases, to browbeat and to bully.[3]

Richard Griffiths, discussing a rather earlier period of Catholic literature than that which I have chiefly in mind here, has written of the French Catholic literary revival between 1870 and the Great War as essentially 'consisting of a hard core of writers in whom, for the first time in two centuries, a deep involvement in religious matters was associated with works of literary value'.[4] If we bear in mind that outside France this revival took place rather later, then this statement is a useful way of saying what is meant by modern Catholic literature. It implies a seriousness, a view of the world coloured by certain beliefs or assumptions, and the ability of a writer to compel the respect and interest of the reader. It would be a sign of the worth we saw in any given writer if his Catholicism, or existentialism, or Marxism, or whatever outlook he held, could, without becoming invisible, never strain our willing suspension of disbelief and never, however strongly it might be present, dominate or exclude our sympathies.[5]

Such a Catholic writer will probably imply that what he is writing about is 'man, the heart of man, and human life', and hope that his conviction and imaginative power will be great enough to sustain the reader's attention and to persuade him to accept, within the framework of the work in question, the writer's view of the world without rejecting his own perceptions or being obliged to protest at intervals. In short, he must convince the reader of the imaginative truth of that view. In an age in which most religious thought, and certainly that incorporated, in fiction, is concerned more with faith than with reason, with witness, or being in or living in the truth than with argument, one would expect to find in the novel portrayal rather than polemics, a situation where, given a certain large-mindedness on the part of the reader, *Brighton Rock* or *The Wild Orchid* is seen as no more tendentious or ideologically suspect that *La Nausée*, *L'Etranger* or *La Condition humaine*.

In this sense, even the most strongly Catholic literature is not, as Gonzague Truc has pointed out, a confessional literature, with the author as simply a preacher or an apologist:

> Il (the Catholic writer) oublie même qu'il est écrivain catholique, et il suffit qu'il le demeure dans son essence et dans les profondeurs ... Il reçoit de sa foi latente et agissante le souffle qui vivifie et transforme toute chose, cette riche doctrine qui s'est inscrite dans tous les mouvements du coeur et de l'esprit, qui a repétri l'humanité. Il n'a pas besoin de le rappel-

---

3    See for example Martin Green's *Yeats's Blessings on von Hügel* (London, 1967), p.124.
4    Richard Griffiths, *The Reactionary Revolution* (London, 1966), p.3.
5    This seems to me to represent the truth of the remark by Camus that all great novels are philosophical novels, that is, the opposite of *romans à thèse*: see *Le Mythe de Sisyphe* (Paris, 1942), p. 138.

er à chaque instant ou de tenter de l'exposer à nouveau. Elle est là, présente. Elle enfante et juge. L'artiste n'a rien à y abjurer de son art.[6]

In other words, Catholic novels, like all other works of literary art which incorporate a specific body of thought or belief, a specific doctrine or system, share in the major advantage which art has over polemics, which is that they present experience rather than arguments drawn from experience. Whatever the message involved, it is the conviction and power of the experience portrayed which will determine what the reader's deepest reactions will be.

In fact, if one were to take apologetics and the direct portrayal of the good (from a religious, a moral or a social point of view) as the criterion for deciding whether a given work was 'Catholic' or not, then much modern literature produced by Catholics would be excluded. This, I think, was perhaps, what was in the mind of Graham Greene when he wrote disclaiming the title of Catholic writer: 'I would not claim to be a Catholic writer, but a writer who in four or five books took characters with Catholic ideas for his material.'[7] Heinrich Böll has of course said the same: 'I am not a Catholic writer. I am a Catholic who writes.'[8] Both, it seems to me, are anxious to claim the freedom to be truthful to experience (even if that experience is Catholic it can still be catholic) rather than conformity to pre-existing dogma. Bernanos made this point much more forcefully and clearly when discussing the subject-matter chosen by Catholic writers: 'Le roman catholique n'est pas celui qui ne nous entretient que de bons sentiments, c'est celui ou la vie de la foi s'affronte avec les passions. Il faut rendre le plus sensible possible le tragique mystère du salut... l'experience vécue de l'amour divin n'est pas du domaine du roman.'[9] The Catholic writer need not necessarily write about, except in the very widest sense, Catholic subject-matter or create Catholic characters. It is an attitude (expressed through character, or situation or comment) on the part of the writer which determines whether a work is Catholic in Bernanos's sense or not. Greene's books other than the 'four or five' he mentioned and Bernanos's *Nouvelle Histoire de Mouchette* may not be Catholic in the narrower sense of the term, but they are nevertheless marked by Catholic attitudes and a Catholic point of view. Indeed, it might be argued that *Mouchette*, where the only obvious religious reference is to the church bells ringing for the Mass to which no one goes any more, is the most deeply Catholic of Bernarnos's novels. It is the underlying stance and imaginative viewpoint adopted which is decisive here.

Within Catholic literature, in the sense in which I have tried to define it, we must be prepared to discover all kinds of sensibilities, all kinds of political and social views, all kinds of personalities. Catholic writers are as interesting for their differences as for the similarities. It is not uncommon to assume that

6    Gonzague Truc, *Histoire de la litterature catholique contemporaine* (Tournai, 1961), p.290.
7    Graham Greene, *In Search of a Character* (London, 1961), p.26.
8    Interview with W.J. Igoe, *Catholic Herald,* 15 May 1973.
9    *Le Crépuscule des Vieux* (Paris, 1956), pp.83-84.

there is (or was) a typical Catholic sensibility and a typical Catholic literature. This assumption may be partly correct, but not, I believe, in the sense implied by John Weightman in his essay on Conor Cruise O'Brien's study of Catholic novelists, *Maria Cross*, where he sees such a sensibility as characterizing certain writers who are fundamentally misguided people, imaginative and with a gloomy view of life, who 'are dramatizing frustrations that result from local or social personal prejudices, that is from non-essential forms of evil, and which would be seen as non-essential by keener intelligences'.[10] For Catholic writers and their readers, the reverse of Weightman's view would be the truth: that is, they would see all local and social evils as arising from an essential and ubiquitous form of evil, from a principle of corruption which for them is a fact of life. It is such views which both unify Catholic views and, in their individual variations arising from local and temporal circumstances, contribute to their diversity. To be fair to Weightman it should be pointed out that he was attempting no more than a concise and stimulating summary of one strand of Catholic sensibility. He does not, however, seem to realize that there are *various* strands, and that, to take a few random examples, neither Dante nor Chaucer, nor Morris West nor Muriel Spark nor Chesterton nor Sigrid Undset can be seen as presenting what he, playing on O'Brien's title in a mildly offensive way, calls the 'sexy cross'. Their work simply cannot be seen as a series of 'frissons' produced by the contemplation of fruit forbidden by their religion. Weightman's implication, of course, is that the whole problem of evil and sin is simply another way of describing sexual tensions, frustrations and neuroses. The idea may be flippant, but it is a tenacious and formative one which distorts the perspective in which Catholic literature as a whole should be seen.

Weightman's rather witty remarks illustrate a point of view which is more fully worked out and illustrated in two essays by Martin Green, entitled *Two Kinds of Catholic Sensibility* and *J.E. Powers and Catholic Writing*.[11] The arguments deployed in these are convincing up to a point, and yet one feels in the end that the truth is perhaps not quite so simple. What is said in them, is however, worth examining, although the examples chosen by Green have been too carefully selected and the arguments illustrated by them pushed too far.

There are, it seems to me, two poles (but more than two kinds) of Catholic sensibility. At one of the poles, as the greatness of God becomes apparent, man becomes more vile. This we would call the sensibility of the mystical and the mysterious, epitomized in certain writers of the French Catholic revival, and emphasized by Weightman and Green. At the other, we have an imagination keenly aware of the ordinary, the normal, the sane and the patently and decently good. This is the imaginative world of *Kristin Lavransdatter, The Wild Orchid, The Burning Bush* and other novels by Sigrid Undset, and of certain novels by Heinrich Böll, where the desire to create a *'bewohnbares land'* is not a

10   *O'Brien's Sexy Cross* in *The Concept of the Avant-garde* (London 1973), pp 270-76. The essay is a review of O'Brien's *Maria Cross: Imaginative Patterns in a Group of Catholic Writers* (London, 1963).
11   Green, pp.65-96 and 97-127.

minor concern. It is also the imaginative world of Chesterton in his poems, his novels, his essays and his journalism. To ignore this strand of Catholic sensibility which includes images of the married woman performing her duties and bringing up her family with love, care, zest and diligence, as well as those of the drunken priest in *The Power and the Glory* and the adulteress in *The End of the Affair*. Green, however, devotes considerable sections of *Yeats's Blessings on von Hügel* to a severe criticism of what he sees as the life-destroying, totalitarian, hectoring aspect of Catholic literature:

> In the world of Catholic literature, on the other hand, the writer's vitality and individualism figure most often as the means of covert bullying, the writer identifying himself with a creed and enforcing himself and it together. No doubt any rigid and massive institutional power is an attractive object of identification for the bully; and there is also a heartiness, a promise that we are the people who know how to really *enjoy life* (unlike those niggardly Non-conformists and greyfaced atheists) recurrent in Catholic sensibility in different periods and places.

Between this kind of sensibility, Green claims, and that of these who are 'at ease in life' there is a radical opposition:

> In the work of these writers (i.e. Claudel, Mauriac, Greene, Bernanos and Bloy) God and religion destroy life, and it is surely not too much to say that the effect of these plays and novels is angrily and proudly to participate in that destruction. The writers are always on the side of those characters who hate the world – who don't belong in it. The sinners differ from the saints in the object of their loves, but both belong in radical opposition to the bourgeois, the property-owners, who are at ease in life. The Catholic-writer syndrome is surely one of the most transparent of all masks for a hateful revenge on life and all who enjoy it; one of the evillest, most distorting of self-disguises.[12]

Apart from the obvious self-contradictions in Green's attack (with Catholics both having the exclusive ability to enjoy life and taking a revenge on those who do enjoy it) such criticism (even from a Catholic who has apparently espoused the cause of bourgeois liberalism) is extreme in its rigidity and exclusiveness. To equate a local (and non-essential) good, that of the comfort of the bourgeois property-owner, exclusively with 'life' and 'happiness' seems shallow at least. That many Catholic writers (with Bernanos and Mauriac figuring prominently amongst them) have said harsh things about the property-owning bourgeoisie is undeniable. What Green does not point out, however, is that such attacks have been made precisely because the concerns of the bourgeoisie have themselves been seen as in some way tending to diminish human life. The land-

12   Green, p.123 and p.125

ed proprietors in Mauriac's novels are attacked not because they enjoy the fullness and richness of human life but because they are so obsessed with property and wealth that they cease to be fully human. Bernanos, in the *Journal d'un curé de campagne* for example, criticizes the bourgeoisie, clerical or lay, not for their possessions or their happiness, but for the pettiness, the aggressiveness and the stultifying conservatism which their preoccupations engender. With their impassioned plea for human dignity – here and now, and not in some distant Catholic heaven – such works as Bernanos's *Lettre aux Anglais, Le Chemin de la Croix des Ames* and *Les Grands Cimetières sous la lune,* as well as the more complex and therefore variously-interpretable novels, should be recommended reading for critics of the persuasion of Martin Green.

We have seen that Green stresses two aspects of Catholic literature which seem mutually incompatible. One is a supposed Catholic exclusivity (if that is not already a contradiction in terms) in the capacity to enjoy life, the second a supposed hatred of those who do actually enjoy it. These contradict each other, as I have already suggested, and at least partly contradict Weightman's emphasis on the gloominess of Catholic literature. Both the enjoyment of life and the gloominess are of course present in such literature. Chesterton and Belloc certainly seem to stress the monopoly of employment, Claudel and Bloy the gloominess. But the important point is that there are other, equally important, elements which both Green and Weightman ignore. The chief of these is the dimension of simultaneous tragic dignity and a desire for ordinary human happiness explored by (for example) Sigrid Undset both in her historical novels and in those set in contemporary life. They could perhaps be seen as examples of a kind of Catholic writing which includes more of the self-contradictory and yet self-contemplatory nature of the two patterns of human experience which Green isolates but does not seem to see as forming a part of a greater whole. Whatever one's personal reaction to them may be, writers such as Chesterton and Undset (and perhaps in our later days Piers Paul Read) have some view of fullness of human life on earth -in ordinary, human terms – with, in certain cases at least, the religious dimension producing the 'expanded personality' of which Green speaks. All that needs to be suggested is that there is another side to Catholic writing which is life-enhancing, and which takes a positive rather than a negative view of ordinary human life. Even the (by implication) 'violent and destructive' Bernanos could write that he had loved the world – 'le doux royaume de la terre' – more than he had ever been able to say. It is also clear that when Green remarks that what Bernanos hated most in life was laughter, irony, and curiosity, he both states a truth and totally misses the point of it, for it is the destructive, negative, vitiating quality of certain kinds of irony, certain kinds of laughter and a certain literariness which is fact a perversion of life that he hated.[13] Nor do his saints – Chantal in *La Joie,* for example

---

13    Quine, Lipotte, Ganse and similar characters are not detestable because they love life, but because they hate it and are made uneasy by it. The images of their anti-life are striking: colourless and tasteless water and a dead, sterile universe.

– despise ordinary human life. It is true that none of his characters is whole-heartedly bourgeois, but it does not need a Catholic writer to point out the dangers facing religion if it becomes a function of a middle-class way of life.

It is also too easy to exaggerate and distort what is sometimes seen as anti-humanism are anti-intellectualism in Catholic literature, and to say that Catholic writers are somehow against the 'fully-expanded personality'. Bernanos's attitude to Proust, for example, was far from being one of scorn or disdain, and he maintained that Proust's influence was beneficial 'par cette espèce d'anxieté qui fait le fond des immenses joies intellectuelles qu'il nous donne. Elle a réveillé le désire de chercher. Elle a ouvert le champ.'[14] The important point is that for Bernanos, and one may suppose also for other Catholic writers, the kind of knowledge which a writer like Proust can give is not an end in itself or complete in itself, for it can be more meaningful, as Bernanos implies later in the same passage, in the light of faith and of a view of man's destiny. In short its importance is increased when it is seen as fitting, with other kinds of knowledge, into a greater whole, each insight illuminating the others rather than invalidating or contradicting them. If it *is* seen as an end in itself, it may well become destructive. For Ouine, for Ganse, for Saint Marin it represents both the chance of power and the chance of creating a protective irony, and is harmful because it is loveless and joyless.

There are, then, varieties of Catholic literature, and it is not a single homogeneous corpus. It may well be that 'attack on human complacency and natural comfort' noted by Green is an important theme in Catholic literature, but it is neither the only one nor necessarily a specifically Catholic one. Such an attack seems in fact contained or implied in a great deal of modern literature, and it may well be that what the agnostic or atheist has discovered about his nature over the last hundred years or so (that his free-will is vitiated, that his is full of dark, mysterious urges, that he is a product of a social pattern and so on) is what the Catholic has always in a sense known. In addition, secular and religious images of man, although different, have in our age at least been subject to common influences, and it would be surprising not to find similarities.[15] Like their agnostic or atheist counterparts, most modern Catholic writers have also attempted to portray a recognizably convincing and credible image of the real world, and however personal that image may be in individual cases, it is on the whole one which seems to carry conviction.[16] Along with this aspect of their work, there is often an element of discursive writing (particularly perhaps in the case Bernanos and Undset), a refusal or an inability to draw a definite line between narrative fiction and overt or implied comment. In other words, like modern writers, they are not exclusively tellers of tales,

14  Bernanos, *Le Crépuscule des Vieux*, p.81.
15  For an introductory survey of this area, see Richard W. Rousseau, 'Secular and Christian Images of Man', in *Thought*, 67 (1972) pp. 165-200.
16  For a development of this point see A.H. Winsnes, *Sigrid Undset: A Study in Christian Realism* (London, 1953) and J.C. Whitehouse, *Le Réalisme dans les romans de Bernanos* (Paris, 1969).

but also commentators on the human condition. There may be similarities in the individual comments, but to see them all as illustrating a common attitude is to over-simplify.

Like most of their contemporaries, they show an abiding interest in concepts of man, and, being of the twentieth century, are unavoidably aware of the proliferaction of such concepts. They are not exclusively concerned, as I have tried to point out, with the anti-humanist, the mysterious, the mystical aspects of human experience, or with the general vileness of man. Some of these concerns are apparent on occasion, but there is a complementary concern for the fullness and dignity of human life.

Catholic writers attempt to communicate a vision of the world rather than to expound an ideology, and are, like Dostoevsky and Melville, philosophical writers rather than writers *à thèse*. Their concern is to show a way of seeing the world rather than to communicate a system of thought and to portray human experience rather than to present arguments based on that experience.

Where they are 'mysterious and mystical' it is because the very nature of their subject-matter precludes, in their eyes a least, simplicity of image and expression. Bernanos states that profundity is a concomitant of their art: 'Un artiste chrétien...c'est d'abord un homme qui va d'emblée plus loin que le pittoresque de la vie, qui en a penetre le sens tragique'[17] and even the most superficial reading of his novels leaves one in no doubt that it is the 'tuf obscur', the central core of being, which is his major concern. This – the profundity and mystery of a basically tragic experience – is probably what Alrik Gustason had in mind when he wrote:

> Some critics have insisted that there is nothing natural in Sigrid Undset's almost morbid preoccupation with the general problem; but this would be to insist on a very limited conception of what constitutes 'the natural'. The most superficial analyses of Sigrid Undset's genius must admit that to her, at least, the *sombre is the natural* – to brood intently is to live deeply, strongly, completely. Though such a brooding preoccupation with the problem of evil might tend to lead other novelists of a spirit of complete disillusionment, to a sense of unrelieved, futile tragedy, even to a state of morbidity which would seem to be the opposite of the natural, it leads Sigrid Undset, in fact, to a grandeur of tragic moral conception which we have been accustomed to identify with great tragedy, with the tragic *katharsis* of the Aristotelian aesthetics.[18]

It is possible to suggest that Undset's novels are not, in fact, particularly concerned with brooding over the general problem of evil, and that the chief impression that they create is one of the essential goodness of creatures striving to become fully themselves and fully human, and that although it is slow

17  'Hommage à Georges Cornelis', reprinted in *L'Herne* (Paris, 1961), p.91.
18  Gustafson, p. 317.

and difficult, there is a progression in their lives towards this end. The main point that Gustafson makes, however – that of the tragic profundity of the novels – is a valid and important one. Undset, like Bernanos, portrays human life in a deep and profoundly satisfying way.

Most of those whom we now consider as Catholic writers (for example, Greene, Bernanos, Mauriac) were at their most productive at a time when there was a definiteness and a conviction in Catholicism (not necessarily to be equated with the triumphalism so suspect today) which now seems largely to have evaporated. It is no longer easy to find the same conviction, the same realistic and yet positive of a Christian concept of man and of human life in the novels of Cesbron, Cayrol or Read as that implied by the images created by the writer of a generation or two ago. Our strictly contemporary culture, where it is not exclusively sociological and political, is much more indefinite, tentative and relative. It seems possible, although time alone will tell, that the writers of the twenties, thirties, forties and fifties represent a high point in Catholic literary revival which has since lost its impetus, or at least changed its direction.

Ultimately therefore such writers are important (and it is here that the views expressed by Green, Weightman and others seem most valid) as examples of a particular cultural phenomenon. We have a group of writers who were active at a time when Catholicism had become the manifestation of religion dominant in literature, taking over and incorporating the remaining strands of modern religious thought and sensibility, a time when it would have been difficult if not impossible to imagine any other variety of Christianity a dominant theme or preoccupation in literature. Twentieth-century Catholicism seems to have absorbed all other Christian sensibilities to such an extent that to consider Christianity and literature means in effect to consider Catholicism and literature. It is difficult to imagine a study of the modern Protestant novel[19] or of twentieth-century Baptist poetry. It is to Catholic writers that we must turn if we are to reflect on the images of man and human life that modern religious sensibility can create. We are concerned then, in Catholic literature, with a group of writers who illustrate one way of looking at human life, and who are important both as individuals and as representatives of a particular movement. It may be a generation, a century, or even longer before we see such a vital and distinct phenomenon again. Whatever their faults, they produced a vital and striking literature, where man was still recognizable as man and of great importance. To stress exclusively, as many critics have done, the sin and squalor apparent in Catholic literature, to ignore its deep humanity and its concern for man's tragic dignity, is to run a serious risk of distortion by simplification.

19  It is at least arguable that even such Anglican writers as Charles Williams and C.S. Lewis are chiefly interesting in so far as they are to a greater or lesser extent 'Catholic' in spirit.

*Papal and Episcopal Reflections*

# On the Pursuit of Literary Studies[1]

## LEO XIII

You fully understand that frequently, and not without reason, We have said that the clergy should make knowledge of sacred teaching a visible mark of their profession. The nature of the times in which we live makes this an even greater need. Wherefore no matter what works and duties occupy the clergy, no matter what the worth of what they are doing, they must never neglect the daily study of Sacred Teaching. For this reason we have been much concerned when dealing with the training of young priests that they should assiduously study Theology and Philosophy, especially the Fathers of the Church and writings of Thomas Aquinas. We are aware that efforts have been made to implement this. And the study of Sacred Teaching is greatly enhanced by the study of Literature, which adds delight to the pursuit of knowledge and is necessary for a fruitful and civilized life. Therefore we have laid it down that such study be increased as far as possible.

In the first place the clergy must realise what Literature does to create beauty and perceive that that is its special glory. Those who have attained skill in Literature greatly contribute to the wellbeing of society. Where good Literature is lacking, the reputation of man is lowered. How great then was the wickedness of the emperor Julian (the Apostate) in forbidding Christians to study Literature. He felt that the future of Christianity would easily be brought into disrepute if it could be made to appear a religion of the illiterate. Thus ignorance of Literature among students of theology can give Christianity a bad name. Since by nature we learn only by proceeding from sense experience to higher truths (there is nothing in the intellect which does not come via the five senses), so only by means of poetic imagery and sensitivity to language do we grow in understanding and intelligence. This adds strength and a certain civilised fittingness to the art of writing. Hence a particular native elegance in speech moves and invites men to hear and read. Thus it so comes about that men are more easily moved to hold with greater conviction truth which is illustrated by the beauty of Literature. Liturgy and the worship of God has a certain likeness to this. A contemplation of the splendour of created things raises up the mind to the Godhead itself. The fruits of such artistic skills are mentioned by Basil and Augustine. Most wisely, Our predecessor, Paul III, ordered Catholic writers to employ elegance of style in order the better to refute heretics. Christians should make it clear that the marriage of doctrine and liturgy beauty is indeed praiseworthy.

But when we say that the clergy should painstakingly apply themselves to

---

1   Letter to Cardinal Parrochi, 20 May 1885, reprinted in *SSi D N Leonis XII allocutiones etc.* (Bruges, 1887).

the study of Literature, we mean not only our own native Literature, but also the Literature, the classics, of Greece and Rome. But there is a special reason why those of us who belong to the Western Church should cultivate the Literature of Ancient Rome. The Latin tongue has been its servant and companion since its inception. There has been a long historical tradition among western Christians of dignified and beautiful writing in Latin. But nor should the treasures of Greek Literature be neglected, for the Greeks excelled in polished and perfect thought. We must never neglect the wisdom of the eastern Churches and their great tradition, nor forget how much Latin Literature depends on Greek, especially in our learned Roman faculty of the Quiritium.

Therefore, having appreciated the value of literary studies for the Catholic Church, we should realise that they should occupy no mean place in our studies, and weigh full well their truth and beauty. Indeed, the ancient Holy Fathers of the Church, according to the amenities of their times, were well learned in such Literature. They gave themselves fully to the study of the old Greek and Roman writers. This too has brought great benefits to the Church. The books of the old Greek and Latin poets, orators and historians greatly influenced our Christian writers. And no one should be unaware that in the midst of fierce strife, war and barbarism, when literary studies could not be engaged in by the populace at large, they nevertheless flourished in monasteries and religious houses. And neither should we forget that among the Roman Pontiffs, Our predecessors, many were noteworthy for their literary skills. Such names as Damasus, Leo, Gregory Silvester II, Gregory IX, Eugene IV, Nicholas V and Leo X are of illustrious memory. Indeed, in the long line of Pontiffs scarcely any can be found who were wanting in a concern for Literature. Through their providential generosity schools and colleges were founded where the young could devote themselves to the study of letters. Libraries and collections of books were founded by bishops. Learned men were rewarded, and literary excellence flourished in the Church. So true is this and so well known that even the enemies of the Holy See have been forced to acknowledge the merits of the Roman Pontiffs in their work for higher literary studies.

Having explored the usefulness of such studies, and following the example of Our predecessors, We therefore decree that such studies should again flourish among the clergy and that past glories should be made to live again. We urge that this be made known in particular to our Roman seminary. We wish that every opportunity of such study be afforded to our young students. The study of Italian, Latin and Greek Literature must be included in the curriculum, under suitable teachers, skilled in these three disciplines. We consequently ask you to choose suitable men for this work.

Therefore, Our beloved son, aware of God's divine gifts and his kindness, We lovingly impart Our Apostolic blessing.

Given at Rome in St Peter's on the XX day of May 1885 in the IX year of our Pontificate.

# On Literary Criticism[1]

## PIUS XII

Our solicitude as Shepherd impels us, Dear Sons and Book Critics, to receive you into Our presence with a special joy. In Our concern to lead the children of Christ toward the verdant pastures of the spirit, today especially found in books, We are much preoccupied with the matter of reading.

We are grateful, therefore, that you have gathered here, because We see in each one of you a competent and faithful fellow-laborer in Our pastoral ministry. All of you are a powerful barrier against the overflowing tide of useless literature. Such reading matter threatens to drag the great dignity of human nature into the mud of error and perversion.

We need not point out here the necessity, and the importance of right criticism. Your own firm persuasion of the great influence of reading on the habits and the lot of individuals and the community, has inspired you to take up the difficult task, which is imposed on the critic by the vast literary production of our day. In a society like our own, so jealous to exercise the right of free press, the criticism of good people, based on a much more sacred right, is certainly one of the most proper means to prevent the spread of evil. This is all the more necessary, because such evil spreads under the appearance of pretext of good. In such matters of the gravest danger to souls, the intervention of some higher authority is justified and necessary. Criticism, however, that is based on the norms of truth and morality is better adapted, perhaps, to the mentality of the modern man, who wishes to judge things for himself, though welcoming the assistance of a critic in whom he has confidence.

You do not confine your work, however, to the moral aspects of a book. Your criticism also takes in the scientific, the literary, and the artistic qualities of a work. Thorough-going criticism, such as expected by the public and by experts, is possible, though it involves much work. Such thoroughness in Catholic critics not only strengthens their authority with the public, but contributes a praiseworthy addition to culture, in line with the perennial tradition of the Church, always ready to assimilate the development of thought and expression. The heights or the depths reached by literature, especially that of the present day, depends largely on the clear judgment, the moral integrity, and the intellectual strength of the critics.

Recognizing this great responsibility resting on the critic, We deem it opportune to point out some fundamental principles to which his work must conform, if it is efficaciously to attain its end of guiding souls into secure paths.

To facilitate the attainment of this end, We consider separately the subject himself, that is, the critic, and, afterwards, the object of his criticism. Today, We

1    From the *Catholic Mind*, 54, 1956.

shall speak about the first point, leaving to another opportunity the discusssion of the other matter (which to Us seems the most important).

## CONFIDENCE OF THE READER

The intention of guiding and advising others in the selection and evaluation of their reading, is to no purpose unless we assume in the readers a disposition of spirit to accept the suggestions of others. Every effort of a critic is useless with people, who of set purpose refuse to admit the critic's knowledge and competence, and who, consequently, have no confidence in him or in his judgment. There are readers with whom the critic has no success, because by nature or through faulty training, they rely on their own superior appraisal of their mental ability. Dominated by the suggestion of their own sufficiency, they expect from the critic only the confirmation of their own judgment, which they take to be certain and unchangeable.

Rejection of objective criticism by such persons, often based on false ideological prejudices, must not discourage the critic. Such rejection only reflects the psychological deficiencies of such persons. With a public of good dispositions, the critic will work much more efficaciously, if he knows how to gain their confidence.

In fact, this is the starting point and the goal of all criticism, whether there is question of an individual critic or of magazines – and here all the more – that make criticism their collective aim. If the reader turns to a critic, it is because he believes in the critic's knowledge, integrity, and maturity, when expounding the contents of a book or passing a well-founded and unanswerable judgment. How is the critic to gain successfully the confidence of the reader? What is the function of the critic, and what can be rightly asked of the public?

## REQUIREMENTS OF THE CRITIC

The first requirement in the critic is the mental ability to read and to properly understand the book in question. The mention of such a norm seems superfluous; it is not however, a rare thing to meet reviewers who do not measure up to this first, elementary requisite. Evidently, a close reading, very often boring and fatiguing, must be free from prejudice; and the critic must be reading in subject-matter that is sufficiently well-known to him. Therefore, the critic must have a many-sided culture; the special knowledge required in a given subject; and a broad general culture that will enable him to place the book properly and to expound its principal contents.

Mere intellectual understanding, however, is not sufficient. The critic must be able to form a judgment which when stated shows his mental competency.

The critic must be able to judge and to evaluate; in other words, to apply wisely his general culture and specialized knowledge to the subject at hand. For this, he must have broadmindedness, versatility; the ability to see and comprehend the relative bearings of a work, and to point out errors, short-comings, and contradictions. From this impartial consideration of the good and the bad in a given work there will come limitation and distinction, the Yes and No in each case. Only then does the criticism reach its final form as ready for publication.

OTHER DEMANDS ON THE CRITIC

In applying the above-mentioned qualities of mind, the critic is influenced by the will, by the sensibility, and by character. This makes it necessary for the critic to have other characteristics.

To prevent the will and emotions from negatively influencing his judgments, the critic must first of all be objective. He must show a liking for the author and confidence in him; unless, for positively grave and certain reasons he is obliged to speak otherwise. A critic habitually subject to partiality should never attempt to write. Nobility of character and goodness of heart are always the best weapons of combat. This holds for the field of criticism, when ideas and opinions are in conflict.

Nobility and kindness, however, are not to be confused with the ingenuity and credulity of a child, whose experience of life has not matured. A critic may have some of the qualities indicated, but they must always be joined to probity, integrity, and firmness of character. The critic must not write to please the author, or the publisher, or the public – often subject to strange sympathies or antipathies – or to follow his own inclination. Against his own better knowledge and conscience, against objective truth, a critic can make a false criticism.

This false judgment may arise from a wrong interpretation of the meaning or of the questionable teaching of the author, or it may come by deliberately omitting important and relevant portions that should not be concealed. To each critic should apply the testimony given to our Redeemer by His enemies, hypocritically: 'Master, we know that thou art truthful and that thou teachest the way of God in truth and that thou carest naught for any man; for thou dost not regard the person of men'(Mt 22:16).

Firmness of character in a critic is shown especially when he writes with serenity and without fear of his own judgment; and when he defends his judgment, keeping always to strict justice. As a judge who lacks the courage to sustain the law should resign; so should a critic, if he loves an easy life more than the truth.

Firmness, however, must always avoid arrogance; for this is an *a priori* presumption of the truth's being in favor of the critic and against the author. Both are subject to the same law in the service of truth; but the critic has the added duty of serving the truth with the maximum loyalty. In every case, the author and the critic should know that the truth is higher than either of them. An unjust criticism, as the word indicates, is not only an error of intellect but a real injury to the author.

In such cases, the reputation of the author may greatly suffer; and, moreover, as is often the case, his rightful interests may suffer loss. In such cases, the critic has a clear obligation of retraction. On the other hand, a justified criticism should not be withdrawn through fear of a powerful opponent. Such action would argue a deplorable lack of character and courage; it would also undermine the necessary confidence of the public, which rightly expects the critic to hold fast to his word, when it has been delivered according to the truth.

These are the common, fundamental principles for the critic and for all criticism, principles worthy of consideration and respect. The better to remember them, a few brief rules are usually given, differently expressed, but substantially in agreement. On some of these, We consider it useful to say a few words, since they are often cited to prove and justify some determined thought or action.

a) The first is the compelling maxim placed by Cornelius Tacitus at the beginning of his celebrated *Libri ab Excessu Divi August,* and afterwards in frequent use: 'Sine ira et studio,' i.e. 'without passion or partiality' (loc. cit., 1,1) Well understood, this maxim not only expresses a criterion for a judge's behaviour, but should be respected in all relations among men. As an admonition it refers particularly to the historian; however, in common estimation, it fits also the critic, who must judge and write *'sine ira et studio,'* without prejudice.

This does not oblige the critic to refrain from manifesting his own right sentiments. Still less is he obliged to renounce his own ideological world, when this is true. A serene and moderate critic has the right, for instance, to express with firmness and veracity his indignation at pornographic literature, which corrupts youth and affects adults. The literacy critic as well as the ordinary Christian cannot be taxed with partiality, when he takes as criterion of judgment the Christian faith in its integrity and purity. For example, Tacitus himself, in spite of the norm laid down at the beginning, sometimes describes in tragic words the despotism of certain emperors, and deplores the corruption found in high places. In his writings, there is personal anxiety for lost freedom, regret for the decline in greatness of the Senate, a looking back to the happy days of the austere Rome of his ancestors.

b) Another maxim, which, in spite of appearance, is somewhat difficult in theory and in practice, is: *'Verbum oris est verbum mentis,'* which means that man says or writes what he thinks. The more obvious meaning is: Speech gets its meaning and content from the inner thought. Therefore, one wishing to know the mind of the author must attend to his words; unless there is real doubt about the words, they are to be taken as natural witnesses to the inward soul.

Accordingly, the personality of the author, his life and his tendencies are not to be the starting point of the critical study; but rather his work itself and what it expresses. This maxim is also a warning to the author that he is to be judged according to his words which, therefore, must faithfully reflect his ideas and his feelings. If these thoughts and feelings are sincere, he will make every effort to express his sound mentality. He will also remember that it is not always easy to thing one way and to write differently; therefore, it is very difficult so to hide his real thought as not to reveal it one way or another.

For the author, then, the maxim is an admonition to sincerity. For the critic, it sets a limit to his study and judgment. He must keep close to the clear, objective meaning of the writing since his strict function is to judge the work and not the author. Therefore, he must honestly interpret what is honestly written. This general rule is necessary for peaceful living together, and for mutual relations between men.

Leaving aside the case where the objective meaning is doubtful – and then it is better to incline toward a favorable interpretation – the critic must bear in mind that the words have their own proper meaning, and that objective meaning is to be presented to the public. This, indeed, is what the critic is to judge. An honest critic gives the objective meaning, even though (perhaps even in the same work) the personal ideas of the author are known to be different.

If on the contrary, the objective meaning of the words contains error or falsehood, the critic must call attention to it, even though one is inclined to think that the author's subjective thought is different and correct. In such cases, a just and benevolent criticism can suggest a correction of the words that will conform to the personality of the author, but the erroneous objective sense will remain manifest.

c) We wish to mention a third maxim: *'Super omnia autem caritas,'* 'but above all charity'. The maxim is usually attributed to St Augustine, probably erroneously. But it does exactly express an idea that We wish to convey, and its purpose is to solve a practical doubt, which often troubles an honest critic: whether to give priority to 'Truth' or to 'Charity'. Theoretically, there is no objective conflict between 'Truth' and 'Charity', if we take the latter to mean the advancement of the neighbor's real good and the avoidance of unjust offense to him. But the difficulty does arise in individual, practical cases.

The literary critic faces a dilemma; to speak the full truth, as seems necessary, and consequently to offend the author or to injure his reputation, which seems contrary to charity; or to follow what seems the dictate of charity, to conceal the truth that should be told, and to ignore serious error. The critic faces the question: charity or truth? His anxiety increases, if he adverts to the divine precepts, wherein respect for truth and respect for charity are strongly and equally recommended.

Our Lord has in fact said: 'The truth shall make you free' (Jn 8:32); the Apostle of the Gentiles teaches: 'Love therefore is the fulfillment of the law' (Rom 13:10); and in another passage (according to the Greek text) *aletheuontes de en agape awesomen eis auton ta panta* (Eph 4:15); i.e. 'adhering to the truth, let us grow up in charity in Him with respect to all things.' The beloved disciple,

John, could hardly find words to express the meaning of charity; and he was accustomed to say: 'God is charity' (1 Jn 4:16); and again: 'In this we have come to know his charity, that he laid down his life for us; and we likewise ought to lay down our life for the brethren' (1 Jn 3:16). Yet this same St John has for us a strong injunction in regard to one who offends against the truth and integrity of doctrine: 'Do not say to him, Welcome' (2 Jn 10).

### A RULE OF CONDUCT

What rule of conduct, therefore, is the literary critic to follow in regard to these precepts of Holy Scripture? How reconcile in his thought and conscience this apparent conflict in precedence: The foundation of all things is 'Truth,' the end and the crown of all is Charity.' The foundation must abide intact, otherwise everything collapses, including the crown and the accomplishment. But like faith, the foundation of truth is not sufficient without charity as stated in the letter to the Corinthians: 'The greatest of these is charity' (1 Co.13:13). In this text, and therefore with an analogous meaning, the maxim: 'But above all charity' is reflected.

Truly, in many cases, a right way can easily be found, if the critic always remembers that the precept of charity holds not only to the author, but also to the reader. He can always find some favorable way to prevent dangerous misunderstandings in the reader, while being tactful toward the author.

We thought it well to mention these maxims because they express, We think, in a more concrete form the general principles that must govern the literary critic's work. These maxims must always be present to his delicate task, subject as it is to oversights, excesses, and deficiencies. They are the foundation necessary to increase the confidence placed in criticism by the public. They set a limit between what is just and unjust in the accomplishment of his important task.

Postponing, as already said, to another meeting, the discussion of the second part (that concerning the object) of Our exposition, We invoke on you and on your work an abundance of light and divine assistance, in pledge of which We gladly give you Our paternal apostolic blessing.

# Extract from an Address to the International Confederation of Societies of Authors and Composers[1]

## JOHN XXIII

As you know, the Catholic Church is happy to encourage international gatherings at all levels. The International Confederation of Societies of Authors and Composers is therefore assured of finding, in the person of those taking part in its twenty-fifth Congress, a most warm welcome with Us. But on this occasion there are special reasons for the warmth of the welcome. On the one hand, the aim of your fraternal and friendly discussions is to pool the exceptional talents and gifts of mind and heart that Providence has bestowed on you. Those gifts have been given to you for the benefit of all and belong, so to speak, to the whole of humanity.

On the other the Vatican, which welcomes you today, lovingly keeps in its galleries, museums, libraries and archives such a collection of masterpieces and mementos that it is one of the most familiar places in the world to scholars and artists. So, in a sense, you are at home here.

You are, gentlemen, members of societies of authors and composers. Apart from the technical and organizational problems your confederation may have to devote itself to, what characterizes you above all in the eyes of the general public is your means of expression, your language. The language of the poet, the man of letters and the musician is particularly apt for laying bare the secret places of the soul, for interpreting its suffering and consoling its suffering. It can lead hearts towards lofty goals, correct errors and purify passions by restraining their plunge into the depths and firing them in their noble thrust towards what is truly good.

Your profession is hardly concerned with encouraging the acquisition of material wealth or economic wisdom. What interests you – and it is the honour of your vocation – is fostering the spiritual impulse that animates all peoples.

It is, in fact, in the voice of its poets and artists that even before it has achieved its economic development, as is the case with so many new countries now beginning to figure on the international scene, a country can, We say, reveal the charm and mystery of the fertility within it.

That is the voice which teaches, educates and consoles, the source of the purest and highest joy. Its message moves over the artificial barriers separating mankind. In times of sadness and humiliation, at the height of fratricidal wars, it has happened that the voice of the poet and musical harmonies of the artist have induced men to reflect and suggested more peaceful projects.

Finally, gentlemen, We should like to say in conclusion that, as a fact of experience that may offer you encouragement in the pursuit of your noble

1   From *Acta Apostolicæ Sedis* 3 (1962) pp 518–20.

activities, it is rare for genius or talent to receive in this world all the under-standing and glory due to them.

It is perhaps more to the generations to come than to the men and women of your time that your message is addressed. We are thinking, as We say that, of the numberless armies of those who have gone before you in your noble career. Their lives were often shot through with inexpressible trials, but their voices are still to be heard bringing consolation and joy to all ages.

The Gospel tells us that one sows and another reaps (Jn 4:37). You are the sowers. Others will reap after you, perhaps from amongst those coming into life before your eyes. What a joy it is for Us – and, We are sure, for anyone with a heart – to hear that the young people of today can sense the presence of a life-giving inspiration encouraging them to be increasingly interested in esteeming and acquiring all the goods the spirit can bring.

So carry out your noble task generously and look ahead with serene con-fidence. That too will help the world to pay heed to your message and direct men and peoples towards thoughts of peace.

In formulating this wish, gentlemen, We call down upon you, your work and your families, the fulness of the divine blessings God is pleased to pour over those who, like you, have in their hearts to make the talents they have received bear fruit by putting them at the service of the noblest ideals of humanity.

# Realism in the Catholic Novel[1]

## THE GERMAN BISHOPS

When we consider the share and importance of Catholic writers in our litera-ture since the end of the last war, we gladly note that – contrary to the situa-tion after the First World War – they are quantitatively and qualitatively in the first rank. Catholic literature no longer leads a ghetto existence. It is read widely and, what is more, is published also by non-Catholic publishers, fre-quently even in the form of cheap pocket editions, the production of which is only worthwhile when a large sale can be expected.

The centre of modern literature is man – his personal life, his relations to his fellow-men, to the world, and, not least to God. It is a joy to see the con-cern of our modern writers with questions arising from religion. We must be grateful that they paint no wishful picture of human existence, its struggles, defeats and triumphs – no sentimentalized, primitive and therefore untrue pic-ture – but that they are concerned to mirror reality.

1    From *The Catholic Mind,* 59, 1956.

The problem now arises that in the choice of their subjects Catholic writers, too, are chiefly attracted by the negative side of reality. Man and sin are the themes which are repeatedly attempted. Now, as the great English Cardinal Newman said, it is a contradiction in itself to produce a sinless literature about sinful man, and we do not fail to see that to call things by their right names, and to recognize the power of evil in the world, is of great value not merely for literature but also for the pastoral duties of our times. This kind of literature gives rise to shocks which can have a wholesome effect.

But we also have cause in this context to express our anxiety. We must demand that such a picture of man in his struggle with evil retains the God-given moral law, the standards of which also apply to writers as artists. The reader must not be allowed to gain the impression that men are hopelessly and irredeemably victimized by the powers of darkness.

Such a false impression may arise through certain ways of depicting sexual life, which is, indeed, as we know, of particular danger. We regret that in this regard the Christian's opportunity to dominate his lower powers in a life of purity, in the sacrament of marriage or in a life of dedicated virginity, rarely finds satisfactory treatment. Instead, certain physical acts which natural shame relegates to an intimate sphere are sometimes depicted in an unsparingly and painfully open manner. Again, certain abnormal dispositions and acts are discussed without offering help towards the mastering of these unfortunate tendencies. We must not condone the surrender of clear moral standards through the deep pity for sinful man which many of these books are capable of awakening.

### CONFUSING MORAL STANDARDS

It is also to confuse moral standards if the case of a man in mortal sin is depicted as if that state were a matter of course, and as if he were deprived of his free decision. The priest, in particular, considering sin as due to personal guilt, will make allowance for the sometimes weighty burden of sins which carry no great guilt, but precisely because he knows that the realm of free responsibility must be left untouched. There is also need to refrain from a false glorification of sin. It is certain that guilt may sometimes contribute towards the growth of sanctity, as in the case of St Augustine. But it remains guilt, and must under no circumstances receive consent afterwards, even if redeemed by genuine conversion and sorrow.

It is, moreover, dangerous if readers with little sense of judgment are given the impression that Catholic authors describe suicide as a solution for a seemingly unsuccessful struggle with the moral law. Certainly there is no earthly authority, not even the Church, which can decide whether or not such a desperate decision is an obstacle to God's mercy. But the impression is not admissible that presumptuous trust in divine mercy gives man a possibility of escaping a life that has become unbearable for him and may yet be acceptable to God.

Criticism of a self-satisfied and materialist *Bürgerlichkeit* [bourgeois way of life] which, despite the fulfilment of religious obligations, is no longer lived from the faith, is certainly justified, and we are grateful to the Catholic authors who raise their voices against it. Such criticism, however, should not be confined to describing the moral decadence which is part of this bourgeois existence, thus giving a one-sided picture. Rather do we expect our Catholic writers to make a diagnosis where there may well be sickness, but where it is also shown that man can make an effort to master his difficulties and get well again.

We are glad to find that literary attempts at depicting man's mastery of life again and again illustrate the means of Grace which Christ, through His Church, provides. But a genuine deep love of truth, of the Church, are the indispensable conditions for a writer who desires to be a Catholic writer. Then he will be able to show also the human weaknesses in the Church and her servants; although he should be mindful of charity and truthfulness.

The Catholic priest is a favorite figure in the modern novel. The dangers to which he is exposed are singled out, as are his temptations to the abuse of his power and possessions, and to unbelief and sensuousness. The struggle between the priestly and the purely human vocation if often depicted, and a false concept sometimes results of the priest who tries hard to overcome his weaknesses. If a sympathetic human picture of an idealized priest is given, his real task of mediating between God and man if often neglected. Not infrequently such a sympathetic priest is confronted by a 'higher clergy' that is depicted as stupid, hard-hearted or pleasure-loving. We would like to see the positive sides abounding in priestly lives given an artistically valid form.

The sacrament of marriage is also treated, besides baptism and confession, in modern novels. Here, too, we note a preoccupation with aberrations and lawlessness. The conflict between sacramental duty and love outside marriage is sometimes emphasized so much that it dominates the struggle against eternal damnation.

SUMMING UP

To sum up, we find that a large section of our Catholic literature prefers the darker side of life. In that case it is in accordance with the literature of our times, and no doubt valuable if it desires to set a wholesome diagnosis of our time against euphemistic descriptions. We would go so far as to speak of the duty of giving such a diagnosis; and there is no need for our writers to feel that their freedom is limited by bourgeois prejudices. But from the point of view of the Catholic faith and the Catholic moral law we must ask that the moral and religious standards which are God-given shall retain their unshakable validity. It would also be desirable if, beyond a mere diagnosis, man in his needs could be helped by literature; if he were saved from the false, fateful impression that there is an unbridgeable gulf between the sober reality of life and the moral law as this is given by God and proclaimed by the Church. We do not speak for a literature of false pieties, but we do speak for a literature which, in addition to making a diagnosis of our times, contributes towards their cure.

So far as our faithful are concerned, we should like to urge them to discriminate in the choice of reading matter, to select what is suitable and what may help them to make their faith more mature, more alive and pure. They should remember that not every book is suitable for everyone, and that, in particular, children and young people must be guarded against a premature choice of literature they are too young to understand.

Our Catholic librarians and their helpers should be mindful of the characteristics of works addressed to readers who are mature and firm in their moral and religious outlook, so that their libraries, the use of which we strongly recommend, should indeed harm no one, but offer each his own fare. Thanks are due to our Catholic writers for their work in the service of the word that ultimately points to God. We feel ourselves through our own divine mission united with them and ask their help in the present tasks of the Church.

# Index